Invoking the Fathers

INVOKING THE FATHERS

Dangerous Metaphors and Founding Myths

in Congressional Politics

———

SARAH KORNFIELD

JOHNS HOPKINS UNIVERSITY PRESS | *Baltimore*

© 2024 Johns Hopkins University Press
All rights reserved. Published 2024
Printed in the United States of America on acid-free paper
2 4 6 8 9 7 5 3 1

Johns Hopkins University Press
2715 North Charles Street
Baltimore, Maryland 21218
www.press.jhu.edu

Library of Congress Cataloging-in-Publication Data is available.

A catalog record for this book is available from the British Library.

ISBN 978-1-4214-4973-9 (hardcover)
ISBN 978-1-4214-4974-6 (ebook)

*Special discounts are available for bulk purchases of this book.
For more information, please contact Special Sales at specialsales@jh.edu.*

To my father

CONTENTS

Preface ix
Acknowledgments xi

Introduction 1
1. Rights and Liberty 49
2. Veneration and Cynicism 86
3. Checks and Balances 120
4. Debate and Bipartisanship 163
5. Losing Faith 192

Notes 209
Index 247

PREFACE

During a 2017 speech that was ostensibly about tax cuts, President Donald Trump bragged that his daughter Ivanka calls him "Daddy." His appeal to fatherhood resonated with the crowd, who cheered wildly in response. In that moment, I heard the mix of fatherhood, power, and politics.

Then, during the early weeks of the COVID-related stay-at-home orders, an extended family member of mine used social media to recirculate the words "I prefer dangerous freedom over peaceful slavery" superimposed over an image of Thomas Jefferson. I was struck by the way this appeal drew upon the authority of Jefferson—a father who enslaved his own children—to protest the pandemic precautions. I was startled by how powerful the memory of Jefferson was in this moment, despite the vast difference between slavery and staying at home. Indeed, in this social-media post, the political power of Jefferson's memory involved an erasure or forgetting—a white-supremacist amnesia of the realities of slavery.

These two moments crystalized in my mind, speaking to each other across time. Trump's appeal to fatherhood and the perennial popularity of the "Founding Fathers" are connected—and this book originated as I traced those connections.

When I began working on this project in earnest, I steered my research away from Trump and presidents because this research is bigger than Trump and bigger than the presidency. Indeed, the reason Trump could successfully appeal to fatherhood is that fatherhood has a larger political resonance in US politics. Still thinking about the recirculation of Jeffersonian quotes and images, I instead focused this research on congressional invocations of the "Founding Fathers."

What I discovered while writing this book is a rhetoric of sovereignty—a rhetoric that establishes what it means to govern in the United States, who can govern in the name of "the people," and who can constitute "the people." What I discovered is that America has daddy issues.

ACKNOWLEDGMENTS

Writing is a palimpsest—a work of art made layer by layer. I have not always written the way I do now, and both my writing and this book have developed over time and under the influence of many lovely people. Peeling back the layers of my palimpsestic writing reveals those influences—the traces of others' kindness, encouragement, and advice. It is only right that I attempt here to acknowledge and thank those whose words, actions, and work are embedded within the layers of my writing.

My spouse is a lovely person; he loves that I love to write. He makes space in our home for my writing. I write at our kitchen counter, and—when I'm in the zone—he steers our household around me like a stream around a boulder. He is the calmest person I know, and to the extent that my writing has any peace or rest in it—any unhurried sentences or patient arguments—it is his influence at work. Our children are inquisitive, and their questions add excitement to my writing. Their interest in this book (in Congress, the Constitution, and rhetoric) helped me remember in the tedious hours that this work is interesting and an important part of our civic life together.

My father read every word of the first draft of every chapter. He had great ideas and questions for each chapter, and he passionately dislikes a single sentence in the first chapter. His support means the world to me. My mother has heard—in exacting detail—all my ideas for every paragraph in this book over countless hours of phone calls. We are the closest of friends, and her patience and support as I verbally process my arguments are the reason this book exists. My sister has the strongest and cleanest sense of right and wrong. She works in refugee resettlement and has no time to write. Her outrage and compassion are twin layers throughout my writing. My family—Matt Roberts, Jacob William Roberts, Geoffrey Kornfield Roberts, Bill Kornfield, Jennie Kornfield, and Claire Kornfield—are layered throughout this book, embedded in every paragraph. Thank you.

In a similar way, I want to thank Devon Schalcher Torchiana and Kristin Summer Mathe Coletta. I met these women in graduate school, and they changed my life. They certainly changed my writing. We've been friends for roughly fifteen years, and their kindness, joy, companionship, and intellectual gifts are layered throughout my life and writing. Thank you.

My dog, Chiaki, died while I was working on this project. He was the world's best Chihuahua and my first love. He was very old and very happy, and every chapter was drafted with his sweet companionship. He didn't care that I was writing; he only cared that I was with him. He was a dog, so he wouldn't have been impressed by this book unless I covered it in peanut butter, but his companionship shaped my writing, and I'm grateful to him. During this project's final stages, I rescued a puppy that I named Honey. He is the most energetic small dog I've ever met, and the final nuances of this book's argument and articulation were worked out on our daily three-mile walks. These dogs have profoundly shaped my daily habits, affecting my writing in tangible ways. I am grateful to them and unbearably sad to have lost my beloved Chiaki.

The majority of this book was drafted during a yearlong sabbatical at Hope College. At the most basic level, then, this book exists because of the support of Provost Griffin, Dean VanderStoep, and my colleagues in the Communication Department and the Women's and Gender Studies program at Hope College, who supported my research through the generous gift of time. I am indebted to Hope College's library and specifically to Jenifer Holman, Michelle Yost, and Tori Longfeld; these librarians supported my research with such consistent professionalism and joy. They scoured databases, managed interlibrary loans, found obscure books, and made this book possible. A special thank-you to my colleagues Drs. Marissa Doshi and James

Herrick, whose friendship and kindness have made my work at Hope College so fruitful.

A number of my colleagues and former faculty have profoundly influenced my writing. Dr. Roger Lundin's writing remains a lasting influence. I aspire to his level of brevity and eloquence. Dr. Rosa Eberly's attention to detail and reality has long influenced my writing, helping me aim not only for clarity but to pay attention to the consequences of my writing within community. I fell in love with rhetoric and writing while learning from Drs. Kenneth Chase and Christine Gardner. These wonderful colleagues have shaped so much of my life and work. I am especially grateful for the support and encouragement derived from the Rhetoric Society of America's mid-career writing workshop. Through this lovely institution and this specific program designed to encourage and support rhetoricians such as me, this work has finally become ready for publication. Namely, I am grateful to Drs. Kristen Hoerl, Alice Johnston Myatt, and Letizia Guglielmo, who have been helping me think about writing for the past year. Dr. Casey Ryan Kelly read this work in its entirety and offered the most helpful advice and support along the way. I am profoundly grateful. Thank you.

The Library of Congress is the most impressive—and perhaps most democratic—of all American institutions. I am incredibly impressed by the rigor and generosity of librarians everywhere and at the Library of Congress specifically. They curate the *Congressional Record*, which is publicly accessible through Congress.gov. Absolutely no part of this book could have been written without their miraculous record keeping. Similarly, the National Archives are unbelievably well maintained and played an important role in this book's development. I am indebted to these librarians, archivists, and institutions. Likewise, the National Constitution Center is the very best resource to learn about the US Constitution and its interpretations—and as I sifted through politicians' rhetoric about the Constitution, I often turned to the expertise available through the National Constitution Center to better understand their arguments. Together, the Library of Congress, the National Archives, and the National Constitution

Center might offer the best defense against fascism and the best resources for democracy and civic education available to those who live in the United States. Thank you.

Throughout this book runs a critique of the way Christianity is wielded within the rhetoric of US sovereignty. This layer of my writing is deeply indebted to those who have shepherded my faith: my grandparents and parents, Sunday-school teachers, camp counselors, Bible-study leaders, chaplains, pastors, and the biblical scholars whose commentaries have made scripture more accessible. A special thanks to the women with whom I co-lead a weekly Bible study and to the Children's Ministry team at my church who entrust me to lead the preschool worship. I am grateful for your witness, your prayers, and your encouragement.

Finally, I am supremely grateful to the editorial team at Johns Hopkins University Press, who have supported this research and published it. This would not be a book without their efforts. Thank you.

Invoking the Fathers

Introduction

THE US CONGRESS HAS A LOT to say about the "Founding Fathers." The leaders and the rank-and-file members of both the Republican and Democratic parties routinely discuss what the "Founding Fathers" would have wanted, what they intended, and what they created—or bequeathed. For instance, when discussing the Senate's then upcoming trial in response to the House's 2019 impeachment of President Donald Trump, Senate Majority Leader Mitch McConnell (R-KY) noted that only the Senate has the authority to remove a sitting president, stating, "The Founding Fathers gave us [the Senate] this task for a reason.... They knew this institution could do what was right for our nation, so I am confident that we can prove our framers right in the days that lie ahead."[1] In counterpoint, Senate Minority Leader Chuck Schumer (D-NY) also invoked the "Founding Fathers," noting that the senators faced a choice to "begin this trial in search of the truth or in service of the president's desire to cover it up" as he charged his colleagues, stating, "the eyes of the nation, the eyes of history, the eyes of the Founding Fathers are upon us."[2] Indeed, whether discussing impeachment, patent laws, gun laws, abortion rights, infrastructure deals, immigration, war, or simply commemorating Bald Eagle

Day, the members of the House and Senate routinely invoke the "Founding Fathers."

The phrase itself, "Founding Fathers," originated in 1916. Warren G. Harding coined "Founding Fathers" during a speech at the Republican National Convention.[3] Throughout his presidential campaign—which he won in a landslide—Harding worked to instill in his generation an "adoration" for the US "founding."[4] His alliterative phrase worked brilliantly, finding its way into school curricula, commemorative biographies, news punditry, and congressional discourse.

The phrase itself, however, mobilizes a gendered metaphor that conflates fatherhood with political power. Indeed, George Washington was the first person named as the "father" of this country—an epithet that had clear precedent in the ways Renaissance writers "often referred to kings as the fathers of their people."[5] Even as those in the founding era rejected governance by monarchy, this metaphor remained politically useful. As both the commander of the Continental Army and the first president, Washington was routinely described as the "Father of Our Country," even during his lifetime.[6] Indeed, Henry Knox persuaded Washington to stand for president, writing that becoming president would "doubly entitle you to the glorious republican epithet—'The Father of Your Country.'"[7]

When Thomas Jefferson became president in 1800, he began rewriting recent history in a way that expanded the title from "father" to "fathers." The loose collection of men who drafted, debated, and signed or declined to sign the Constitution were largely well-educated, wealthy male enslavers who vehemently disagreed on the meaning of the Constitution they had written.[8] During his presidency, Thomas Jefferson revised this history, imagining they agreed that the Constitution's role is to protect the states' and individuals' liberties from federal interference.[9]

Reimagined as a unified body, these men could be invoked as a cohort—and allusions to "the fathers" joined the references to Washington as the "father of our country." For instance, by the time Abraham Lincoln delivered the Gettysburg Address, his usage of "fathers" was commonplace as he stated, "Four score and seven years ago our *fathers* brought forth on this continent, a new nation, conceived in Liberty, and dedicated to the proposition that all men are created equal."[10]

As such, when Harding coined "Founding Fathers," he referred to a cohort that was regularly invoked but that did not exist as a cohort. Only one man, Roger Sherman, signed all four of the founding documents: the Continental Association, the Articles of Confederation, the Declaration of Independence, and the Constitution. Moreover, of the fifty-five delegates who hammered out the Constitution, only thirty-nine of them signed it; three delegates refused to sign it, and another thirteen delegates were absent when the document was signed and made no arrangements for it to be signed by proxy.[11] The Bill of Rights, meanwhile, although originally drafted by James Madison, was significantly changed by the newly elected senators and then ratified by the states' legislators. To speak of the "Founding Fathers" as if they were a cohort or even an identifiable group of men is a vast oversimplification that paves over their many ideological differences.

And yet, Congress reverberates with the phrase. The *Congressional Record* is a verbatim transcript of the remarks made in the House and Senate chambers. Curated by the Library of Congress, its records are arranged into "entries," and those from 1995 to the present are publicly available online. The *Congressional Record*'s entries are uneven: a given entry within the *Congressional Record* might contain just one one-minute speech, might contain two speeches that are approximately thirty minutes each, might contain a slate of fifty speeches of varying length given by different congresspeople, or almost any other combination. Since 1995, the phrase "Founding Fathers" has been used in over 4,450 entries—often occurring multiple times in the various speeches within an entry. To put this into a frame of reference, Congress is only in session for approximately 120–190 days per year, which means that even if the phrase "Founding Fathers" occurs only once in each of the 4,450 entries, it would still be frequent enough to have been said in Congress every single day that Congress has been in session since 1995.[12]

This book takes political fatherhood seriously by analyzing "Founding Fathers" as a metaphor within contemporary congressional discourse. Metaphors are not innocent. This is not an ethereal endearment that symbolizes a gender-neutral respect toward the founders. Rather, as scholars such as I. A. Richards and Leah Ceccarelli have amply demonstrated, metaphors merge two disparate concepts, wrapping one term in the other, to create a new combined meaning.[13] In so doing, metaphors "select some aspects of a subject to emphasize, while deflecting our attention from other aspects of that subject."[14] Metaphors are not simply figures of speech; they profoundly affect meaning-making. As George Lakoff and Mark Johnson noted, we "live by" metaphors, using them to both create and control reality.[15] Metaphors that control a culture's perception and construction of reality are often clustered—meaning a whole host of word choices and stylistic techniques come into play to support and seemingly naturalize the metaphor at hand.[16] It is the work of this book to "wake up" the metaphor of fatherhood in US political discourse—to make it visible, to interrogate the sovereignty it imagines for the United States, to analyze its clustered terms and stylistic techniques, and to assess the reality it creates.[17]

Focusing on Congress rather than the presidency, this research attends to the pervasive, established, longstanding—even mundane—rhetorical norms that govern US politics. Typically, presidential candidates have short-lived moments in the national spotlight, but congresspeople routinely serve for decades. By studying congressional discourse, this research is able to, first, survey the norms of US political discourse rather than becoming ensnared by the personalities and unique rhetorical styles of US presidents and presidential candidates. Second, this research focuses on the discourse that governs US democracy. Congress designs, debates, and discusses the laws and policies that govern everyday life in the United States. The assumptions, myths, and metaphors that circulate in Congress, then, play an outsized role in US governance. As such, this book analyzes the gendered metaphor of "Founding Fathers" in congressional speeches, working to understand how this metaphor shapes the myths of the founding era, the premise of US governance, and the assumptions of what it means to be American.

The focus here is on contemporary politics. While this work is informed by the history of the founding era and historic interpretations of the founding documents, I am primarily concerned with how contemporary politicians employ the metaphor of the "Founding Fathers." As such, this research surveys the congressional discourse that invoked the "Founding Fathers" during recent election cycles—namely the 2016 and 2020 elections.[18] During these election cycles, all 435 members of the US House of Representatives were elected as was one-third of the Senate. The 2016 and 2020 election cycles were also presidential election cycles. I selected these election cycles rather than midterm elections because of the intricate connections between congresspeople, party politics, and the heightened partisanship of presidential politics. That is, while congressional members are individually elected, they derive significant power from their party's backing and typically participate in their party's brand.[19] Focusing on these months of heightened partisanship, I narrowed my research to the 382 entries in the *Congressional Record* that use the phrase "Founding Fathers" at least once. This amounts to several hundred speeches that invoke the "Founding Fathers" since the *Congressional Record* typically contains multiple speeches within a single entry. What follows then is not a close analysis of each congressional speech that invokes the "Founding Fathers," but it is a representative account, focusing on the metaphorical clusters, themes, and strategies as well as the cracks and counter discourses at play within this congressional discourse.

This book ultimately demonstrates how the rhetoric of "Founding Fathers" imagines a *real* America—an America that is *inherited* from the "Founding Fathers" by their true heirs. By positing the imagined founders as fathers, this metaphor equates the United States with a family. Americans become the founders' children, and the United States itself becomes something the fathers *birthed*—for lack of a better term. As such, this metaphor mixes a version of masculinity—an idealized fatherhood that is associated with whiteness and "family" values—with political authority. It draws upon and reinforces the supposed naturalness of fathers being preeminent, authoritative leaders. Indeed, mobilizing the same commonsense logic that equates masculinity with kingship in the colloquialism "a man's home is his castle," this fatherhood metaphor assumes that fathers are rightfully preeminent.

This metaphor has several consequences. First, this metaphor renders women seemingly irrelevant to the nation. Despite women's procreative capacities—and fathers' general lack thereof—this metaphor imagines that the United States and Americans descend only from the fathers. Second, this metaphor situates the United States—and Americans—as white. If the founders *fathered* the United States, then it is the exclusive creation of white men. This privileges white culture as the United States itself and naturalizes white Americans as true Americans. The metaphor renders white Americans as the fathers' obvious descendants while racialized others are rendered suspect—despite the reality that many Black Americans can trace their lineage to the founders. Moreover, this book demonstrates how the metaphor of "Founding Fathers" steeps the US Congress in the assumptions that fatherhood connotes power and authority, that the founders created that which is true or good about the United States, and that this "real" America is a legacy passed down from the fathers to their true heirs—real Americans.

This metaphor's work is pernicious. It sets up a real and fake America, tilting US "equality" toward patriarchy, white supremacy, and "family" values, ultimately creating and reinforcing a legislative system in which some are more equal than others.

By analyzing the metaphor of fatherhood in US politics, this monograph explicitly extends George Lakoff's "nation as family" metaphor, going beyond the "strict father / nurturing parent" dichotomy that he mapped onto Republican and Democratic presidencies.[20] Indeed, rather than assessing what sort of "father" a Republican or Democratic president attempts to project, this research demonstrates how the "Founding Fathers" metaphor renews a patrilineal and propertied conception of sovereignty within US politics, creating a logic of inheritance in which the "Founding Fathers'" most obvious descendants—white men who espouse Christian values—function as the first among equals.

Fatherhood, however, is not the only way in which contemporary congresspeople discuss the founders: indeed, members of the Congressional Black Caucus and occasionally others counter this discourse, most fully by voicing cynicism. As such, this book analyzes the ways in which cynicism charts a path away from inheritance-based governance. Cynicism, as Mary Boor Tonn and Valerie A. Endress explain, is a discourse of "tragic alienation" or a loss of "faith" in something: in this case, the "Founding Fathers."[21] In contemporary congressional politics, cynicism expresses both a lament (rendering the founding myths as tragedies) and a sort of promise—that having cleared away the false myths, the United States might begin again.

Here, I see considerable overlap between the rhetoric of cynicism and the related concepts of racial realism, prophetic pessimism, and Afropessimism as discussed by scholars such as Derrick Bell, Andre E. Johnson, Anthony J. Stone Jr., and Frank B. Wilderson III.[22] These concepts all pertain to a recognition rooted in empirical observations that challenge dominant narratives—such as the narrative of progress. For instance, Derrick Bell argues that "racial equality" is not a "realistic goal" for Black Americans and that aiming for this "unobtainable" status in "a perilously racist America" leads Black Americans to "face frustration and despair."[23] Instead, Bell recommends an approach of "racial realism." This approach recognizes the "permanence" of Black Americans' "subordinate status" in the United States, thus avoiding despair, and instead opens new imaginaries and potentialities for implementing "racial strategies that can bring fulfillment and even triumph."[24] Essentially, Bell counters the "progress" narrative with empirical observations (realism) which then lead him to form different goals and strategies than would be possible within a progress narrative. Studying how members of the Congressional Black Caucus counter the metaphor of "Founding Fathers," I highlight the language of cynicism in order to draw attention to the ways in which this counter discourse seeks to reveal American exceptionalism as *myth*. Indeed, this counter discourse is focused on the past (both real and imagined) rather than the realistic present. In so doing, it expresses a necessary loss of faith in the received mythology of American exceptionalism and voices a new faith—one founded in Black resistance. While this is not the only discourse to counter the fatherhood metaphor in Congress, it is the most comprehensive.

Analyzing the metaphor of fatherhood in contemporary politics, this book ultimately works to make visible a rhetoric of sovereignty. Sovereignty is often theorized in relation to borders. As Stephen J. Hartnett and Bryan R. Reckard write, sovereignty has to do with how "nation-states create borders, organize space, and wield power over particular areas."[25] Indeed, as Anne Demo has argued, borders—both real and imagined—symbolize a claim of "authority," or sovereignty, "over a territorial entity."[26] Within democracies, sovereignty is not only tied to the land and symbolized by borders, but it is tied to the will or consent of "the people."[27] That is, democratic governance ostensibly derives its authority from "the people."

As such, this book uses the metaphor "Founding Fathers" as both a case study and the prima facie example of the rhetoric of sovereignty in the United States. That is, as a case study, this book explores how the "Founding Fathers" are used and abused; how counterfactuals, nostalgia, American exceptionalism, and selective amnesia about the nation's founding ground and reinforce Christian nationalism, white supremacy, and patriarchy—and how some congresspeople speak back and resist these interpretations. But at another level, this book is theorizing the rhetoric of sovereignty, demonstrating how invocations of the "Founding Fathers" conceptualize US governance, including who can govern in the name of "the people" and who can constitute "the people."

Indeed, as rhetoricians and political theorists such as Paul Elliot Johnson and Nadia Urbinati demonstrate, "the people" is quite clearly a "social construct."[28] "The people" are imagined, described, and called into being through rhetorical appeals. For instance, studying "freedom-soaked, populist" Republican and conservative rhetoric, Johnson focuses on how this rhetoric identifies "the people" by differentiating them from others who are considered not the "real America."[29] Tracing this rhetoric's identity politics, Johnson demonstrates how this version of "the people" is ideologically comprised by capitalism, individualism, white supremacy, and patriarchy. In a similar vein, Michael J. Lee and Jarrod Atchison analyze secessionist rhetoric, exploring the rhetoric at play when groups differentiate themselves from "the people."[30]

Since democratic governance derives its sovereignty, or authority to rule, from "the people," the way "the people" are rhetorically constituted bears significant weight. That is, Western post-Enlightenment eras have largely disavowed governance through "naked sovereign violence" in response to "humanist expectations" that "direct violence is verboten."[31] Describing this "humanist" governance through theories of biopower, Foucault differentiated between the "ancien régime" of governance as the right to kill and more modern conceptualizations of governance as the ability to produce and regulate life.[32] For example, within US politics it would make no sense for gubernatorial candidates to threaten their would-be constituents with the death penalty if not elected—indeed, if not elected they would not be in a position to wield the death penalty. Instead, gubernatorial candidates attempt to woo voters with promises of lowering taxes, providing support for childcare, supporting farming, and so on. Unfortunately, this shift in governance does not "eliminate the role of violence in producing political order."[33] It merely obfuscates such violence, compensating for the "challenges made by various entities to the legitimacy of naked sovereign violence."[34] For instance, this type of governance rationalizes the "distribution of inequality," enacting violence against a portion of the population—often in the name of "the people."[35] Here, the lines between "sovereign and subject" become complicated since "democratic authority" is derived from the imagined social contract between "the people" and the government, but clearly the whole population rarely constitutes "the people."[36] Instead, the idea of "the people" is often wielded on behalf of some people and against others.

Analyzing the metaphor of the "Founding Fathers," then, this book theorizes the rhetoric of sovereignty, demonstrating how this metaphor functions to establish who has the right to rule in the name of "the people" and who can constitute "the people." Specifically, I demonstrate how invoking the "Founding Fathers" works to contain or delimit what it means to be American, preserving the nation for its "proper heirs" and nullifying alternative claims to sovereignty.

This introductory chapter proceeds by first attending to the ways in which the "Founding Fathers" are publicly remembered in the United States—and how this public memory frames the founders as good fathers and as Christians. Next, I discuss the theory of whiteness as property and social contract theory, applying the concept of inheritance to the fatherhood metaphor and then exploring its explicit connections to hegemonic masculinity and Christianity. Next, I discuss this book's methodological contribution, charting a pathway for public address criticism that is informed by critical theory and foregrounds tropes—such as metaphors—rather than a speaker-based approach. Finally, I offer a case-study example of contemporary congressional discourse, demonstrating how this discourse's fatherhood metaphor animates and reinforces the structures that naturalize the United States as a patriarchal and white-supremacist country—with Christian or "family" values. Throughout this case study, I demonstrate how the metaphor of "Founding Fathers" shapes and informs a rhetoric of sovereignty.

Remembering the "Founding Fathers"

Americans today have no true memories of the men who drafted, debated, or signed the founding documents. Yet the United States is replete with memories of the founders. They are featured in an endless array of biographies, documentary films, biopics, television mini-series, museums, archives, tourist sites, memorials, monuments, Broadway musicals, and so on. They are enshrined in school curricula and children's books. Their portraits grace US currency, and their words echo across popular culture. As such, while Americans have no true memories of these men, Americans have a collective memory of them. This collective memory informs the "Founding Fathers" metaphor, but the metaphor also informs the collective memory.

"Collective memory" is a people's agreed-upon recollection, or the common knowledge of historical events. Barbie Zelizer describes collective memory as "the recollections that are instantiated beyond the individual by and for the collective."[37] Unlike a person's individual memories that accumulate and dissipate over time, collective memory is knowledge of the past that is *created* through speeches, artwork, sculptures, monuments, elementary curricula, and so on, and filters down into tourist guides' banter and pop-culture references.

As a creation, collective memory is always chosen. For instance, those with power and authority decide what figures and events are deserving of monuments and whose faces should appear on currency; and then those figures, events, and faces enter the collective memory of the people who routinely encounter those monuments and handle that currency. Since it is chosen, collective memory is always partial, and some facts are largely omitted from collective memory. No one can "account for the entirety of the past"; they must "select and omit, emphasize and elide," making these decisions profoundly political.[38]

For instance, the history that George Washington was infertile has been omitted from collective memory.[39] Likely a complication from tuberculosis, George Washington sired no children. His spouse, Martha was clearly fertile: she celebrated four live births in eight years with her first husband. Washington adopted Martha's surviving children, Martha "Patsy" Parke Custis and John "Jacky" Parke Custis, and after Jacky's death they adopted two of his children. It is these adopted grandchildren, Eleanor and "Washy," who appear alongside George and Martha in the famous oil painting by Edward Savage, *The Washington Family* (1789–1796).[40] Remarking on how rarely historians and biographers "discuss Washington's infertility," John Amory—a medical doctor specializing in male reproduction—notes that this reticence reflects a cultural taboo, as if "infertility would diminish" Washington in Americans' minds.[41] Amory's observation makes the links among political power, fatherhood, and male fertility explicit: the lack of biological children jeopardizes Washington's role as a father, which in turn compromises his political standing. Indeed, the metaphor of fatherhood powerfully shapes Americans' collective memory of George Washington, rendering him a father despite having sired no children.

Similarly, although the founders are generally remembered as mostly having been rich men, the extent of that wealth and the rigid social hierarchies of the colonial and revolutionary eras are largely omitted from collective memory. Typically during these eras, however, one's family—and lack thereof—quite rigidly predestined one's role in society.[42] For instance, the "slave laws codified the most rigid dimensions of this inheritable social order" by denying the rights of family such that children belonged to their enslavers rather than their parents.[43] Meanwhile, the "doctrine of coverture" subsumed women's legal status into that of their husband's status; thus family fixated women's roles, first in relation to their father and then their husband.[44] Even free white men, if "lacking sufficient land, family connections, and reputations," learned "their place" in the social order.[45] Indeed, these "lesser sort," as the likes of Thomas Jefferson, James Madison, George Washington, Patrick Henry, and George Mason referred to them, encountered a "raft of laws" that reminded them of their low rank.[46] For instance, "sartorial statutes" policed their clothing, forbidding them from "wearing certain fabrics and colors."[47] Family—and the lack thereof—played a consequential role in the social hierarchy. While free white men sometimes changed rank by squandering an inheritance or making (or marrying) a fortune, the vast majority of people derived their rank and role in society from their family connections and inheritances—or the lack thereof.[48]

By forgetting the ways in which "politics and family" were "indelibly linked in the revolutionary age," Americans lose sight of the ways in which, under the colonial order, plantation patriarchs were expected to serve in governmental roles.[49] That is, the ruling fathers who oversaw the "great houses" were expected to oversee matters for the local social order.[50] This pattern continued in the founding era as these plantation patriarchs became the "Founding Fathers," shepherding "the rebellion against England," commanding the Continental Army, leading the "early continental governments," and drafting the Declaration of Independence, the Constitution, the Bill of Rights, and many of the early states' constitutions. They also dominated Congress, the federal judiciary, and the presidency during the early constitutional era.[51] Indeed, as Lorri Glover argues, these plantation patriarchs became founders because "they were fathers."[52] Their position as plantation patriarchs was predicated on fatherhood, which—in their minds—entailed the right to rule and a responsibility for "the well-being of their communities, the wealth and power of their relatives, [and] the preservation of social order and civic justice."[53] None of this history—from the doctrine of coverture, to the laws dictating what working-class white men could wear, to the importance of family and the expectation that government positions belonged to plantation patriarchs—is common knowledge. None of it is part of Americans' collective memory.

Collective memory is, then, as Carole Blair argues, an "overtly political and emotionally invested phenomenon."[54] Which is to say, power and powerful emotions are at work in deciding what a people will collectively remember—and what a people will collectively remember is emotionally resonant and politically charged for those people. Here, then, it warrants pausing to consider four key ways in which Americans collectively remember the founders.

First, the founders are collectively remembered as a united cohort. Indeed, the language within this book—"fathers," "founders," and "Founding Fathers"—mobilizes this collective memory despite noting that this unity has been superimposed upon these men. This collectively remembered unity is a foundational principle behind judicial "originalism," or "original intentionalism," wherein justices believe the founders' original intent in the Constitution can be discerned and then must be applied to contemporary cases. Famously, Supreme Court Justice Antonin Scalia held this position, as do Clarence Thomas, Neil Gorsuch, Brett Kavanaugh, and Amy Coney Barrett. Yet "intent" is hard to discern in many cases. For instance, there is no documentation of the Senate's debates regarding the First Amendment; more importantly, those who drafted the Constitution and the early congressmen and presidents had very different interpretations of the Constitution, and many of its phrases are opaque in order to satisfy competing demands during its drafting.[55]

Indeed, studying the founding era, historian David Sehat asserts that the founders "agreed to separate from Great Britain," and they "agreed after much compromise, at least some of them, on the text of the Constitution," but "beyond that, they had vast and profound differences."[56] Sehat concludes that "the founding era was, in reality, one of the most partisan periods of American history."[57] These men were deeply divided, disagreeing on the nature of the federal government and of power itself. This ideological difference generated a range of vicious schisms during the founding era that ultimately laid the groundwork for the two-party system that now dominates US politics. Yet these men are collectively remembered as a unified group: the "Founding Fathers." Here, the metaphor of "Founding Fathers" directly contributes to this collective memory. The metaphor not only succinctly groups them together, but it attributes a joint or unified fatherhood to the group as a whole. The metaphor gives Americans an easy and unified way to refer to these men while creating a shared ontology for them: "fathers."

Second, Americans collectively remember the founders as the architects of democracy. This perspective infuses not just these men but the United States itself with a grandeur of historic importance. It also ignores the history of ancient Greek democracies, fundamentally misrepresents the nature of the US federal government—which is a republic—and overestimates the founders' opinions of everyday US citizens. Unlike what is now known as direct democracy, the Constitution ensures that US citizens do not vote on federal laws nor do they decide who becomes president—those powers belong to Congress and the Electoral College, respectively. Indeed, until the Seventeenth Amendment was ratified in 1913, only the members of the House were directly elected by citizens; under the founders' design, senators were chosen by state legislatures.[58] As such, instead of a direct democracy, the Constitution creates a representative democracy in which citizens select a class of politicians who then govern on their behalf. This system of government expects citizens to vote "and then keep quiet," as James Madison summarized in a letter to Thomas Jefferson, describing the citizenry as "too much uninformed, and too inert to speak for itself."[59]

Far from advocating for a democracy in which the common person meaningfully shapes the laws of the land, the founders largely ensured that only the richest and most educated white men would have a role in US governance. Yet the metaphor of "Founding Fathers" directs attention away from differences between direct and representative democracies while directing attention toward the founders as creators. The focus is on the founders as innovators, as men who created something brand new. The metaphor directly draws upon and reinforces the collective memory of the founders as the architects of democracy.

Third, in collective memory, the founders appear to be above the fray. The early presidential speeches especially evoke a sense of dignity and magnanimity that goes beyond the charm of their now antiquated turns of phrase. Indeed, although these early politicians involved themselves in partisan politics almost from the beginning—Jefferson's election in 1800 signified a clear shift into a party system—the presidents' personas were designed to appear above the fray.[60] As Jeffrey Tulis recounts, early US politicians were deeply concerned about demagoguery, wanting to avoid a situation in which presidents answered to the people, becoming beholden to their popularity and thus reliant "on the mob's fickle and often ill-informed views."[61]

Although the early presidents occasionally skirted these "old way" norms, the tide began to change in earnest during the progressive era as William McKinley and then most significantly Theodore Roosevelt and Woodrow Wilson circumvented Congress, appealing directly to "the people" on behalf of particular bills they wanted Congress to pass.[62] This "new way" is known as the "rhetorical presidency," calling attention to the way presidents speak to "the people": they speak often, at length, and in impassioned, partisan ways. They advocate for specific policies, hoping to gather popular support for their policies so that "the people" will then pressure Congress into supporting these bills. This rhetorical presidency is now typical. Presidents are expected to have their own political agendas—proposing policies—and are expected to speak to "the people," not to Congress. As a result, the founders and early presidents indeed appear above the fray compared to the politicking of "rhetorical presidencies." Here, I suggest that the metaphor of fatherhood plays a role in heightening the collective memory of the founders' supposed dignity and magnanimity. Fatherhood is idealized as good, right, and supremely wise—and these are the associations activated in Americans' collective memory of the founders.

Finally, the founders are collectively remembered as Christians who founded a Christian nation. To be sure, the Bible is the most frequently cited work of literature in the "political rhetoric of the American founding era."[63] This is no surprise considering that the Bible was the "most accessible" text during this era.[64] Americans were so familiar with the King James scriptures that quote marks and chapter and verse citations were unnecessary in published works; politicians drew upon the Christian scriptures because this was the discourse that resonated.[65] The men collectively known as the "Founding Fathers" include both "pious" Christians such as Samuel Adams, Patrick Henry, and John Witherspoon and "skeptical" men such as Thomas Jefferson, Benjamin Franklin, and Thomas Paine. The more skeptical founders hardly "believed the Bible was god's revealed word," but as they incorporated scripture into their writing and framed their arguments through Biblical allusions and references, it wrapped their political designs in language that certainly sounds *faithful* to contemporary Christian audiences.[66]

While the collective memory of the founders as Christians fails to capture the differing beliefs these men held, it hints at what Daniel Dreisbach describes as the revolutionary connection between Protestantism and the United States' founding. Protestantism—with its vernacular scriptures—is a "liberating" movement or religious tradition, fostering both "egalitarian" and "libertarian impulses."[67] That is, Protestantism is egalitarian because its doctrines announce all believers to be equally capable of a relationship with God and equally responsible for their own souls and devotion. It is libertarian as it empowers each person to "think for themselves about the matters most vital to their consciences."[68] Of course, some founding-era Protestant doctrines (e.g., about who can be ordained, family hierarchy, and slavery) created and reinforced sexist and racist hierarchies that empower white men as pastors, fathers, and overseers. Within the founders' context, then, Protestantism deputized white men as individuals who were morally responsible for others but who answered to no one but their own conscience.

Again, I suggest that the metaphor of fatherhood plays a significant role in the collective memory of these men as Christians and their venerated place in US mythology. That is, Christian divinity is imagined as fatherhood, and US Christians routinely pray to God the Father. Moreover, God the Father is understood as the creator of both the universe and humanity. This close association of fatherhood and the Christian God provides a matrix or framework that I suggest is then transferred to the "Founding Fathers," imbuing these men with an aura of Christianity and the authority of the creator.

Together, these elements combine in US collective memory, creating a picture of the "Founding Fathers" in which they are not just unified, democratic, nonpartisan, and patriotically Christian, but practically utopian. Largely by design—and shaped by the metaphor of fatherhood—this collective memory omits many of the messy realities of the founding era. Yet it informs contemporary US politics: congresspeople routinely activate and reinforce this collective memory, using it to advance their legislative goals as they invoke the "Founding Fathers." Even as the metaphor shapes and is shaped by this collective memory, however, it operates in political discourse by turning policy debates—about which reasonable people might disagree—into purity tests, discriminating between the fathers' supposed heirs and the un-American.[69]

These purity tests are both explicitly and implicitly gendered. After all, Americans began referring to the founders as "fathers" with George

Washington, making the gendered aspect explicit. At the same time, however, gender works implicitly within this discourse. That is, the obviousness of gender is often swept under the rug through disavowals that refuse to "recognize the sexism implicit in language which does not include women."[70] Here, "fathers" is shrugged off with the same sort of logic that insists "that everyone knows 'man' includes women, that 'he' includes she," and so on.[71] Indeed, this is an analogous move to US Christian communities' insistence that masculinist language (e.g., "mankind") is gender neutral even while reviling any attempt to adopt "truly generic language" (e.g., "humanity").[72] Thus, as Helen Sterk demonstrates, "truly generic language shocks because it removes maleness as the definitional criterion for being 'generic.'"[73] Understood in this way, "fathers" is obviously masculinist, and yet because maleness is considered the norm, "Founding Fathers" largely passes for neutral in US society. As such, the founders function in US society in both overtly and implicitly gendered ways: venerated as fathers—creators of a nation—their memories and words, especially the Constitution, operate not just as the family's rule book but as its seed.

Inheritance and Social Contract Theory

To inherit something is to receive it—intact—from someone else, usually upon their death or retirement. The "thing" that is inherited need not be a tangible thing. People inherit tangible items such as land, furniture, and jewelry, semi-tangible items such as the balance in a bank account, and intangible items such as positions, titles, and intellectual property—for instance, inheriting an author's estate.

During the founding era, the ability to inherit was not enjoyed by all people. Enslaved Black people were prohibited from owning or inheriting property. Likewise, Native Americans' relationship with land was ignored and discounted to grant inheritance rights to white men. Moreover, under the doctrine of coverture, a free married woman's rights were subsumed into her husbands', and she could not own property, sign a contract, represent herself in court, or receive a salary in her name.[74]

During the colonial and early republic eras, then, inheritance was a privilege exclusively available to some citizens—white men—and it provided them a clear advantage through generational accumulation. White fathers labored with the knowledge that their efforts would help their descendants, and white sons started with a legally ensured foundation upon which they could build. The laws of inheritance—both common law and, later, the laws Congress wrote—were explicitly patriarchal and, given the way colonists and later the founders equated Blackness and enslavement, these laws of inheritance were also explicitly white supremacist.[75]

Historically, the United States has privileged white people in relation to property through the oppression of Black people and Native Americans. For Black people, this primarily involved the "seizure and appropriation" of their labor, bodies, and sexuality; for Native Americans, this primarily involved "the seizure and appropriation of land."[76] Both of these seizures and appropriations are oriented toward property and ownership—and both were "implemented by force" and then "ratified by law."[77] That is, during the United States' founding, whiteness was culturally and legally understood as including the right to own Black people and to own Native American land. Only white people were granted these rights of "possession and occupation," and this dual history—the possession of bodies and land—has fundamentally shaped "the construction of whiteness as property."[78] Here, legal scholar Cheryl I. Harris demonstrates how whiteness itself functions as property within the United States.

That is, not only have property laws favored white men (e.g., making it impossible for many white women, enslaved Black people, and Native Americans to possess land during the colonial and founding eras), but whiteness in the United States "shares the critical characteristics of property."[79] Here, "property" refers not just to "things" that can be "owned" but to a larger framework or worldview that grants persons rights in relation to things—even intangible things. That is, land is not property until someone conceives that persons have the right to possess land. Thus, property is "said to be a right, not a thing."[80] James Madison clearly understood property through this framework, defining property as encompassing "every thing to which a man may attach a value and have a right."[81] Again, this definition transforms many intangible, nonphysical things into the purview of property. Indeed, copyright and patent laws make it clear that the idea of property is about rights, not things. Conceiving of property as the relationship between persons, rights, and both tangible and intangible things, Harris demonstrates that whiteness not only provided privileges of ownership but that whiteness itself functions as property—creating a society in which white people *own* whiteness.

Demonstrating the "conceptual nucleus" that unites whiteness and property, Harris outlined four key characteristics: the "right to exclude, the right to use and enjoyment, the rights of disposition, and reputation and status property."[82] First, the right to exclude can be commonly seen in No Trespassing signs, but can also be seen in whiteness through laws such as the Naturalization Act of 1790 that limited citizenry to white people, the post–Civil War segregation and antimiscegenation laws, contemporary immigration policies, and de facto school, church, and housing segregation.

Second, the right to use and enjoy property encompasses significant terrain, including the ability to use property by putting it up as collateral. Whiteness is something that white people can use and enjoy. Whiteness provides white people with a wide range of privileges, such as consistently seeing people who look like them featured in cinema, television, and educational curricula.[83] Moreover, white people can use their whiteness as a type of collateral, leveraging their whiteness when applying for loans, encountering police officers, lodging complaints with a store manager, and so on.[84]

Third, the right of disposition refers to the right to transfer ownership—to decide who gets to inherit. Here, whiteness ensures that "those who do not fit the parameters of what it means to be white do not easily access, or inherit, whiteness and its privileges."[85] Essentially, the right of disposition ensures that whiteness remains exclusive to the people socially and legally considered white. In prior years, this was violently enforced through slave laws that reversed the "usual common law presumption that the status of the child was determined by the father," so that—as those laws put it—when "children got by an Englishman upon a Negro woman" were born, the children's status as slave or free was "according to the condition of the mother."[86] These slave laws demonstrate the right of disposition, the right to determine who can inherit whiteness and its privileges. This right of disposition was later enforced through anti-miscegenation laws and continues to be enforced through lynching and—less overtly—through inequities in education, immigration policies, incarceration, and voting rights that ensure the privileges of whiteness are not shared with those racialized as other.

Indeed, the right of disposition draws attention to race as a "virtually pure construct, with none but the most superficial biological stratum."[87] That is to say, "races" exist because societies imagine them and organize social, economic, and legal structures of exclusion. The laws defining the children of enslaved Black women as both Black and enslaved are clear examples of how race is constructed, as are the so-called one-drop rules and the later anti-miscegenation laws. To be clear, then, when I refer to race throughout this book (e.g., "white" men), I refer to historically, socially, and rhetorically created racial identities, not supposedly "natural" categories. Moreover, I work throughout this book to attend to the ways in which racism racializes bodies: racism makes certain types of difference consequential, and racism imagines race as a natural category.

Finally, the right to reputation and status refers to the ability of property to confer a reputation or status upon the owner, and for the owner to trade based on that reputation. For example, a business mogul's reputation for owning several real-estate properties often makes it easier to generate start-up funds for a new enterprise—even enterprises outside of real estate. John Locke theorized each man's own self as property, stating that "every man has a 'property' in his own 'person,'" and this thinking undergirds the idea of reputation as property—which directly informs the way slander, libel, and defamation laws are written.[88] Here, not only do individuals own their own reputations, but whiteness itself is a reputation that is owned and that confers status: to be "seen as white is to be seen as a whole person that has value to the nation."[89]

During the founding era, the patriarchy and white supremacy that infused the legalities of inheritance also shaped the concept of sovereignty. That is, not everyone was part of "we the people." Not everyone was considered to have been born with inalienable rights or to be free enough to freely enter a social contract as imagined by Enlightenment thinkers such as John Locke. Indeed, not all people were considered people. Only free white men were involved in the US social contract—only they counted as rational subjects with rights and freedoms who could self-govern, manage property (including land seized from Native Americans and enslaved Black people), and, as the Constitution puts it, "ordain and establish" their own sovereign governance.[90]

In some ways, the exclusionary nature of the founding era's social contract theory was undone by social movements (e.g., abolition, women's suffrage, the Civil Rights Movement, Women's Liberation Movement, and so on) that culminated in constitutional amendments and sweeping congressional legislation. For instance, the Thirteenth Amendment abolished slavery; the Fourteenth Amendment extended citizenship to women and Black people; the Fifteenth Amendment established that the right to vote will not be denied by race; and the Nineteenth Amendment allowed women to vote. Similarly, the Civil Rights Act of 1964 and the Voting Rights Act of 1965 together prohibited discrimination in public spaces such as schools, swimming pools, and libraries as well as in businesses such as restaurants and hotels. The acts also banned discrimination in employment and outlawed the policies, such as literacy tests and poll taxes, that disenfranchised Black people.

As social contract theorists like Carole Pateman and Charles W. Mills explain, however, the original exclusions were designed around biological assumptions.[91] That is, most Western Europeans and American colonists believed white men had biological capacities—such as intelligence, rationality, and so on—that women and people of color did not.[92] It was on this assumption of biological capacity that white men derived the theories of their own political rights—which included the right to dominate white women by containing them to the so-called private sphere, and to dominate people of color through the control of their labor, reproduction, and land. As Pateman and Mills argue, because the original political inequities were built on deeply ingrained patriarchal and white-supremacist assumptions of biological capacity—of personhood—undoing such inequity is not as easy as writing new laws.[93]

If it were, the constitutional amendments and civil-rights legislation would have eradicated sexism and racism in the United States. Instead, both patriarchy and white supremacy continue to shape the United States, as seen in pay gaps, unequal divisions of household labor, global industries rooted in sweated labor, police brutality against people of color, incarceration practices, immigration policies, de facto school, church, and housing segregation, voting discrimination, and so on.[94] Essentially, as social contract theorists demonstrate, US sovereignty is tied to concepts of personhood, and personhood remains informed by the intertwined logics of patriarchy and white supremacy, creating a sovereign territory in which freedom seemingly inheres more in some than others.[95]

Indeed, detailing the historic injustices enacted against enslaved Black women, Hortense J. Spillers traces these relations among property, inheritance, racism and sexism, political subjectivity, sovereignty, and the social contract to a "symbolic order" that she describes as an "American grammar."[96] Grammar is a language's rules that dictate how its symbols and entities interact and relate to one another. As such, Spillers identifies sexist racism (or racist sexism) as the foundational rule of relations in the United States—sexist racism is "America's grammar book," dictating who is human (a noun or subject) and who is not.[97] Spillers outlines this grammar's rules, noting the ways in which the rights—and lack thereof—of political subjectivity, property, sovereignty, family, and inheritance are derived through racism and sexism.

For instance, responding to Daniel Patrick Moynihan's infamous "report" accusing African American families of "fatherlessness" and "matriarchy," Spillers explores how enslaved Black women were denied the "rights" of family, explicitly linking forced reproduction and

Introduction   23

the disruption of family to property and inheritance.[98] As Spillers notes, the legalities of family, or "kinship," in the United States involve "property" such that "offspring" *belong* "to a mother and father," and male offspring can inherit the father's estate.[99] If Black enslaved people were understood to have kin—to be families—this would "undermine" the "property relations" in which enslavers benefited from Black women's exploited reproduction. That is, if Black enslaved people were allowed to have "kin," children would *belong* to their parents rather than belonging to a white enslaver. Moreover, if Black enslaved people were allowed to have "kin," the enslaved sons of white men could have made familial claims of inheritance.

Here again, Spillers emphasizes how sexism and racism bind together family, property, sovereignty, and inheritance in "America's grammar book," where "family" is mythically imagined and celebrated as "the *vertical* transfer of a bloodline, of a patronymic, of titles and entitlements, of real estate and the prerogatives of 'cold cash,' from *fathers* to *sons* and in the supposedly free exchange of affectional ties between a male and a female of *his* choice."[100] The rights of property and inheritance are reserved for "families," and only the "free and freed" could attain them.[101] The point cannot be overstated: in Western conceptualizations, "family" is a prerequisite for "human"; everyone is someone's child—even if orphaned. The denial of "family" for enslaved Black people was a denial of personhood, and therefore a denial of the rights of property, inheritance, and sovereignty that accrued to persons—who again, were perceived most fully as propertied and male.

Indeed, by juxtaposing the "nature" of free white men and enslaved Black people, free white men conceptualized themselves as individuals who could *possess*, welding individualism and possession together. As Saidiya V. Hartman demonstrated, the "invocation of rights" and the justifications of "freedom and liberty" are at play in the basest enactments of "violence and domination."[102] Enacting sexist or racist domination has become the hallmark of what it means to be human—where "human" is tacitly understood as white and masculine. Again, this is not a flaw that can be easily corrected by new legislation. Indeed, Hartman traces the effects of such new legislation during the Reconstruction era, noting that "benevolent correctives and declarations of slave humanity" only "intensified the brutal exercise of power upon the captive body rather than ameliorating the chattel condition."[103] Reconstruction failed not only because of poor legislation and "flagging commitments to black rights" but also because of US conceptualizations of personhood and sovereignty, such that "emancipation" was less a "grand event of liberation" and more a "point of transition between modes of servitude and racial subjection," as the "whip" was replaced by the "compulsory contract."[104]

These subordinations, embedded in what it means to be an individual, a human, and a citizen, continue to operate in the United States, shaping pay gaps, de facto segregation, inequalities in household labor, gendered and racial inequalities in local, state, and federal representation, and so on. These subordinations continue to affect the very conceptualization of US sovereignty. Democratic sovereignty—rightful authority over terrain—is dependent on the will or consent of the governed. Sovereignty is derived from "the people." Who gets to constitute "the people," then, is of the utmost importance to US sovereignty. By tracing the metaphor of "Founding Fathers" throughout congressional discourse, this book examines the rhetoric of sovereignty, demonstrating how US politics wields the concepts of family, property, and inheritance in ways that delimit "the people."

Property, inheritance, possession, and the imagined social contract are important to this research not because people of color and women are still legally prohibited from inheriting property or voting, but because congresspeople routinely use the metaphor of fatherhood in such a way that the United States becomes the property of whiteness and patriarchy. Indeed, this metaphor imagines the United States as bequeathed by the "Founding Fathers" and thus inherited by their descendants—their families.

Whiteness, Masculinity, and Family Values

Within the contexts of the US social contract and whiteness as property—both of which are tied to ideas of family—it is worth exploring the resonances of hegemonic masculinity and Christian or "family" values. In the United States, hegemonic masculinity links "male identity" with five specific "traits," elevating those traits "above other stereotypical gender or sexuality traits."[105] Essentially, idealized manhood in the United States embodies: (1) physical force and control; (2) occupational achievement; (3) familial patriarchy; (4) frontiersmanship; and (5) heterosexuality.[106] The extent to which a man embodies these traits—even if he cannot achieve mastery of all five—affects his social and often legal standing. Meanwhile, the extent to which women support, compliment, and reward men's displays of these traits affects their place in the hierarchy. Notably, the traits of physical force and control, familial patriarchy, and frontiersmanship overlap with property: to a large extent, to exert physical control is to *own* one's self, the space, or land around oneself, and—potentially—to enact ownership over others; embodying familial patriarchy renders one's family as one's domain, and—more directly—fathering children ensures the workings of inheritance; and frontiersmanship is the enactment of white ownership—an embodiment of the spirit of conquest and survivalism modeled in the US invasion and ongoing settlement of Indigenous lands.[107]

Hegemonic masculinity has a history: its traits were shaped and developed through cultural processes. And here, there is a specific confluence between US Christianity and hegemonic masculinity. Victorian ideals for devout men in the 1800s involved gentility and restraint; however, Christianity became more "muscular" as the progressive era unfolded and white men across the country turned to displays of athleticism and virility to assert their superiority over Black and immigrant men who could now (legally) vote, own property, run for office, earn wages, and enjoy other privileges that had largely been the exclusive property of white men.[108] Perhaps no figure better exemplifies this shift from white gentility to white frontiersman than Theodore Roosevelt, who went from being teased as the "exquisite Mr. Roosevelt" to being known for his rugged, cowboy-esque demeanor—which he used to advocate for imperialism.[109] Christian evangelists such as Billy Sunday used this rugged masculinity to appeal to white men, calling them back into Christian devotion. Here, women were typically blamed for having driven men out of the church by feminizing it with their soft "womanly virtues."[110] As Kristin Kobes Du Mez notes, by the 1950s John Wayne had become the ultimate role model within this "burgeoning evangelical culture."[111] This is curious since John Wayne had no "born-again experience" and was known for drinking and adultery.[112] As such, the "affinity" between Christians and John Wayne was born not of theology but rather "a shared masculine ideal."[113]

The 1970s saw an explosion in Christian politics that—trading on an unspoken assumption of whiteness as property—comingled whiteness, nationalism, and Christian culture in the United States. Paul Weyrich and Jerry Falwell, who cofounded the Moral Majority, whipped up momentum for their movement, galvanizing white Christians by framing Bob Jones University, a white Christian institution, losing its "tax-exempt status" after refusing to retract its racially discriminatory policies as an attack on religious liberty.[114] Calling the white church to arms, Falwell preached that "the idea that religion and politics don't mix was invented by the devil to keep Christians from running their own country."[115] Falwell's statement conflates whiteness and national ownership: assuming that Christians are white and that the United States is "our" country.[116] His assumptions and activism echoed the logic of early colonists, intertwining whiteness, Christianity, and property. For instance, the Colony of Virginia legally determined that no Black enslaved people could be Christian, making Christianity the exclusive property of whiteness during the founding era.[117]

Within this framework, however, those called to "run their country" are not just white Christians, but white Christian *men*. Indeed, US Christians are among the most ardent supporters of patriarchal family structures.[118] Weaving together whiteness and hegemonic masculinity's core trait of "familial patriarchy," Christian communities routinely tout "family" values. In direct response to feminist activism in the 1970s, evangelical leaders such as John Piper and Wayne Grudem worked during the 1980s to establish men's "unique leadership role," founding the Council on Biblical Manhood and Womanhood and drafting the Danvers Statement in 1987. The Danvers Statement codified a doctrine now known as Complementarianism—a term coined in 1988 to summarize the Danvers Statement.[119] Complementarian doctrine asserts that men are divinely appointed leaders, exclusively qualified for authority in the church and the home—and by logical extension, everywhere else as well.[120] Women, meanwhile, are imagined as divinely created for submission and nurturance. This perspective makes the nuclear family—headed by a strong heterosexual father—of paramount importance.

The Christian discourse of "family" values, then, developed out of patriarchy and white supremacy. It builds upon the historic "one-drop" laws that insisted on the "purity" of the "white race" and the legal denial of marriage and family to enslaved Black people, even as it works to control white women's procreation in the contemporary era.[121] Indeed, the links among male domination, white supremacy, and Christianity are well established in the decades-long Christian political campaigns to prevent comprehensive sex education and to overturn *Roe v. Wade*—an accomplishment that will be felt most painfully among poor communities and communities of color, and that will likely reverse the declining birth rate among white women.[122]

To put it bluntly, patriarchy, white supremacy, and Christianity have collaborated in US politics, constructing a system of ownership wherein white men own—or seemingly ought to own—both their country and their families. Here, again, the principle of inheritance comes into play. One of the defining features of ownership is the right to disposition: the right to transfer ownership from one generation to the next. Drawing on the understanding of whiteness as property and its reinforcing pillars of patriarchy and Christian "family" values, this book examines the ways in which the United States is rendered as an inheritance through the metaphor of fatherhood in congressional discourse.

Analyzing invocations of the "Founding Fathers" within the *Congressional Record*, I attend to its Christian appeals through the framework of Christian nationalism—drawing attention to this rhetoric's ideological impact—rather than attending to religiosity per se. That is, first, it is beyond my capacity to assess the sincerity of a congressperson's religious assertions. Second, as the above account demonstrates, there is more than religiosity at play in Christian political activism such as the Moral Majority. Christian nationalism, as sociologists of religion Andrew L. Whitehead and Samuel L. Perry describe it, is an ideological and political framework that mobilizes voters' fear of moral decline while suggesting that "Christian values should inform public policy."[123] Christian nationalism, then, typically intertwines hegemonic masculinity, traditional gender roles, opposition to abortion rights, anti-LGBTQ+ activism, and white-supremacist norms under the banner of "family-friendly" and conservative values. Moreover, Christian nationalism often frames its policies as "restoring" the United States to its original "Christian" values.[124]

Essentially, when discussing congressional Christian appeals throughout this book, I want to be especially precise—not the least because I typically identify as an evangelical Christian. But more broadly, precision is important because Christian religiosity and Christian nationalism are overlapping realms: some Christians are also Christian nationalists and vice versa, but other Christians want nothing to do with Christian nationalism—and some Christian nationalists are deists, agnostics, atheists, spiritualists, or the like who want very little to do with Christianity.[125] As such, in this book I track Christian nationalism as the confluence of Christian symbolism, appeals to Christian morality, hegemonic masculinity, patriarchy, and white supremacy—especially as it engages in the rhetoric of restoration and inheritance within the *Congressional Record*.

A Critical Approach to Public Address Scholarship

Before turning to a case study of how the logic of inheritance operates within congressional discourse and enacts a rhetoric of sovereignty, I want to pause for a brief discussion of three methodological contributions I make throughout this book.

In this book I trace the metaphor or trope of fatherhood *across* congressional discourse. In so doing, I model an approach to rhetorical criticism and public address scholarship that accounts for meaning and agency within diffuse, fragmented, layered, and multi-voiced discourses—such as congressional discourse. Rather than locating meaning and agency in a single politician's genius or even within a single rhetorical act, my first contribution is to model an approach that highlights the agency of tropes themselves—of how a metaphor, or such, saturates a discourse community, structuring and organizing thought.

Focusing on the trope of the "Founding Fathers," I analyze hundreds of congressional speeches in this book. Many of these speeches were only sound bites, but some lasted hours. Sometimes the metaphor of "Founding Fathers" suffused the entirety of a speech—as it does in this chapter's case study—but often the "Founding Fathers" were invoked only for a specific point within longer speeches. Rather than narrowing my analytical focus by speaker or policy topic, I have narrowed it by focusing on the trope itself: analyzing when, how, and to what effect this trope is deployed within congressional politics. As such, this book presents a methodological approach that foregrounds how a trope functions within a discourse community. I attend to the work the trope does—within the context of speakers, political parties, policy debates, and ideologies—but the trope rather than any given speech or speaker takes center stage.

To be sure, humans have (limited) agency, and the rhetorical tradition of studying rhetors rightly recognizes the ways in which humans harness the available means of persuasion to affect or attempt to affect change in their communities. Yet at the same time, some of those available means of persuasion are pre-existing tropes within discourse communities. Tropes, especially metaphors, come with built-in connotations, logics, ideologies, and assumptions. Essentially, when a discourse community relies on a trope so frequently and so consistently, it warrants discovering how the trope itself functions. As such, this book's first methodological contribution is modeling an approach that helps critics understand how deeply embedded tropes—some might even call them ideographs—function within a discourse community.

Second, this book models a methodology that is well suited to studying public address that is fragmented, layered, and multi-voiced—and public address is fragmented, layered, and multi-voiced in the United States. For instance, outside my research, I cannot recall the last time I watched, heard, or read a political speech in its entirety. I routinely watch, hear, and read sound bites and fragments from political speeches, however, through social media, news outlets, and micro-video platforms. Usually, I interact with these fragmented speeches in layered and multi-voiced ways—I watch several short clips on YouTube in a single sitting or watch a compilation of opposing viewpoints on a given policy issue. While anecdotal, my example is telling. Indeed, as Megan Foley recounts, even the length of sound bites in "presidential election news coverage" has dropped from approximately forty-three seconds in the 1960s to between seven and nine seconds in the contemporary moment.[126] Political oratory, which is the "traditional object of public address scholarship," has been "squeezed" into ever smaller "sonic segments," leading to some considerable hand-wringing among academics.[127] As Foley argues, however, shorter does not mean less important: public address "has not been dissolved but instead condensed."[128] That is, political rhetoric has adapted to news outlets' and social-media platforms' systems of truncation, repackaging, and recirculation. Politicians prepare sound bites and "viral" moments within their speeches such that "campaigns can plan their whole day around which snappy one-liners" will go viral.[129]

Focusing on the trope of the "Founding Fathers," this book models an approach that works with the largely fragmented, diffuse, and multi-voiced nature of contemporary public address rather than against it. In the case study below, I offer an analysis of a representative speech, setting the scene with a close reading of the metaphorical clusters, themes, and rhetorical techniques that animate the metaphor of fatherhood within contemporary congressional discourse. In the subsequent chapters, however, I move from fragment to fragment and speaker to speaker as they invoke the "Founding Fathers," demonstrating how this metaphor functions within congressional politics.

In many ways, congressional rhetoric is an ideal site for this methodological approach: much of its rhetoric is already fragmented. It is fairly common for representatives to be given only one minute of time in which to make their statements in the House, rendering their statements already more sound bite than speech. In the Senate, such draconian time restrictions are not an issue, but senators—especially the majority and minority leaders—often present omnibus-style speeches. These are speeches that move from policy to policy and topic to topic, holding forth on one matter and then another. These are less speeches than compilations of several short speeches—and it is not uncommon for senators to largely repeat themselves day after day.

However much scholars might bemoan the fragmentation of our culture, both politicians and citizens assemble meaning from scraps and fragments—from sound bites and clips—and this book models an approach that works within the fragmentary nature of public address. Indeed, only by tracing the ways in which the "Founding Fathers" are invoked *across* congressional discourse does the full impact of this rhetoric take shape. That is, the rhetoric of sovereignty at play within these invocations is clearest when seen en masse.

Third, this book models a critical approach to public address scholarship that centers a critique of sexism and racism within its analysis. Here, I join a burgeoning cohort of scholars such as Ersula Ore, Paul E. Johnson, Michael Lee, and Jarrod Atchison in working to demonstrate how political rhetoric so often relies on myths, assumptions, and collective memory—many of which are sexist and racist.[130] This book specifically problematizes the narrative of American exceptionalism at work within the appeals to the "Founding Fathers." In so doing, I model a healthy skepticism, demonstrating one way to grapple with the hegemonic metaphors that organize US political discourse—even when those metaphors, like "Founding Fathers," are so pervasive and commonplace they can be easily mistaken for benign. Ultimately, this book models an approach to public address criticism that is informed by critical theory, foregrounds tropes such as metaphors, and works across fragmentary discourses.

The Congressional Discourse of Inheritance: A Case Study

The House and Senate chambers are governed by clear rules and strict norms of decorum. Even when bitingly condescending, congresspeople respect their time limits, use one another's proper titles, and address their remarks not to one another or the US public but to their chamber's presiding figure—the Speaker of the House or the president of the Senate. The vice president of the United States is the president of the Senate but presides over it in name only, typically appointing the most senior majority party member as the president pro tempore.[131] The Speaker of the House, meanwhile, wields considerable authority as both the "leader of the majority party and the chamber's presiding officer."[132] Presiding over a much larger body, the Speaker enacts much stricter control, and the House chamber follows well-defined "practices of recognition" and "precedence" in determining who can speak and in what order.[133]

As such, when Representative Barry Loudermilk (R-GA) rose to address the House on June 18, 2015, he spoke with considerable authority as the House majority leader's official designee. Indeed, he was granted a full sixty minutes.[134] Speaking at the beginning of the 2016 campaign season—during which he and nearly every other House member were campaigning for re-election—Loudermilk offered a speech about the nature of US governance titled "Our Documents of Freedom."

This speech presents a tour de force of the clusters, themes, and rhetoric that animate the metaphor of fatherhood within contemporary congressional discourse. Analyzing Loudermilk's "Our Documents of Freedom," then, I offer a sort of case study demonstrating how the metaphor of fatherhood (1) constructs us-other binaries between the "real" America and the un-American; (2) frames this real America as exceptional; (3) imagines a possessive relationship in which the fathers belong to "us" and "we" to them; (4) uses material appeals to frame this exceptional America as "real"; and (5) assumes that this real America is *inherited* by real Americans—the "us." Together, these appeals constitute a rhetoric of sovereignty, establishing both what it means to govern in the name of "the people" and who can be "the people."

These appeals are not unique to either this speech or Loudermilk's discourse—although Loudermilk is especially effective at deploying these appeals. Instead, these appeals will appear throughout the rest of this book because they appear throughout the vast majority of congressional discourse. By foregrounding these appeals in this introductory chapter, I hope to offer a coherent summary or overview before turning in the subsequent chapters to address how these appeals function when congresspeople champion "rights and liberties," commemorate the United States, call for "checks and balances," and appeal to bipartisanship.

Elected in 2014 to represent Georgia's Eleventh Congressional District, which includes Atlanta's northern suburbs, Representative Barry Loudermilk (R-GA) ostensibly began his part of the 2016 election cycle with "Our Documents of Freedom." Speaking just days after Trump had announced his presidential candidacy, Loudermilk began by acknowledging that congresspeople typically "come before this body" to "recognize someone" from their district or to "speak about a bill," a "piece of policy," or "an issue."[135] Befitting a new campaign cycle, however, Loudermilk's purpose was different. Thus, he stated that his sole agenda was to remind "those of us who are here of why we are here."[136] Situating his speech as explicitly about the nature of US governance, Loudermilk framed his speech by asking two related questions: "Why do we attend sessions here in this body day in and day out? What is the purpose for our being here?"

Having thus begun, Representative Loudermilk immediately interrupted himself, stating, "Before I begin remarks, Mr. Speaker, I would like to personally extend my thoughts and prayers on behalf of myself and my family, as well as those in the Eleventh Congressional District in Georgia, to those victims of the horrific attack that happened last evening in Charleston, South Carolina."[137] This opens an eight-sentence sequence in which Representative Loudermilk recognizes the immediate context of his speech: the day before, Dylann

Roof murdered nine African Americans, wounding many others, at the Emanuel African Methodist Episcopal Church in Charleston, South Carolina. Loudermilk, however, does not name the Black church that was targeted, does not name Dylann Roof as a white supremacist despite Roof's manifesto—which was already widely circulating—and Loudermilk does not mention that the victims were racially targeted.

Instead, after offering "thoughts and prayers," Representative Loudermilk pivots to cite his own authority, stating, "I am a member of the Committee on Homeland Security"; continuing, he states that he spends "a lot of time studying terrorism and the terrorist attacks against this nation."[138] With his ethos thus established, Loudermilk here equivocates from the Emanuel African Methodist Episcopal Church and Black victims more broadly to the *nation*, implying that this was a terrorist attack against the nation as opposed to an attack by a white nationalist against a Black church. Loudermilk then generalizes about terrorism, arguing that the "consistent" thing about "terrorist attacks" is that terrorists do not know who we are, what our names are, who our families are, or what we believe.[139] Here, Loudermilk shifts away from the specific oppressions, violence, and terrorism visited upon Black people and people of color because of racism. Instead, he substitutes "we" in the place of the victims and "this nation" instead of Black communities and communities of color. Ignoring the violence of racism, Loudermilk posits an us-other reality in which terrorists attack *us*—the nation.

This shift is completed as Loudermilk describes a failed attack during the prior month in Garland, Texas. Two gunmen, one of whom had tweeted he had ties to ISIS, attempted to ambush an event center featuring "controversial cartoons of the Muslim Prophet Mohammed."[140] The gunmen injured one security guard before they were killed by police officers.[141] Describing this attack, Loudermilk argues that terrorism is an attack on "freedom," specifying that "in Garland, Texas, it was an attack on the First Amendment, our freedom of speech."[142] Having framed terrorism as an attack on freedom, Loudermilk circles back around to Charleston and invokes the "Founding

Fathers." He states, "Last night it was an attack on the most fundamental right that *our* Founding Fathers *gave to us*, and that is *our* freedom of religion, a right that, as they said, was *given to us* by God and cannot be taken away."[143] Here, Loudermilk characterizes freedom as a material thing, a gift that was *given* to Americans by both the "Founding Fathers" and by God.

Moreover, just as Loudermilk used the first-person plural pronoun "we" to shift focus from Black experiences of racism to a universalized—white—experience, he also uses the first-person plural possessive pronoun "our" when referring to the "Founding Fathers." The phrase "our Founding Fathers" not only maintains the us-other dichotomy but marks a possessive relationship in which "we" have the founders. The "Founding Fathers" belong to us: they are *our* fathers, and "we" are the United States. Similarly, Loudermilk used this plural possessive pronoun to describe "*our* freedom of religion," and his speech's title, "*Our* Documents of Freedom," also reinscribes this sense of ownership.[144]

This opening interlude folds Black people—the victims of the Charleston attack—into the "us" by erasing Blackness. Loudermilk never acknowledges the racism that motivated this attack or the oppressions and violence Black communities and communities of color experience. Loudermilk likens this attack to the attack against the Garland event center. Indeed, Loudermilk sweeps the obviousness of the racist attack under the rug by reframing Dylann Roof's white-supremacist violence as an attack on freedom of religion. While Loudermilk recognizes Roof's violence as terrorism, he simultaneously ignores the racist nature of white-supremacist terrorism and the way it targets Black people and people of color.

Moreover, Loudermilk uses the attack to further his agenda: the rest of the speech focuses on a governance of freedom. This freedom agenda is, however, clearly a white agenda. There is no consideration of Black freedom in Loudermilk's speech—no consideration of what it would take for Black parishioners to worship in peace and safety in the United States. Instead, Loudermilk acknowledges only that violence was committed in Charleston and then uses that violence as a symbol to suggest that the "Founding Fathers'" vision is in jeopardy—that the United States and freedom are under attack. Here, Black people participate in the national "us" only by ignoring racism—ignoring the needs and oppressions created by the violence of white supremacy—and Black people's pain is invoked only to further an argument for (white) US freedom.

Indeed, as Representative Loudermilk turns to his prepared remarks, he deploys exceptionalism, ascribing a sense of grandeur to the founders and the Congress they designed. He states, "As I walk down the Halls of this building and I point out the statue of Thomas Jefferson that we have right outside the Chamber, or even as I stand here, the image of Moses is looking at me as he is looking over the Chamber, as I see the statues of *our* Founding Fathers, they have left us reminders of why we are here."[145] Again deploying possessive pronouns, Loudermilk fuses together the founders and religious icons as he describes the "statue of Thomas Jefferson" and the "image of Moses" presiding over the House chamber. Seemingly, Loudermilk stands in their shadow, and his authority is blessed by their oversight: they have "left us reminders of why we are here." Moreover, the sense of grandeur in this sequence enshrines Congress—and the nation more broadly—as an exceptional nation, a nation blessed by God and by the "Founding Fathers." Loudermilk's appeals here are also material: he is pointing to a statue of Thomas Jefferson and a marble relief of Moses that is directly across from the rostrum in the House chamber.[146] This forms a material appeal: he is pointing to *real* things even as he claims the founders "left" something to remind us of "why we are here."

Loudermilk then explains that his speech will offer "two phrases that you can find in Washington, DC, that remind us not only of why we are here, but what it takes to *preserve* the freedom that we have been *given*."[147] Freedom, again, is a gift from the founders. A gift that we are beholden to "preserve."[148]

To aid us in preserving this gift, Loudermilk introduces the first phrase, calling attention to its materiality as he notes that the words "In God We Trust" are inscribed above the Speaker's rostrum in the House's chamber. While Loudermilk does not directly say that the founders were responsible for the inscription, he strongly implies it—noting that this phrase "goes back" to the Declaration of Independence.[149]

Loudermilk expands upon this first phrase, "In God We Trust," by offering a geographically marked interlude that again evokes a sense of grandeur and American exceptionalism. He describes walking through the Mall to the National Archives and then finding in that building "the most hallowed of all of our documents": the Constitution, the Bill of Rights, and the Declaration of Independence.[150] The geography and material markers throughout this speech create a fusion of Americana and reality.

That is, there is a very palpable sense of *reality* in this speech: Loudermilk takes his audience on a geographical tour through the capital and draws their attention to statues, buildings, and words etched in stone and written on parchment. At the same time, the reality—or materiality—he draws attention to celebrates the United States by seemingly glorifying its founding. In actuality, these material items were created over the better part of two centuries; for instance, the phrase "In God We Trust" was etched into the House chamber in 1962 as a Cold War–era rebuke to the Soviet Union. Regardless, Loudermilk frames these items as pertaining to the US founding and foregrounds the "Founding Fathers" as instituting this reality.

Having mentioned the Declaration of Independence, Loudermilk pauses to explain that "in that Declaration, our Founding Fathers expressed" their "vision," their "faith," and their "philosophy about this new Nation."[151] Again, Loudermilk fuses Christianity and the founders, collapsing their "vision" and "philosophy" into their "faith" and vice versa. He argues that this vision-faith-philosophy was "revolutionary" because for the "first time in the history of mankind" a "government existed with emphasis on the freedom of [the] individual, empowering the individual."[152] Loudermilk continues by doubling down on this sense of exceptionalism, contrasting the founders' government with "every other government on the face of the Earth," claiming that all the rest focused their attention "upon a group" or "collective" by using "their race or their religion or aristocracy or their family line" as delineating factors.[153] In contrast, according to Loudermilk, "our Founding Fathers sensed something different," believing that "if we [the founders/government] empower the individual, if we recognize the rights that God has given them [individuals] and we give them the freedom to excel and exceed, then our Nation, as a whole, would excel."[154]

In this passage, Loudermilk first frames humanity in masculine terms, stating that the United States was revolutionary in the "history of *mankind*," and then directly ignores the whiteness that explicitly and legally delineated the nation—which he possessively refers to as "*our* nation." That is, while Loudermilk claims that "our Founding Fathers" gave freedom to the individual and empowered the individual, the government created by the founders gave freedom and empowerment only to individual white men. Perhaps for Loudermilk—a white man—there is no incongruity with representing the raced and sexed diversity of actual individual Americans with the universalized white male who operates as the "we" throughout this speech and is the recipient of "*our* Founding Fathers'" gifts of freedom. Yet not only is it impossible for white men to represent all of humanity, it is also fundamentally dishonest to imply that the founders designed a country that only saw individuals—not race, sex, class, or family.

Next, Loudermilk extols George Washington and the "ragtag rabble of Washington's soldiers" for prevailing against "the most powerful military force in the history of the world."[155] He circles back, reinforcing the importance of his first phrase, "In God We Trust," by arguing that "Washington's soldiers" prevailed because they identified the importance of the words etched "in marble above the rostrum . . . In God We Trust" as essential to their success.[156] He then claims that the phrase "In God We Trust" reflects the spirit in which "our Founding Fathers wrote" the closing words of the Declaration of Independence, which he quotes in full, saying, "And for the support of this Declaration, with a firm Reliance on the Protection of divine Providence, we mutually pledge to each other our Lives, our Fortunes, and our sacred Honor."[157] This again fuses the founders and

Introduction   39

Christianity, suggesting that Washington and "Washington's soldiers" owed their military success to their trust in God and God's "divine Providence."[158] Here, Loudermilk not only reinforces the sense of American exceptionalism—a "ragtag rabble" won against the "most powerful military force in the history of the world"—but frames this success as proof of God's particular blessing upon the United States.

Loudermilk then moves to the second phrase he claims the founders identified as crucial for Americans "to preserve the freedom that we have been given."[159] Again, noting the physicality of these words, Loudermilk identifies his second phrase as the words displayed on the exterior of the National Archives, "Eternal vigilance is the price of freedom."[160] Having just quoted from the Declaration, he links this phrase to it, arguing that freedom is a sacred honor that demands the pledge of our very lives in a commitment of eternal vigilance. Ironically, Representative Loudermilk misquotes this second phrase, which is one of several inscriptions on the exterior of the National Archives. This quote is inscribed beneath a statue known as *Guardianship*. The statue, created by James Earle Fraser, depicts a muscular man holding a centurion-style helmet and sword, and the inscription reads, "Eternal vigilance is the price of liberty," not "freedom."[161]

Even more ironically, although Loudermilk ties both phrases, "In God We Trust" and "Eternal vigilance is the price of freedom [liberty]," to the founders, neither originated with them. As already noted, "In God We Trust" was added to the House chamber in 1962, and the *Guardianship* statue and its inscription were added to the National Archives' entryway during 1934–1935. The phrase "Eternal vigilance is the price of liberty" is often spuriously associated with Thomas Jefferson, but there is "no evidence" that "Thomas Jefferson ever said or wrote" those words.[162]

Given the ways in which collective memory frames the founders as Christians, however, it comes as no surprise that Representative Loudermilk connects the explicitly religious phrase "In God We Trust" to the founders and that he uses the deistic clause in the Declaration's conclusion, "the Protection of *divine Providence*," to baptize his second phrase while connecting it to the founders.[163] Yet in both instances, Loudermilk reads Christian sentiment retroactively onto the founders even as he attributes their military success against the British to their Christian faith—in God they trusted.

Moreover, within this framework, US freedom was achieved through the Christian faith—and thus can only be preserved through Christianity: in God we trust. As such, although Loudermilk had previously extolled "freedom of religion" as the "most fundamental right that our Founding Fathers gave to us," there is a tautology operating within this logic wherein the Christian faith both originally granted this freedom of religion and preserves this freedom of religion.[164] Thus "freedom of religion" is a hallmark of the United States based on the prerequisite that the United States is a Christian nation.

Finally, Loudermilk moves into his conclusion by telling a story about visiting the beaches of Normandy and collecting some of its sand in a bottle. He makes a direct biological link, bolstering his right to take this French sand by stating that "my dad was in World War II and served in that theater."[165] Reflecting on his bottled sand, he notes that it "absorbed the blood of American patriots," and thus at a forensic or biological level it holds those soldiers' DNA.[166] He then makes the metaphorical leap to claim that the sand holds "not just [the] DNA of the soldiers, but the DNA of our entire nation."[167] Here, Loudermilk exclaims—quoting the preamble to the Declaration of Independence—that the blood-absorbing, DNA-infused sand testifies, "We hold these truths to be self-evident, that all men are created equal and they are endowed by their Creator with certain inalienable rights; that amongst these are life, liberty, and the pursuit of happiness; that to ensure these rights, governments are instituted among men, deriving their just powers from the consent of the governed."[168]

The materiality in this speech—its statues, buildings, etched marble, and bloodied sand—foregrounds the logic of inheritance. Like an heirloom or a parcel of land, US freedom is passed down from the fathers to the sons. To close, Loudermilk calls upon his congressional colleagues, asking them to "reflect on why we are here" and reminding them that their duty is "to preserve freedom."[169] Representative Loudermilk then closes his speech, fulfilling the norms of the House by yielding back the balance of his time.

Throughout this speech Loudermilk focuses on what we must do to "preserve the freedom that we have been given," directly tying freedom to the "Founding Fathers": they designed US freedom and then left it as a gift for "us."[170] Freedom is an inheritance—a gift handed down from the "Founding Fathers." Yet as this speech makes clear, Loudermilk's "us" does not encompass every American. Instead, its appeals situate white men with Christian-nationalist worldviews as the "Founding Fathers'" descendants: they function as the universalized "us" and "we" pronouns that mark this speech. Indeed, considering how this speech applies its principles, it becomes clear that freedom of speech matters when it is anti-Muslim speech. Terrorism matters when it targets freedom of religion, not Black people. Freedom of religion matters, but not in a way that would ensure the rights of Black parishioners. The individual matters, then, when the individual is a universalized white Christian-nationalist man because they are the *fathers*' heirs.

Drawing on Cheryl I. Harris's conceptualization of whiteness as property and the attendant and reinforcing structures of hegemonic masculinity and Christian religiosity in the United States, I argue that when congresspeople present the founders as fathers—embracing the metaphor of fatherhood—it turns a loose association of white men into authority figures and imagines the United States as their offspring. Here, a contractual or perhaps even covenantal logic of inheritance sets in: *if* the founders are "our" fathers, *then* "we" inherit their property. This contract—covenant—forms the nucleus of US sovereignty as mobilized in this rhetoric.

This if-then formulation stipulates the "right to disposition," the right to determine who inherits.[171] In regard to property, this right—as Harris points out—has clearly and legally been reserved for white people. My analysis demonstrates how the metaphor of fatherhood activates this inheritance-based logic in congressional discourse so that the United States, democratic institutions, and US freedoms are primarily inherited by white men with "family" values and the women who support them.

Ultimately, the metaphor of fatherhood works by positioning the "Founding Fathers" as the fathers of the United States. The United States, then, is a family with no mothers. Instead, the "Founding Fathers" birthed or created the nation, their authority presides over the American family, and they bequeath this nation to Americans. As Loudermilk's speech, "Our Documents of Freedom," so amply demonstrates, this metaphor is supported and reinforced by metaphorical clustering and five strategic moves. First, this fatherhood discourse constructs us-other binaries that are structured by whiteness and patriarchy; second, it frames "us" as exceptional; third, it creates a possessive relationship with the "Founding Fathers," in which they are *our* fathers; fourth, it uses material appeals to frame the United States and US values as *real*; and finally, it assumes that the real United States is *inherited* by real Americans. Loudermilk's speech is a tour de force, but this trope and its clustering techniques are found throughout Congress. The trope's power is best understood in its diffusion across congressional discourse—as demonstrated in this book's ensuing chapters.

Overview of the Book

When I began this research, I was intrigued by the questions of when, how, and to what effect congresspeople invoke the "Founding Fathers" in the House and Senate chambers. Taking Loudermilk's speech as a microcosm of the broader congressional discourse, I have already briefly demonstrated how—or through what appeals—the majority of Congress invokes the founders, and it is apparent that the effects are largely pernicious. This discourse imagines a "real" United States that descends from the "Founding Fathers." It voices a rhetoric of sovereignty, creating and reinforcing a legislative system in which some are more equal than others.

Reading through the *Congressional Record*, I discovered that the answer to "when" congresspeople invoke the "Founding Fathers" is better understood thematically than chronologically. That is, Congress invokes the "Founding Fathers" almost daily and sometimes hourly. Chronology, then, seems to provide little if any analytic insight. Likewise, Democrats and Republicans and members of the House and Senate invoke the "Founding Fathers" with similar regularity. There is a clear thematic pattern, however. Congresspeople invoke the "Founding Fathers" primarily (1) when they champion "rights and liberties"; (2) when they venerate the United States—or express cynicism in its founding myths; (3) when they call for "checks and balances"; and (4) when they extol debate and bipartisanship. Moreover, within these four themes there exists some variation in how the founders are invoked and thus what type of effect this discourse has. As such, the ensuing chapters are organized around these themes, analyzing how and to what effect the "Founding Fathers" are invoked as support for a particular set of policies—for example, rights and liberties, checks and balances, and so on—but more importantly, this book overarchingly demonstrates how this discourse articulates who possesses the right to govern in the name of "the people" and who counts as "the people."

Rights and Liberty: Congressional politicians routinely invoke the "Founding Fathers" when championing rights and liberties. This extols freedom as a central US value, but—through the metaphor of fatherhood—frames freedom as an inherited right. Analyzing how congressional Republicans champion the "right to life" and "freedom of religion," this chapter demonstrates how the possessive and material appeals within this discourse coalesce into the logic of inheritance, curtailing the very possibility of what freedom is and who has rights in the United States. In contrast, exploring how Democrats advocate for the "freedom of the press" and the "right to vote" provides a first and partial glimpse at how congresspeople counter this metaphor and its exclusive rights of disposition. Here, I demonstrate how Democrats in Congress deviate from fatherly veneration; this leaves the founders' fatherhood intact, but clusters the metaphor more toward leadership than inheritance.

Veneration and Cynicism: In passing asides during policy speeches and in ceremonial speeches entirely dedicated to celebrating the United

States, congressional Republicans and Democrats routinely venerate the founders as wise fathers. Placing this rhetoric within its socio-religious context, I demonstrate how this veneration invokes the covenant of American exceptionalism, positioning the founders either as secular gods of the covenant or as dignitaries within an explicitly Christian covenant. Moving from origin to telos, the covenant of American exceptionalism depends on the veneration of the founders as fathers who birthed a glorious nation. This glorious destiny, then, becomes possible only for true descendants—only for Americans who seemingly remain true to the founders' wisdom by espousing patriarchal, white, Christian "family" values as good governance. This veneration is not unchallenged, however. Members of the Congressional Black Caucus—and occasionally others—invoke a counter discourse of realistic cynicism. This counter discourse asks Americans to rethink the covenant of American exceptionalism, revoking the founders' fatherhood. Analyzing these moves, I argue that this counter discourse offers the clearest off-ramp or exit from the metaphor of fatherhood's inheritance-based reasoning.

Checks and Balances: Congressional politicians consistently invoke the "Founding Fathers" when calling for "checks and balances." These speeches commend a "separation of powers" and rail against the other branches or chambers within the federal government. For instance, congressional Republicans called for "checks and balances" when President Obama issued executive orders regarding gun control during the 2016 election cycle, and members of the Senate criticized the House, claiming its impeachment of President Trump was blindly partisan during the 2020 election cycle. The majority of this discourse—by Republicans, Independents, and Democrats—escalates the logic of inheritance by launching a *defense* of the United States. This relies on implicitly masculinist appeals and hallows us-other politics as essential to "our" survivance. But a cadre of Democrats—again, typically from the Congressional Black Caucus—instead voice realistic cynicism, rejecting the metaphor of fatherhood even as they call for checks and balances.

Debate and Bipartisanship: Congresspeople routinely invoke the

"Founding Fathers" when calling for debate and bipartisanship. This largely relies on veneration, enshrining debate and bipartisan collaboration as the ideal form of government. Here, I demonstrate how inheritance-based reasoning transforms even appeals for bipartisanship into partisan politicking. That is, this bipartisan rhetoric is largely disingenuous, designed to publicly shame the other party rather than create bipartisan deals. Here, I demonstrate the rhetoric at play within Congress as these parties jockey for the imagined moral high ground. Moreover, I articulate how these appeals to the founders—as fathers—ultimately delineate the American family, affecting who is seen as worthy to take up the mantle of bipartisan governance and reinforcing the exclusionary nature of that governance.

Losing Faith: To conclude, I explore the repercussions of fatherhood as a metaphor within US politics. Specifically, I attend to the way inheritance structures US democracy and the implications this has for men's rights groups, white-supremacist groups, and Christian political groups—especially as these groups overlap. I specifically note how Congress's venerating rhetoric normalizes the logics and frameworks that are violently taken up and activated through conspiracy theories such as "replacement theory." I conclude by returning to realistic cynicism, arguing that this counter discourse offers a way out of the United States' structurally exclusive democracy.

Analyzing the hierarchies of gender and race at work within the longstanding assumptions of what it means to be an individual, a human, and a US citizen, Charles W. Mills argues that incremental policy changes will not suffice—piecemeal legislation has not and will not accomplish equality. Instead, Mills argues that if the United States is to actually become a "liberal idea for everybody" and not just for "a privileged minority," these founding hierarchies, oppressions, and subordinations must be acknowledged, and their ongoing influences must be rooted out.[172] *Invoking the Fathers* makes precisely such an attempt. In this book, I work to acknowledge the hierarchies, oppressions, and subordinations at work within the commonplace phrase "Founding Fathers." I work to make plain how this rhetoric of sovereignty operates and the deleterious effects it has upon so much of the US population—upon people who almost never get to comprise "the people" in political rhetoric.

Ultimately, *Invoking the Fathers* demonstrates that venerating the "Founding Fathers" enacts a rhetoric of sovereignty, biasing US democracy toward whiteness, patriarchy, and the "family" values typically espoused in Christian nationalism. Imagining that US rights and liberties are property bequeathed by the "Founding Fathers" and that they must be defended at all costs creates a framework of paranoid scarcity. Paranoid because it perceives potential attacks and risks at every turn and scarcity because it imagines that America's exceptionalism is only possible for a select few: "the people" who keep the covenant of American exceptionalism, who are true descendants—both inheriting and defending the "Founding Fathers'" gifts.

It is my contention that this congressional discourse sets the stage for and stokes the fires of patriarchal white-supremacist violence and conspiracies such as replacement theory. Consider, for instance, how white nationalists chanted, "You will not replace us," in Charlottesville, Virginia, in 2017; how Patrick Crusius killed twenty-two people in a Walmart in El Paso, Texas, in 2019, publishing his manifesto on the "great replacement" moments before he opened fire; and how the mass shooter who killed ten in Buffalo, New York, in 2022 published a similar "replacement theory" manifesto.[173] When top-ranking politicians routinely describe the United States as if it were created by white fathers and bequeathed to white men with "family" values, there can be very little mystery as to why white men with "family" values routinely attack people of color, publishing manifestos about preventing the white "race" from being replaced. Understanding how the metaphor of fatherhood functions as a rhetoric of sovereignty in US politics explains much of how patriarchal white supremacy operates in US discourse and explains the ongoing contemporary crises of structural inequality and violence. Indeed, this book demonstrates the conceptual links between how contemporary politicians invoke the "Founding Fathers" and how white supremacists understand the United States as a white nation.

Discerning how this metaphor works also highlights the importance of studying counter discourses and alternative ways of imagining the founders and the myths of US democracy. This book highlights those counter discourses, especially focusing on the language of cynicism—or realism—as voiced by members of the Congressional Black Caucus. This counter discourse expresses a loss of faith in the "Founding Fathers," revealing the falsity of the founding myths. Moreover, this counter discourse offers a new faith, one that traces every ounce of democracy and freedom this country enjoys not to the white fathers, but to Black resistance.

CHAPTER ONE

Rights and Liberty

IN 1826, James Madison wrote to Thomas L. McKenney, who was then the superintendent of Indian Affairs, warning that "next to the case of the black race within our bosom, that of the red on our borders is the problem most baffling to the policy of our country."[1] This quote illustrates at least five things. First, Madison and others were grappling with slavery and conquest as fraught policy considerations. Second, common sense presumed that white people owned the United States: the *our* in "our borders" and "our country" is presumed white. Third, race was a determining factor: race was not only seemingly obvious but also determined if one owned the country, was enslaved, or displaced and massacred. Fourth, races were clearly understood in contrast with one another. That is, within Madison's framework, white people are *not* "the black race within our bosom" or the "red on our borders," and vice versa. Finally, Madison wrote this approximately three decades after drafting the US Constitution, suggesting that the federal government's design had ongoing policy problems regarding "race," slavery, and the borders—and here, even a quick glance at contemporary politics suggests that these design problems remain.

When Madison penned this letter, he had already been president

(1809–1817) and was now an elder statesman—advising politicians from his plantation, Montpelier, where he enslaved approximately three hundred people. Madison's brief letter to McKenney demonstrates his ongoing political importance: McKenney had asked him to advocate on his behalf to President John Quincy Adams, a request Madison declines in the letter's opening lines. The remainder of the letter focuses primarily on questions of "new-modelling the Indian character."[2] By "new-modelling," Madison means the "civilizing" efforts that—when not explicitly violent—involved relocating and evangelizing Indigenous populations while converting them to agriculture-based economies.[3] While Madison supposes that some Indigenous people in Mexico and Peru might be part of an "advanced" civilization, his letter is full of the sort of casually overt racism that most contemporary audiences abhor: Madison refers to the Indigenous people who live near the United States' "white population" as "inferior tribes," refers to large swaths of Indigenous people as occupying "the most savage state," and assumes that white men are in a position of authority to determine—through research—the "precise condition" of Indigenous people's "political, legal, social, intellectual, and moral" capabilities.[4]

What is evident throughout this letter and its broader cultural and political context is that the United States is "a white settler state established on what is originally Amerindian territory" and that "race is central to its formation and identity."[5] Indeed, in 1790 Congress made "whiteness a prerequisite for naturalization," rendering Black people, Indigenous people, and people of color as "permanent aliens or outsiders" who exist beyond the social contract articulated in the US Constitution.[6] Thus, when Madison writes of "our country" in 1826, he explicitly and legally meant a white nation whose borders enclosed land that was claimed and inherited by white men.

This chapter specifically explores the idea of possession—*ours*—that structures congresspeople's invocations of the "Founding Fathers." Implicit within the language of possession—*ours*—is a number of inclusions and exclusions based on identity. That is, for there to be an "ours," there must be an "us" who are in possession and conversely a "not-us," or more precisely an "other," who are not in possession. How "we," "us," and "ours" are identified—and how "not-us," or "other," are identified—becomes especially relevant to this discourse since these distinctions determine who can possess and who cannot.

Here, I draw on Edwin Black's and Philip Wander's conceptualizations of the Second and Third Personae, respectively.[7] The First Persona is understood as the person a speaker "projects" or "strategically" implies in their speeches.[8] This is the identity a speaker cultivates and embodies or attempts to embody during the speech. The Second Persona is, then, the "implied auditor"; it is the identity the speaker hopes the audience embodies and which the speaker invites the audience to become.[9] The Second Persona differs from the "real or actual" audience who "heard, or read, or saw the speech," and identifying the real audiences does not identify who the speaker "wished to reach" and certainly does not capture the "persona commended through the speech."[10] If the First Persona is a discourse's "I," then the Second Persona is the "you" a discourse invites the audience to become—and thus to enact.

Here, Black argues that the Second Persona is characterized by its ideology—by the "network of interconnected convictions" that function epistemologically, shaping identity and determining how one views the world.[11] Black continues, demonstrating that this identity-shaping ideology is rarely laid bare by "substantive claims"; instead, a speech beckons to audience members, inviting them into the Second Persona—adopting its identity-shaping ideology—through its style.[12] Studying a discourse's style, its metaphors and repeated rhetorical techniques, reveals the human "archetype" with which a discourse beckons its audience.[13] Focusing on the metaphor of "Founding Fathers," then, this chapter attends primarily to the logic of possession. In so doing, I trace the figure or Second Persona characterized within this congressional discourse, mapping it onto the rhetoric of sovereignty as it delineates who *we* "the people" are and, thus, to whom the nation belongs—who can claim it as *ours*. Indeed, given congressional rhetoric's repeated use of plural pronouns, "we," "us," and "ours," I suggest that this discourse offers a conflation of the First and Second Personae, a shared identity rooted in lineage and possession, an identity based in claiming the founders as "our" fathers.

As Philip Wander argued, however, for every discursive "us" there is a "not-us," or for every Second Persona there is a Third Persona—an audience that is "rejected or negated through the speech."[14] A discourse constructs its Third Persona by the way it implies the "characteristics, roles, actions or ways of seeing things" that are "to be avoided."[15] The Third Persona is "negated," becoming an "object," an "it" in relation to the "subject" positions of the First and Second Personae.[16] The Third Persona is almost never spoken of or directly commented on. Instead, it is "fashioned" by its absence. Implied and obliquely suggested, it is often represented as a sort of "cancer" or "parasite" that preys upon society—or more precisely, that preys upon the Second Persona.[17]

While this negation occurs within discourse, Wander is clear that its exclusions and objectifications translate into "the world of affairs" through laws, traditions, prejudices, and the denial of rights in the "public sphere," wherein the negated, objectified Third Persona is measured against the idealized "human beings" who comprise the Second Persona.[18] And here, Wander noted that this negation is typically enacted against people categorized by "race, religion, age, gender, sexual preference, and nationality" as "non-subjects" within the "established order."[19] Indeed, combining Wander's conceptualization of the Third Persona with social contract theory and whiteness as property as discussed in the introduction, it becomes clear that the "established order" has long divided US political subjectivity and objectivity, or the Second and Third Personae, along sexist and racist distinctions.

At stake within the metaphor of the "Founding Fathers" and the rhetoric of sovereignty it deploys are the questions of who gets to be "us" and what "our" rights and freedoms are—and who is negated as an "it" and alienated as "un-American." Focusing on congressional speeches that champion rights and liberty, this chapter notes starkly partisan differences. That is, unlike the upcoming chapters on American exceptionalism, checks and balances, and bipartisanship where there are few differences between Republicans' and Democrats' congressional discourse, there are significant differences at play when Republicans and Democrats invoke the "Founding Fathers" in relation to rights and liberty.

Republicans have far more to say on the topic of rights and liberty. Analyzing this discourse and highlighting its possessive and material appeals, this chapter traces how Republicans render freedom as an *inherited* right. Specifically, I demonstrate, first, how this discourse imagines freedom as if it were birthed by the founders—in coordination with the Christian God—and second, how this discourse links America's exceptionalism to inheriting these rights and liberties. Since Republican congresspeople are especially profuse in championing rights and liberty, this chapter analyzes some of the most heated and recurring topics, focusing on speeches that champion "freedom of religion" and the "right to life." Through this analysis, I trace how the logic of inheritance curtails the very possibility of what freedom is and who has rights in the United States.

Yet this discourse is not monolithic. Indeed, while it is far less common for Democrats to champion rights and liberty, when they do engage in such discourse, they typically present a counter frame that reimagines the founders' fatherhood less in material terms of possession and inheritance and more in terms of leadership and expansion across time—not land. To demonstrate how this counter discourse operates, this chapter analyzes how congressional Democrats advocate for the "right to vote" and "freedom of the press." To be clear, this counter discourse is a small minority compared to the much larger and louder rhetoric that links the privileges of "rights and liberty" to the founders' most obvious heirs—to white men with "family" values and the women who support them—but it forms an important counterpoint, providing alternative ways of conceptualizing the founders.

Freedom of Religion

The Constitution's first ten amendments are known collectively as the Bill of Rights. They were drafted by James Madison, rewritten and approved by Congress in 1789, and ratified by state legislatures in

December of 1791. Madison drafted—and the House approved—seven other amendments as part of this Bill of Rights, but the Senate rejected five of them, and the states refused to ratify the remaining two, leaving the Bill of Rights with the now-familiar ten amendments.

These amendments were a contentious issue for the early congressmen. Anti-Federalists (such as Jefferson) wanted "power to remain with the state and local governments" and thus wanted a specific "bill of rights" that would enumerate what the federal government could *not* do.[20] Federalists (such as Hamilton) argued that "the Constitution did not need a bill of rights" because by default "the people and the states kept any powers not given to the federal government" in the Constitution.[21] Essentially, the Anti-Federalists feared federal overreach and wanted to put safeguards in place to prohibit such overreach. Meanwhile, the Federalists objected to amendments they saw as redundant. For instance, Federalists argued that since the Constitution made no mention of religion, religion was by default left to state and local governance—and as such, the First Amendment's religion clause was unnecessary.

Ultimately, however, the congressmen and state legislators voted in favor of safeguards, and thus the Bill of Rights functions as a clearly delineated list of rules enumerating what the federal government cannot do. As such, the Constitution and the Bill of Rights exist in a sort of tension with each other: The Constitution establishes the federal government as a ruling body, and then the first ten amendments explicitly limit its rule. Moreover, the arguments of suspicion and the fear of federal overreach that swayed these early politicians remains as a beating heart within the Bill of Rights. Far from a celebration of US freedom, the Bill of Rights was drafted as a line of defense. Indeed, its creation in 1791 assumed that—unless prohibited—the federal government would attempt to violate states' sovereignty and white men's individual sovereignty.

The right referred to as "freedom of religion" or "religious liberty" is derived from the first two clauses of the First Amendment. The first clause is known as the Establishment Clause and reads, "Congress shall make no law *respecting an establishment of religion.*"[22] The second clause is known as the Free Exercise Clause and adds, "Congress shall make no law respecting an establishment of religion, *or prohibiting the free exercise thereof.*"[23] Although the words "freedom," "liberty," and "rights" are absent from these opening clauses, the First Amendment continues by using such words interchangeably as it states, "Congress shall make no law . . . abridging the *freedom* of speech, or of the press; or the *right* of the people peaceably to assemble, and to petition the Government for a redress of grievances."[24] Taken together, the First Amendment is known to grant five "rights": freedom of religion, speech, press, assembly, and petition.

During the founding era, these opening clauses regarding religion generally prohibited the federal government from creating a "nationally established church," such as the colonies had experienced under British rule. This was especially important to the "southern colonies" where the Church of England had required colonists to "pay religious taxes and (often) to attend church services," and had "appointed and disciplined" the clergy.[25] As such, these clauses had a fairly narrow application during the founding era. Indeed, the courts routinely punished "blasphemy" during the founding era and up through the nineteenth century, demonstrating that while "Congress shall make no law respecting an establishment of religion, or prohibiting the free exercise thereof," the courts certainly used Christian religious norms to regulate criminality.[26]

In the contemporary era, however, these clauses are taken more broadly and have become known as the "separation of church and state." They are used as the basis of legal arguments on a wide variety of issues such as preventing public schools from requiring children to participate in religious prayers or exempting ill children's parents from facing charges of medical neglect if they "do not believe in medical treatment."[27]

Within this broader interpretation of the Establishment Clause and the Free Exercise Clause, Republican congresspeople routinely invoke the "Founding Fathers" as they champion "freedom of religion." Representing this vast discourse, I analyze a series of speeches by Senator Orrin Hatch that broadly champion "religious liberty" and a speech by Representative Alexander Mooney that specifically pitches religious freedom against the Affordable Care Act. These speeches define religious freedom as the most important US right even as they claim that Christianity created this freedom. Here, Christianity operates as the master religion; it is the religion that ensures religious liberty. For the United States to be a nation of religious liberty, then, it must be a Christian nation.

These speeches emphasize material appeals and a sense of possession, rendering religious liberty as *ours*. The material appeals emphasize a sense of *reality*. The assumption is that the founding documents are not just words; they are real—or at least, they create real things. Together, these appeals position religious liberty not just as a thing, as property, but as *our* property. This raises significant questions about this discourse's Second Persona, about who is imagined as and invited to become the "us" that operates within these speeches.

For instance, early during the 2016 campaign, on October 7, 2015, Senator Orrin Hatch (R-UT) spoke on the Senate floor as part of his "series of speeches about religious freedom."[28] Hatch begins with claims of American exceptionalism, insisting that "religious freedom" makes the United States unlike any other nation throughout "world history."[29] He then situates "freedom of religion" as the foundational concept, stating, "freedom of religion undergirds the very origin and existence of the United States."[30]

Arguing that religious freedom is the most important of US freedoms, Hatch cites material documents prodigiously. For instance, in a single speech, Hatch quotes from the Declaration of Independence to define the idea of "inalienable rights," and then quotes from James Madison's more obscure documents, including the Virginia Declaration of Rights, Madison's 1785 Memorial and Remonstrance against Religious Assessments, and Madison's 1810 State of the Union Address. He also cites the 1649 Maryland Toleration Act, the 1853 Senate Foreign Relations Committee's resolutions, President Franklin Roosevelt, Supreme Court Justice Arthur Goldberg, the Universal Declaration of Human Rights, the Helsinki Accords of 1975, the 1992 International Covenant on Civil and Political Rights, the 1993 Religious

Freedom Restoration Act, the 1998 International Religious Freedom Act, and—of course—the First Amendment. As Representative Hatch cites these documents, he describes when they were established and often by whom, and cites the exact section(s) of the document he refers to. For example, when dealing with the Helsinki Accords, he states, "The United States signed the Helsinki Accords in 1975. Section VII declares that signatories 'will recognize and respect the right of the individual . . .'" Similarly, referencing the Universal Declaration of Human Rights, he notes that the United States became its signatory in 1948 and then specifically references Article 18 as he begins to quote from the document.

This is more than attention to detail. It renders these documents *real*. They have material heft. By demonstrating that he can turn to chapter and verse in seemingly any document from any part of US history and point out how the First Amendment's Establishment and Free Exercise Clauses were upheld, Orrin Hatch is also demonstrating that there *is* a chapter and verse in seemingly any document from every part of US history that upholds the First Amendment's freedom of religion.

Despite the *reality* of US religious freedom, Hatch argues that it is no longer a guaranteed inheritance. He bemoans the Supreme Court ruling in *Employment Division v. Smith* (1990), which he argues led to the federal government compromising, burdening, and even prohibiting "the exercise of religion not by overt assault but by covert impact."[31] Here, Hatch stipulates that his "remarks are very important because a lot of people don't realize that religious freedom is not as free as the original Founding Fathers expected it to be."[32] In so doing, Hatch invokes the "Founding Fathers" to raise the alarm, alerting the other senators that they have gone off course—have strayed away from the founders' intent. This activates the inheritance logic that was seeded in this speech's opening lines: the United States is an exceptional nation—unlike any other in "world history."[33] This exceptionalism is real—it is a US birthright—and it is under attack. Chastising his audience for slipping away from the "Founding Fathers'" expectations, Hatch calls on the Senate to change its ways.

Rights and Liberty

Hatch ultimately concludes this speech by stating that current legislation is "not enough" to function as a "true and noble protection of religious freedom," and finally insists that "we need to change these things and get religious freedom the preeminent position it really holds as the first clause of the First Amendment."[34] Here, Hatch supports his closing argument with a material appeal: "religious freedom" is preeminent because it is "the first clause of the First Amendment." This is an argument that literally turns on page numbers and page layout. Citing a phrase that never occurs in the First Amendment, Hatch argues that because "religious freedom" is positioned at the top of the page, it deserves a more expansive interpretation and more enforceable protections than he believes it currently enjoys.

Senator Hatch made a number of speeches as part of his series of speeches on religious liberty. One of these, on December 1, 2015, refers to religious liberty as a "legacy" while employing the possessive pronoun "our" to describe "*our* Founding Fathers."[35] Speaking shortly after Thanksgiving, Hatch's speech clearly intertwines this sense of possession and inheritance. For instance, Hatch describes Thanksgiving as "the holiday we commemorate in remembrance of *our* Pilgrim *ancestors*" and then stipulates that "freedom of religion" was especially "precious" to "*our* Pilgrim *forebears*."[36] Here, the Second Persona is clearly white. Hatch's speech situates the United States as a white nation: *we* are the descendants of the Pilgrims—*we* are not the descendants of the Indigenous people who were violently removed or of the Black people who were enslaved. A clear negation is at work, signaling the Third Persona.

In this speech, Hatch next moves into what he describes as a discussion of "the most tangible benefits religion brings to society."[37] He begins by recounting that the Declaration of Independence recognizes the "inalienability" of these rights since "they are 'endowed *to men* by their creator.'"[38] Here, Hatch adds the phrase "to men" into his quote from the Declaration. The Declaration reads, "We hold these truths to be self-evident, that all *men* are created equal, that they are *endowed by their Creator* with certain unalienable Rights, that among these are Life, Liberty, and the pursuit of Happiness."[39] As such, Hatch is not wrong that the Declaration recognized the inalienability of *men's* rights, but it is telling that given the opportunity to remove this gender-specific language, Hatch chose to reinforce it instead. In contrast, for example, Representative Sheila Jackson Lee (D-TX) paraphrases this passage of the Declaration by saying, "we are all created equal, with certain inalienable rights."[40] Hatch, however, reinforces a masculinist framework—again, outlining the Second Persona— even as he quotes a document that does not mention religious freedom. He leans on the Declaration's deistic reference to a "Creator" to argue that the founders believed that men's "rights" were "religious in nature."[41]

Continuing his tour of "the most tangible benefits of religion," Hatch turns to "abolition," which he ties to the "Second Great Awakening," and then to the "civil rights movement," chastising his audience for forgetting that "before [Martin Luther King] was a doctor he was a reverend."[42] He concludes this "tangible" historical tour with a discussion of the religious charitable giving without which "our government welfare system would be overwhelmed."[43] Again, Hatch makes a reality-based argument, attempting to present material realities (e.g., abolition, civil rights, charity—all of which he frames through Christianity) as evidence for his claims regarding religious liberty. Moreover, this sequence clearly negates any consideration of racism, deflecting attention away from anti-racist activism and toward Christian evangelism instead. Here, the Second and Third Personae are clearly traceable. Throughout this speech, the Second Persona has been characterized by whiteness, masculinity, and Christian values. The Third Persona in contrast is negated as people of color, women, and those who agitate against racism rather than primarily evangelizing.

After quoting considerably from George Washington, John Adams, and Alexis de Tocqueville, Orrin Hatch concludes this speech with a personal story of growing up in the Church of the Latter-day Saints— which "still teaches" that the Constitution is "the product of divine intervention in history," and which Hatch situates as a Christian denomination.[44] This personal story is generationally marked. He focuses on his father's hard work building a family home, and then notes that he and his wife, Elaine, are "so grateful that we have been able to raise our six children, all of whom are married now, all of whom have children, and many of whom have our great-grandchildren."[45] This closing story again underlines the generational, inheritance-based logic that operates throughout this discourse of "freedom." Religious freedom was secured for (white male Christian) Americans through the "Founding Fathers'" wisdom and is generationally passed down—from the fathers to true sons who comprise the Second Persona.

These same appeals are on display in Representative Alexander Mooney's (R-WV) speech against Obamacare on behalf of the Catholic organization Little Sisters of the Poor.[46] Representative Mooney first announces "one of *our* founding principles, *our* freedom of religion, is being taken away."[47] Implying the Second Persona, this opening pronouncement clearly relies on the assumption of possession: freedom of religion belongs to *us*, and *we* are clearly sympathetic to Catholic and evangelical religious politics.

Moreover, by imagining freedom of religion as *ours*, Mooney imagines it as a thing—as a property—and he immediately follows this with a material appeal. Displaying a painting, Mooney states, "I have here a beautiful picture of the Constitutional Convention, the signing of the Constitution at Independence Hall in Philadelphia on September 17, 1787."[48] Mooney visualizes the *reality* of the constitutional signing while naming its physical location and date. Seemingly, the utility of this material appeal outweighed the fact that it visualized the Constitution, which is explicitly *not* the First Amendment. Undeterred, Mooney—like Hatch—argues that because "freedom of religion" is the first part of the First Amendment it deserves special attention. He states, "[In] the very First Amendment to that Constitution, the very first one, *our* Founding Fathers solidified *our* citizens' right to freedom of religion," and then he quotes the entire First Amendment.[49] Mooney's appeals rely on and activate a logic of inheritance: The "Founding Fathers" left us a birthright; it is *ours*; and someone (the Third Persona) is trying to take it away. For Mooney— and his voting bloc in the 2016 election cycle—the Affordable Care

Act represents an affront to the freedom of religion. The Third Persona is characterized as President Obama, Democrats, and "the Left," which is constituted by its supposed secularism. Here, a number of binaries are at play. Mooney characterizes "us," or the Second Persona, as Christian, American, and upholding the founders' principles of freedom of religion. In contrast, then, the Third Persona is secular, un-American, and attacking or undermining freedom of religion. Or to put it more succinctly, the Second Persona abhors the Affordable Care Act, and the negated Third Persona promotes it.

The Affordable Care Act is religiously offensive primarily among evangelicals—conservative Catholics and Protestants—who find its coverage for contraception against their religion. As such, when Mooney argues that the Affordable Care Act cannot stand because "*our* Founding Fathers solidified *our* citizens' right to freedom of religion," he is largely equating "us" and citizenship with evangelical Christianity. In so doing, Mooney ties the "Founding Fathers" to Christianity—under the guise of religious liberty. Within this equation, by defending Christianity, "we" defend US religious freedom.

Championing religious freedom, these speeches use possessive appeals as they invoke the founders as fathers. This constructs a lineage in which "we" are their children, and freedom is a legacy passed down from them to "us." Describing page layouts, bringing portraits to the lectern, and prodigiously citing from founding documents, these speeches' material appeals give religious freedom heft—making it tangible, making it "our" property.

Clearly, however, not all Americans participate in the "us" these speeches imagine. For instance, curtailing access to contraception makes it harder for women to achieve bodily autonomy. This discourse pits religious freedom against women's freedom, declaring that religious freedom is the legacy from *our* "Founding Fathers" and the most foundational right without which all other rights would crumble. Within this framework, women's freedom is not only irrelevant; it is a problem—it is preventing the United States from fulfilling the founders' exceptional design for religious liberty.

Indeed, the recent ruling in *Kennedy v. Bremerton School District*

(2022) demonstrates that when political discourse champions religious liberty it is largely championing Christianity as a cultural norm. The ruling in *Kennedy v. Bremerton School District* argues that the principle of "separation of church and state" does not require the government to be hostile to religious expression and thus permits public-school employees—such as a football coach—to publicly pray at school events while defining such public Christian prayers as not coercive to students.[50]

Within this context, it becomes especially clear that when Senator Orrin Hatch called on Congress to "change these things and get religious freedom the preeminent position it really holds as the first clause of the First Amendment," this privileging of religious liberty is largely a privileging of Christianity as a cultural norm—as such, it is in line with Christian nationalism.[51] In so doing, it privileges a patriarchal version of Christianity, subordinating women's freedom and the rights of those of other faiths or no faith. Indeed, women's freedom and the right to choose not to experience Christian morality or Christian culture are framed as antagonistic to the "legacy" of US religious liberty. Again, these speeches invite audience members into an identity-shaping ideology. They beckon to audiences, and their style—the gendered metaphor of "Founding Fathers" and its associated possessive and material appeals—posits an "us" who are "the people" and by contrast and negation a "not-us" who are fundamentally un-American. Those who oppose Christianity's political preeminence, who put women's bodily autonomy before some interpretations of Christian doctrine, Black people, and those who trace their lineage to Indigenous people are clearly negated in this congressional discourse. Comprising the Third Persona, they are largely unspoken and yet they are implied by their absence and exclusion at every turn.

The Right to Life

During the recent election cycles, congressional Republicans routinely decried abortion as a breach of Americans' "right to life." Since then, the Supreme Court overturned *Roe v. Wade* (1973), making these congressional arguments all the more relevant. Now that states can once again fully legislate abortion, the "right to life" is even more pertinent in US politics. When advocating for the "right to life," congresspeople ground their legal claim not in the Constitution or the Bill of Rights, but in the Declaration of Independence. While the Constitution is a living, legal document—open to amendment—the Declaration "stands on its own" and was "designed to justify breaking away from" the British government.[52] Drafted by Thomas Jefferson in 1776, the Declaration of Independence contains three parts: the preamble, the list of grievances against King George III, and finally a declaration of independence from Britain. Of little importance at the time of writing, the preamble is now famous for containing "the entire theory of American government in a single, inspiring passage."[53] Its opening reads,

> We hold these truths to be self-evident, that all men are created equal, that they are endowed by their Creator with certain unalienable Rights, that among these are Life, Liberty and the pursuit of Happiness.—That to secure these rights, Governments are instituted among Men, deriving their just powers from the consent of the governed,—That whenever any Form of Government becomes destructive of these ends, it is the Right of the People to alter or to abolish it, and to institute new Government, laying its foundation on such principles and organizing its powers in such form, as to them shall seem most likely to effect their Safety and Happiness.[54]

Jefferson drew the concept of "natural rights" from Enlightenment philosophers (e.g., John Locke, Jean-Jacques Burlamaqui, Francis Hutcheson, Montesquieu) and resistance theology—a Protestant theology popular during the founding era that identifies tyranny as "satanic" and thus claims that "rebellion to tyrants is obedience to God."[55] Within the framework of this social contract, white propertied males are assumed to have "natural rights" by the simple virtue of "being human."[56] Moreover, some of these rights—specifically, the rights to life, liberty, the pursuit of happiness, and to alter and abolish one's government when necessary—were considered "unalienable," meaning that they could not "be surrendered to government under any circumstances."[57] This political framework—the confluence of social contract theory and resistance theology is still active today. For instance, it provides (white) Christian men's groups and Christian gun corporations a sense of divine purpose by equating resistance toward imagined tyranny as obedience to God.[58]

Writing for the National Constitution Center, Jeffrey Rosen and David Rubenstein note that the Declaration "made certain promises about which liberties were fundamental and inherent, but those liberties didn't become legally enforceable until they were enumerated in the Constitution and the Bill of Rights."[59] Indeed, Rosen and Rubenstein conclude that the Declaration "didn't give any rights to anyone."[60] Rather than having a legal function, the Declaration was "propaganda" that advertised "why the colonists were breaking away from England."[61]

Even though the Declaration is not a legal document, and the phrase "right to life" does not occur in the Declaration—nor does it occur in the Constitution or its amendments—congressional Republicans use the Declaration to link a "right to life" into the founders' legacy when advocating against abortion. Analyzing this discourse, I demonstrate how fatherhood circulates throughout these speeches in possessive and material appeals that create explicitly Christian and implicitly white-supremacist arguments. Invoking the founders as *our* fathers, these speeches position opponents to abortion rights as the fathers' heirs and the Second Persona. This is especially marked as these speeches imagine missing descendants—implicitly white missing descendants—who are absent due to abortions. The Second Persona then is constituted by a "pro-life" ideology.

For example, Representative Brad Wenstrup (R-OH) argued that since *Roe v. Wade* (1973), "fifty-four million human beings" have been denied the "natural and inalienable right to life that *our* Founding Fathers enshrined in the Declaration of Independence."[62] Representative John Ratcliffe (R-TX) opened a speech, stating, "the Declaration of Independence contains a passage that every student in America learns at an early age. It explains that each of us are endowed by *our* Creator with certain inalienable rights, chief among them the right to life."63 Continuing, Representative Ratcliffe states that "protecting unborn life" is among the "highest honors" he has as a representative and then celebrates his constituents, whom he claims work tirelessly to create a "culture of life" not for the notoriety but simply to protect "the inalienable right to life, which *our* Founding Fathers spoke of."64 Similarly, Representative Steve King (R-IA) argued that "innocent babies" should be able "to enjoy that first right, that right to life that comes before the right to liberty, which comes before the right to the pursuit of happiness, as *our* Founding Fathers prioritized those rights in the Declaration of Independence."65 Here, just as his colleagues argued that "freedom of religion" deserved special attention because it was listed first in the Bill of Rights, so too Representative King reinforces his argument with a material claim regarding how the words lie on the actual page of the Declaration of Independence: life is listed first and thus deserves special attention.

This discourse routinely links the "right to life" to Christian appeals. For instance, Representative Ted Yoho (R-FL) concludes a speech—given as part of the annual series of speeches celebrating the March for Life—with the circular statement, "*Our* Founding Fathers were grounded in the Christian principles this Nation was founded on," and then quotes 2 Chronicles 7:14 in its entirety, saying, "If my people, who are called by my name, will humble themselves and pray and seek my face and turn from their wicked ways; then I will hear from heaven, and I will forgive their sin, and will heal their land."66 Here, Representative Yoho moves from the possessive (*our* "Founding Fathers") immediately into two land-based metaphors ("grounded" and "founded") and then ends by conflating the United States with the Israelites and their land. The verse Yoho quotes is a promise from the Israelites' God, Yahweh, to King Solomon after the completion of the Temple. In this passage, Yahweh promises to dwell in the Temple, confirming that he will hear the people of Israel and will "heal their land" after droughts, locusts, and plagues. Lifting the verse from this context and using it to conclude his speech, Yoho materially fuses the "Founding Fathers"—and "their" land—with Christianity.

Similarly, Representative Barry Loudermilk (R-GA) opened a

speech by describing the House chamber, noting the "effigies of great philosophers and lawgivers" that adorn the "beautiful building."[67] He then states, "one of those [effigies], to my right, is that of Sir William Blackstone. Now, Blackstone had great influence upon *our* Founders, especially that of Thomas Jefferson. In fact, it was Blackstone who influenced the three enumerated rights of life, liberty, and the pursuit of happiness."[68] Here, Loudermilk begins with a material focus—the physical effigy to his right—and then links the Declaration of Independence to what sounds overtly Christian while emphasizing its position on the page, saying, "Mr. Speaker, let me read from Blackstone's Commentary, the very document which influenced Thomas Jefferson to make life *the very first* right that is given by government. Blackstone said: 'Life is the immediate gift of God, a right inherent by nature in every individual; and it begins in contemplation of law as soon as an infant is able to stir in the mother's womb.'"[69]

Although phrases such as "Life is the immediate gift of God" sound overtly Christian in the contemporary context, Loudermilk is lifting this quotation from Blackstone's multivolume *Commentaries on the Laws of England*, which offers only a deistic framework. Moreover, Blackstone puts the legal contemplation of "life" at the "quickening," which is the moment a woman feels a fetus "stir" within her—usually around 18–20 weeks into a first pregnancy and around weeks 15–17 for subsequent pregnancies.[70] Loudermilk skips over the difference between the quickening (when a woman feels movement) and conception (when egg and sperm meet), however, announcing, "that is one of the foundations of this Nation, that life begins at conception. And *our* Founding Fathers understood that it was a great philosophy and that is when the protection of law begins."[71] Tying life to conception, Loudermilk parrots many US Christian institutions rather than following Blackstone's philosophy or contemporary scientific discourses.

Loudermilk concludes by attempting to quantify—in material terms—the number of people who might have been born. Claiming that *Roe v. Wade* "literally changed the landscape of America," Loudermilk announces that the number of lives "equivalent to the population of Georgia, Florida, Alabama, Mississippi, Kentucky, South Carolina, Louisiana, and Tennessee" has been taken.[72] Using Southern land, Loudermilk visualizes the lives he claims were denied their right to life.

In addition to this discourse's usual techniques—possessive pronouns, materiality, American exceptionalism, and inheritance-based logic—Representative Trent Franks (R-AZ) offered an analogy from slavery in a pair of speeches. Speaking first to condemn Planned Parenthood and second to condemn what he describes as "born-alive abortion," Representative Franks reprises the classic features of these "freedom" speeches. He extols the United States, describing it as "an exceptional nation" with a "unique core premise," and he draws upon the Declaration of Independence.[73] Then, in both speeches, he describes "America's Founding Fathers" using a quote from Abraham Lincoln, saying that they held the "enlightened belief that nothing stamped with the divine image and likeness was sent into the world to be trodden on or degraded and imbruted by its fellows."[74] His speech condemning Planned Parenthood additionally quotes Lincoln, saying, "Those who deny freedom to others deserve [it] not for themselves; and, under a just God, can not long retain it."[75] His speech condemning "born-alive abortion" directly likens the abortion debate to the debate regarding "the effort to end human slavery in America."[76] Even assuming that these speeches express Franks's earnest belief that an inseminated ovum is the spiritual and legal equivalent of an adult human person, the slavery analogy demonstrates an opportunism that is rooted in white supremacy as Franks uses the memory of emancipation in a way that limits Black women's liberties.

That is, as legal scholar Adrienne Davis explains, the US economy of chattel slavery was a sexual economy carried out through the rape and forced impregnation of Black women who then birthed the next generation of enslaved people.[77] Likening women's ability to terminate a pregnancy to the generational enslavement of Black people—without directly mentioning Black people—Franks demonstrates a white-supremacist ignorance or callousness as he advances policies in direct opposition to the reproductive-justice politics led by Black women collectives.[78] Indeed, this negation characterizes the Third Persona as Black and female.

Finally, in Franks's speech condemning Planned Parenthood, he quotes both the Fifth and Fourteenth Amendments. This is an unusual move in these "right to life" speeches; typically, these speeches cite the Declaration of Independence alone. Franks quotes from the Fifth Amendment, however, stating, "No person shall be deprived of life, liberty, or property without due process of law," and quotes from the Fourteenth Amendment—which was drafted and ratified in the wake of the Civil War and specifically applies the Fifth Amendment's mandate to the states. Given the way these amendments echo the Declaration (substituting "property" for "the pursuit of happiness"), one might imagine that congresspeople would use these amendments more often when supporting their "right to life" arguments.

The Supreme Court, however, used the Fourteenth Amendment to guarantee a right to privacy in *Griswold v. Connecticut* (1965), even though privacy is not an enumerated right in the Constitution or its amendments.[79] Here, the right to privacy was inferred from other rights, such as the First Amendment's right to assembly, the Third Amendment's right "to be free from quartering soldiers during peacetime," and the Fourth Amendment's right "to be free from unreasonable searches of the home." Based on this right to privacy, the ruling in *Roe v. Wade* (1973) granted the right to abortion. At the time of Representative Franks's speech, then, the jurisprudence on the Fourteenth Amendment held that it granted the right to abortion, along with the rights of interracial couples to marry (1967), of unmarried individuals to use contraception (1972), of same-sex sexual conduct (2003), and of same-sex couples to marry (2015).[80] As such, even as Representative Franks asked Congress to protect "the lives of all Americans and their constitutional rights" by opposing abortion, he cited an amendment that at the time constitutionally conferred upon women the right of abortion.[81] Again, this speech constitutes the Third Persona by its omissions, negations, and erasures. In this instance, it becomes clear that "all Americans" and "their constitutional rights" do not include women who choose to exercise the right to an abortion.

Ultimately, this congressional "right to life" discourse uses the language of rights and liberty to curtail women's freedom. Drawing on possessive and material appeals, this discourse establishes a Second Persona, an "us" who receive rights from *our* "Founding Fathers." The "we" at play, however, certainly invokes an ideology of patriarchy, conservative Christianity, and white supremacy. Moreover, not only were all these speakers white, but they all demonstrate the privileges of white supremacy, ignoring the ways in which race-based oppressions place Black women under additional risks for poverty and sexual violence—both of which factor into women's decisions to terminate pregnancies.

Women's freedom does not enter into the equation as these congresspeople champion a "right" that not only curtails women's bodily autonomy but subsequently affects women's careers, lives, and civic engagement. That is, women who delay the birth of their first child are able to achieve higher educational outcomes and command greater earnings in high-wage occupations.[82] They are also more likely to identify as liberal and vote for Democrats.[83]

Moreover, this "right to life" discourse slides into explicitly white-supremacist politics. White-supremacist groups are galvanized by the proposition that a white "race" and a uniquely white civilization exist—and are dying out. The idea here is that white women are having too few white children, and thus the "race" is committing suicide. White-supremacist groups have been terrorizing abortion clinics and doctors for decades.[84] By prohibiting abortion, white women will be forced to birth far more children. Indeed, while Black women are often scapegoated for having abortions, the Centers for Disease Control and Prevention notes that in 2019 approximately thirty-eight percent of Black women reported having an abortion, and thirty-three percent of white women reported having an abortion—indicating that the rates are fairly similar.[85] Since approximately fifty-eight percent of the US population is white, and only approximately twelve percent identifies as Black, the vast majority of abortions are procured by white women.[86] As such, when Representative Barry Loudermilk (R-GA) used the material appeal of mapping the number of abortions since *Roe v. Wade* to the "population of Georgia, Florida, Alabama, Mississippi, Kentucky, South Carolina, Louisiana, and Tennessee," he was largely lamenting the loss of white life—and using geography with strong white-supremacist politics to visualize how many (white) people could be added to the population by criminalizing abortion.[87]

Anti-abortion activism also demonstrates the overlaps between white-supremacist politics and the culture-wars politics that conservative and evangelical Christians are known for. Clearly, many Christians and Christian political organizations believe that life begins at conception and that abortion is tantamount to murder. Their motives in ending abortion are driven by this religious belief—not by a desire to build an Aryan super-race. Yet conservative Christians have not always believed that abortion was a sin: as late as 1976—three years after *Roe v. Wade*—the "conservative evangelical Southern Baptist Convention (SBC) passed resolutions affirming abortion rights."[88] Indeed, as discussed in the introduction, conservative Protestants became politically galvanized by leaders such as Paul Weyrich and Jerry Falwell Sr. only after Bob Jones University lost its tax-exempt status by refusing to "rescind its racially discriminatory policies."[89] It was white supremacy—cloaked as religious liberty—that originally mobilized the Moral Majority. Conservative Protestants adopted anti-abortion politics as they formed political coalitions with conservative Catholic groups and white-supremacist religious organizations such as Christian Identity.[90]

Congressional discourse often uses explicitly Christian appeals but largely avoids overt white-supremacist arguments. Congresspeople are not always careful outside the House and Senate chambers, however. For instance, Representative Steve King (R-IA) tweeted in 2017, "We can't restore *our* civilization with somebody else's babies," and in 2018 he opined that "if we continue to abort *our* babies and import a replacement for them in the form of young violent men, we are supplanting *our* culture, *our* civilization."[91] Likewise, Representative Mary Miller (R-IL) greeted the overturning of *Roe v. Wade* in 2022 by stating it was a "historic victory for White life in the Supreme Court."[92] Ultimately however, whether or not congresspeople directly stated white-supremacist arguments or parroted white-supremacist conspiracies such as "replacement" theory, this congressional discourse fundamentally positions whiteness, patriarchy, and Christianity as the Second Persona's ideology and as the most valid expressions of US citizenry. Positioning the founders as *our* fathers and the "right to life" as *our* inheritance, this discourse makes it clear that white men with Christian-nationalist ideologies—and the women who support them—are the true heirs, the true Americans, and have the right to curtail others' freedom. As such, this discourse enacts a rhetoric of sovereignty as its Second Persona imagines "the people" as white, patriarchal, and Christian nationalist, and it beckons its audience to identify with this ideology.

The Right to Vote

Compared to Republican congresspeople, Democrats are far less likely to advocate for rights and liberty while invoking the "Founding Fathers." During the recent election cycles, however, Democratic members of the Congressional Black Caucus invoked the founders as fathers when advocating for the "right to vote." In so doing, these politicians used fundamentally different appeals from their Republican colleagues. Instead of foregrounding a logic of inheritance—with its possessive and material appeals—this discourse attempts to frame the founders' fatherhood in terms of leadership and features a recurring attention to time rather than materiality. This constructs different Second and Third Personae, and it enacts a slightly different rhetoric of sovereignty.

The Constitution only briefly describes voting. In a clause known as the Election Clause, the Constitution makes each state's legislature responsible for deciding the "Times, Places, and Manner" through which the citizens of that state shall elect federal congresspeople. But the Election Clause also permits Congress to "make or alter such Regulations." As such, although the states are "responsible for regulating congressional elections," they do so on the Constitution's authority—not their own state authority—and federal laws "automatically displace" or "preempt" any "contrary state statutes."[93] Congress can also institute regulations that the state has "not addressed."⁹⁴ As constitutional experts Michael T. Morley and Franita Tolson explain, the Elections Clause was included in the Constitution because the founders were "concerned that states might establish unfair election procedures or attempt to undermine the national government by refusing to hold elections for Congress."⁹⁵ Thus, the Elections Clause functions as a sort of "self-defense mechanism," guaranteeing that the federal government can regulate federal elections as needed to ensure its own continuance.

There is, however, a caveat to Congress's power regarding elections since Article I, Section 2 of the Constitution establishes that those who are eligible to vote for a state's larger legislative body are eligible to vote for the US House. This leaves the states in control of who can vote. At the time the Constitution was ratified, this "allowed roughly two-thirds of white men" and "very few others" the right to vote for US representatives.⁹⁶ Meanwhile, US senators were appointed by state legislators—not direct elections—until 1913.

Although the Constitution gives states the power to decide who can vote in federal elections, four constitutional amendments have been passed to prohibit states from certain types of discrimination as they decide who is eligible to vote. Namely, the Fifteenth Amendment "prohibits racial discrimination"; the Nineteenth Amendment "prohibits discrimination based on sex"; the Twenty-Fourth Amendment "prohibits the use of poll taxes in national elections"; and the Twenty-Sixth Amendment "prohibits denying the vote to those over 18 years of age."⁹⁷

In 1965, Congress began attempting to enforce the prohibition against racial discrimination through the Voting Rights Act. This law enacted many provisions, such as prohibiting literacy tests. Most notably, however, it required a preclearance process for any election policy changes in jurisdictions that—in 1964—had voting tests and lower than fifty percent turnout in presidential elections. During the preclearance process, a jurisdiction must prove to the US Department of Justice or a district court in DC that its "proposed change" does not deny or infringe "on the right to vote on account of race or color."[98] In 2013 the Supreme Court largely obviated this portion of the Voting Rights Act in their *Shelby County v. Holder* decision. The Supreme Court ruled that the criteria used to determine whether a jurisdiction required preclearance was out of date and thus created an unconstitutional burden upon that jurisdiction. Functionally, this means that no jurisdiction can be required to engage in the preclearance process until Congress adopts new criteria. Congressional Democrats have made several attempts to enact such legislation, such as the John Lewis Voting Rights Advancement Act of 2021, which clearly updates the criteria used to trigger the preclearance process. Although the House passed this legislation, it stalled in the Senate.

When Representative Terri A. Sewell (D-AL) invoked the founders to support voting rights in December of 2015, it was on behalf of the Voting Rights Advancement Act, which was renamed for John Lewis after his death. She began her speech by noting that she was speaking on the "sixtieth anniversary of the Montgomery Bus Boycott" and then directly pivoted to her topic, stating that since *Shelby County v. Holder* (2013) there has been a "renewed and relentless assault on our sacred right to vote."[99] Sewell—a Black woman—then makes an embodied appeal, addressing the Speaker as she states, "So I stand before you and this august body today in hopes of giving a voice to those who have been excluded from our political process" and asks every representative in the room to support the proposed legislation.[100] Stipulating that the Voting Rights Advancement Act would provide "more protections to more people in more states," Representative Sewell invokes the founders, stating that this legislation is "what our Founding Fathers would have wanted when they declared that our electoral process would be fair."[101]

Representative Sewell's claim regarding the "Founding Fathers" is, however, tenuous at best. Her appeal is based more in the US collective memory of the founders as "fair" men who were passionate about democracy than in historical reality. Indeed, the historical reality demonstrates the vast majority of the founders were enslavers who had every intention of establishing a white nation where voting rights applied exclusively to propertied white men. For instance, John Adams wrote in 1776 that it would endanger the nation if others could lay "claim" to the right to vote—specifically decrying the idea that "women," "lads from 12 to 21," and men who had "not a Farthing" might "demand an equal Voice" in the "Acts of State."[102] Seemingly, then, John Adams could not even fathom a world in which Black people and Native Americans might "demand an equal Voice" in the "Acts of State."[103]

Like her Republican colleagues, Sewell uses possessive pronouns, referring to the founders as "*our* Founding Fathers." But she does not foreground material and geographic features: there is no mention of land or description of monuments and engraved epitaphs, nor does she take her audience on a citation tour of previous legal documents or cite the page layout for any part of the Declaration of Independence, the Constitution, or the Bill of Rights. Indeed, she does not mention the Declaration, Constitution, or Bill of Rights. Neither does she imagine voting as an inheritable right. Instead, she imagines that the "Founding Fathers *would have wanted*" these protections put in place.[104] This is substantively different from arguing that the founders put these protections in place and that we—as heirs—have inherited them.

Indeed, rather than foregrounding inheritance-based logic, Sewell's speech foregrounds time. Not only does she mark time by recognizing the "sixtieth anniversary of the Montgomery Bus Boycott," but she notes that she rises to speak on a Tuesday, and that since "elections are held on Tuesdays," her "colleagues in the Democratic House Caucus" have declared "every Tuesday" a "Restoration Tuesday."[105] She then discusses the "events of last week," when she celebrated the "381 days" during which people boycotted segregation on buses in Montgomery. She returns to mark time by noting that it was "sixty years ago" when Rosa Parks "refused to give up her seat on a segregated bus."[106] Finally, she closes with a repeated "Tuesday" refrain. Again referring to "Restoration Tuesday," Sewell mentions that we can restore voting rights "today" by "remembering that on Tuesdays across this country, people go to vote, and they should do so without barriers, knowing that their polling stations will not be changed, knowing that if they are disabled, they will still be able to get into the ballot box in order to vote."[107] Finally, Sewell states, "we cannot return to the days where only some votes matter."[108] Sewell's time-orientation charts a path from "what the Founding Fathers would have wanted" to an expansion of voting rights. This loosely builds on the associations between fatherhood and leadership, positioning the "Founding Fathers" as leaders who pointed a direction through time.

Similarly, in 2019 Representative Sheila Jackson Lee (D-TX) invoked the "Founding Fathers" to support a bill to strengthen electoral cybersecurity and address Russian (and other foreign) interference in US elections.[109] Jackson Lee eschews possessive pronouns, instead referring to "*the* Founding Fathers," and largely omits material appeals, refraining from any discussion of land, landmarks, and the like. She does, however, briefly allude to the Constitution and the *Federalist Papers*, before noting that the Republic had to be perfected through the Voting Rights Act. Jackson Lee concludes by asking her audience to support the bill in question and then ends with an ominous reference to Benjamin Franklin, stating, "Remember, Benjamin Franklin said [the United States] is a republic, if we can keep it." Here, Jackson Lee engages in inheritance logic: the founders created and bequeathed a republic—and it is up to us to "keep" it.

Jackson Lee's speech, however, does not posit the founders as geniuses, nor does it frame the US republic as a world wonder. Instead of exceptionalism, Jackson Lee—also a Black woman—specifically notes that the original construct was flawed and that "we have had to perfect it" through "the Voting Rights Act," which she further notes Democrats are "trying to reauthorize."[110] Moreover, like Sewell's speech, Jackson Lee opens with a focus on time and a sense of urgency. She notes that "in many of our jurisdictions, there are local elections going on" and that "in a couple of weeks" the 2020 primaries will commence.[111] She then states twice, "Time is of the essence."[112] These appeals add nuance to the speech's inheritance logic, creating a framework in which Americans inherit a good but flawed system and emphasizing the idea that congresspeople must—once again—quickly intervene to correct that system.

These speeches are relatively unusual. During the recent election cycles, Democrats only occasionally invoked the "Founding Fathers" when discussing voting rights. And although Jackson Lee's speech features inheritance logic, neither Jackson Lee nor Sewell relied on the tactics Republicans routinely used when advocating for rights and liberty.

Instead, even as Jackson Lee suggests that the Republic is inherited, these speeches counter the idea that voting rights are inherited. Although white Americans now commonly assume that the right to vote is inherited—derived from one's ancestry and from one's possession of the land—the speeches by these two Black congresswomen suggest otherwise. It was not until the Fourteenth Amendment (ratified after the Civil War) that the US Constitution established criteria for citizenry, stating, "All persons born or naturalized in the United States, and subject to the jurisdiction thereof, are citizens of the United States and of the State wherein they reside." Read in this context, Sewell's and Jackson Lee's speeches bear within them the memory that being born in the United States and born to parents living in the United States has not always conferred the rights of citizenry—and the rights of citizenry have not always included the right to vote.

Indeed, Black men and most non-Indigenous women living in the United States first qualified for citizenship during the 1860s when the Fourteenth Amendment was ratified. The Fourteenth Amendment, however, did not effectively expand rights. Women did not receive suffrage for approximately another sixty years; the "jurisdiction" clause in the Fourteenth Amendment largely prevented Native Americans from receiving full citizenship until the Snyder Act of 1924; and both Native Americans and Black people were largely disenfranchised by Jim Crow laws until the Voting Rights Act of 1965.[113] Far from inheriting the right to vote from the "Founding Fathers," these speeches loosely position the "Founding Fathers" as leaders and urge current politicians to act—intervening in time—to expand and secure voting rights for the currently disenfranchised.

As constructed in this discourse, the Second Persona is idealized as someone who supports democracy by expanding voting rights and voting access. This is framed as important and timely work and as advancing or extending the founders' vision. In contrast, the negated Third Persona is constructed as someone who wants to "return to the days where only some votes matter."[114] These speeches use time as a key stylistic element. The Second Persona moves forward with time, adapting and expanding the founders' supposed vision to match the current moment. The Third Persona, meanwhile, would reverse time, dragging the United States back into the past.

Freedom of the Press

During the 2020 campaign, Democrats championed "freedom of the press" in the Senate, specifically bewailing the way Trump's administration and foreign governments punished journalists through threats, tax-based retaliations, imprisonment, torture, and murder. Like the "voting rights" discourse by Democratic members of the Congressional Black Caucus, this "freedom of the press" discourse foregrounds time and the founders' leadership, but it also employs a masculinized war metaphor.

"Freedom of the press" is one of the five freedoms enumerated in the First Amendment. Specifically, the First Amendment circumscribes the federal government's power, stating, "Congress shall make no law . . . abridging the freedom of speech, or of the press." For over a hundred years, this clause of the First Amendment was understood to forbid the government from placing "*previous restraints* upon publications," meaning that the government could not outlaw certain types of content, such as anti-government publications.[115] For instance in 1907, Justice Holmes observed that while the First Amendment forbids the government from placing a prior restraint upon the press, it does "not prevent the subsequent punishment of such as may be deemed contrary to the public welfare."[116] In practice, this meant Congress could not preemptively outlaw certain types of expression, but it could and did punish them after the fact—indeed, the courts routinely punished expressions of blasphemy.[117]

After World War I, however, the Supreme Court began moving toward its current jurisprudence, which holds that the First Amendment not only prohibits the government from placing prior restraints on the press but also "means that the government may not jail, fine, or impose civil liability on people or organizations based on what they say or write, except in exceptional circumstances."[118] Put simply, with few caveats, the government can neither prohibit expression nor punish expression. Currently, those caveats involve items such as child pornography, defamation, and commercial advertising (misleading commercial advertising can be banned—but misleading political speech cannot). Additionally, government employees, especially those with access to classified information, can be prohibited from some speech, and the government can issue "content-neutral restrictions," such as "reasonable" noise restrictions if they apply neutrally to all parties.[119]

Similarly, the Supreme Court broadened the First Amendment's application by ruling in *Gitlow v. New York* (1925) that although the First Amendment specifies Congress ("Congress shall make no law"), it applies to other branches of government. Current jurisprudence holds that the First Amendment protects against "all government agencies and officials: federal, state, and local, as well as legislative, executive, and judicial."[120] Despite this broad application, the First Amendment restrains only the government. Private individuals and organizations, such as "private employers, private colleges, or private landowners," are free to impose prior restrictions on expression and to reasonably reprimand those who violate either the letter or the spirit of those regulations.[121]

When advocating for a "free press" during the 2020 election cycle, some Democratic senators invoked the founders as fathers. For instance, on May 1, 2019, Senator Robert Menendez (D-NJ) introduced a bipartisan resolution to commemorate World Press Freedom Day and then spoke at some length. Senator Menendez states that Thomas Jefferson "recognized the importance of the press in a constitutional republic," and he then quotes Jefferson without a specific citation, saying that Jefferson "wisely declared, 'Were it left to me to decide whether we should have a government without newspapers, or newspapers without a government, I should not hesitate a moment to prefer the latter.'"[122] Menendez then emphasizes the importance of freedom of the press, stating, "freedom of the press is a fundamental human right, a foundational pillar of democracy, and an indispensable check on authoritarian overreach."[123] His speech then offers a litany of crimes perpetrated against journalists in different countries by different regimes.

Rather than taking the audience on a tour of Washington, DC's landmarks and monuments or working through documents and their page layouts, Senator Menendez names the journalists who have died or been imprisoned, where they were attacked, and the crime they were reporting. For example, Menendez states, "Slovak journalist Jan Kuciak and his partner Martina Kusnirova were gunned down in their home after investigating organized crime in his country and in alleged retaliation for his reporting of tax fraud on a businessman with close ties to Slovakia's ruling party."[124] Menendez also discusses the violence against journalists—and the crimes those journalists were reporting—in Afghanistan, Saudi Arabia, Burma, Nicaragua, Turkey, the Philippines, Bangladesh, China, and Venezuela. This geographic tour focuses on violence around the world rather than on land itself.

Menendez punctuates this tour by bringing it back to the United States at the beginning, middle, and end of his speech. At the beginning of his speech, Menendez states, "Today, press freedom is under assault across the globe—including in the United States."[125] In the middle of his speech, after most of his global tour of atrocities, Menendez states, "But the threat to press freedom isn't limited to foreign lands—it is something we've had to increasingly contend with here at home in the United States."[126] Finally, Menendez closes his speech by calling on the Trump administration to "reverse course" and choose to advance "press freedom" both "at home and abroad."[127] Here, Menendez's vocabulary focuses not on land but on war. He uses the words "assault," "threat," "reverse course," and "advance." Throughout the rest of his speech, he repeatedly speaks of "danger," "threats," "defending," and "hostility," and describes an "unprecedented assault on the free press" and the need to be "constantly fighting" on behalf of a free press.[128] Menendez's speech, then, frames "freedom of the press"

Rights and Liberty   79

not as inherited property but as a hotly contested battle. While this avoids the exclusive logic of inheritance, it keeps freedom closely associated with masculinity by drawing on the longstanding associations between masculinity and war. Indeed, this constructs the Second Persona in a masculinized way.

Like his colleagues who foregrounded time when advocating for the right to vote, Menendez also attends to time throughout his speech. The whole resolution is about "commemorating World Press Freedom Day," and Menendez draws attention to temporal markings throughout. He notes that "today, press freedom is under attack," and then recounts that "since 2009" over six hundred journalists have been killed in retaliation for their work and that "2018 marked the worst year on record for deadly violence and abuse toward journalists."[129] He again marks the time when invoking the "Founding Fathers," stating, "Over two hundred years ago, our Founding Fathers had the foresight to recognize the importance of a free press to a fledgling democracy, enshrining it in our first amendment."[130] Here, Menendez uses the possessive "our" and offers a sense of American exceptionalism—but he does not directly quote the First Amendment. Instead, he links back to a sense of chronology by stating that "today" the importance of freedom of the press "cannot be overstated."[131] He continues by describing an ongoing need to defend "brave journalists," making it clear that "freedom of the press" is not a right birthed by the founders and passed down from father to son but rather a freedom created across time through an ongoing fight. Likewise, Menendez's closing statement intertwines this temporal orientation and war metaphor, declaring, "On this World Press Freedom Day, I call on the Trump administration to reverse course and recommit to advancing press freedom—both at home and abroad."[132] Within this perspective, freedom of the press is not a thing that can be inherited, it is a continual fight—it can be advanced and fought for but not established or bequeathed.

In a similar way, Senator Ron Wyden (D-OR) spoke in support of "freedom of the press," specifically calling for the Trump administration to conduct investigations and publicly release intelligence reports regarding the murder of journalist Jamal Khashoggi, who was a US resident and wrote for the *Washington Post*. In this speech, Senator Wyden argues that the Trump administration's refusal to publicly recognize that the Crown Prince of Saudi Arabia was involved in the murder, while the administration continued to do business with the Saudi government, amounts to "open season on journalists."[133] That is, Wyden argues that the Trump administration's refusal to admit Saudi wrongdoing—much less to impose any type of response or sanction—sends a "horrendous message" to other regimes that they too can murder US journalists when it serves their interests to silence the press.[134]

Like Senator Menendez, Senator Wyden uses a masculinist vocabulary focused on violence, repeatedly using words such as "brutal," "kill," "killing," "threats," "dangerous," and "atrocity." Instead of a geographic tour of violence around the world, however, Wyden offers what he describes as a "record" of President Trump's statements regarding the press. Here, rather than providing a tour of documents and citing page numbers and layouts as his Republican colleagues so often do when advocating for rights and liberties, Wyden's "record" is a freewheeling list of offenses. For example, he describes how the White House and Pentagon stopped having "press briefings," how Trump "threatened to use the taxation and antitrust powers of the government to punish the media when they dare to criticize him," how Trump whips up the crowds at his rallies to threaten the "journalists in attendance" and dismisses critical news as "fake news."[135] Most of all, Wyden repeatedly describes how Trump "ominously" calls "journalists enemies of the people."[136] Describing all this as "public statements," Wyden offers no citations or documentation.[137] This list is not concerned, then, with proving its reality or describing its materiality. For this speech's Second Persona, Wyden's list needs no citational support.

After presenting this "record," Wyden then invokes the "Founding Fathers"—without possessive pronouns—saying, "I don't know of any such provision in the First Amendment about which the Founding Fathers felt so strongly. They thought freedom of the press was almost as important as anything else people could imagine."[138] Wyden continues, stating, "The Founding Fathers didn't in any way suggest the First Amendment applies to discussing only nice things about someone who is a public official."[139] Here, Wyden offers no documentation that the founders felt "so strongly" about freedom of the press: he does not read the First Amendment; he cites no supporting materials; and he does not directly quote any of the founders—but he does make a claim about original intent. Rather than offering proof, Wyden assumes the First Amendment has a commonsense interpretation that is readily available to the Second Persona operating in this speech. His target audience or the type of person he invites his audience to become is the sort of person who assumes that the founders felt strongly about press freedom.

Like his Democratic colleagues, Wyden sidesteps inheritance-based logic and instead foregrounds time. Having already begun a time-based metaphor with his "open season" statement, Wyden describes the "brutal, premeditated murder of Jamal Khashoggi" as "the canary in the coal mine for press freedom," and then announces that "these are dangerous times for journalists."[140] Continuing, Wyden proclaims that "it is time for the American people, the Congress, and everyone around the world fighting for press freedom to see the reports" of the Saudi government's role in Khashoggi's death.[141] Finally, Wyden concludes with repeated calls for urgency, stating, "The US Congress must demonstrate that the fight for press freedom does not die in the Nation's Capital," and he personally commits himself, saying, "I am not going to rest," and "I will use . . . every tool at my disposal to finally get this long overdue information about the death of Jamal Khashoggi to the American people."[142] The orientation around time coupled with the battle metaphors rejects the idea of freedom as an inheritance, although it maintains patriarchal associations that privilege masculinity. In this speech, freedom of the press is not a thing that one can have and that can be passed down; instead, freedom of the press requires an ongoing fight—one Wyden feels is "overdue" in the United States.

Advocating on behalf of a free press, these speeches invoke the

"Founding Fathers" but largely avoid inheritance-based reasoning. The founders are not commended for giving the United States a precious heirloom, but rather they are positioned as leaders who started a particular course of action. Together with the "right to vote" discourse by their Democratic colleagues, this discourse offers a counter example to the profuse Republican rhetoric of rights and liberty. The rhetoric of sovereignty within this discourse on the right to vote and the freedom of the press does not entail the hoarding of rights as the property of a select few. Instead, this discourse attempts to expand sovereignty, attempts to expand rights through ongoing, timely intervention.

Conclusion

Republican congresspeople routinely invoke the founders as fathers, speaking vociferously on behalf of rights and liberties. Indeed, contemporary Republican politicians are far more likely to invoke the "Founding Fathers" when championing rights and liberty than Democrats. During the recent election cycles, Republicans emphasized "freedom of religion" and the "right to life," using possessive and material appeals that frame US rights as property while ideologically circumscribing who can inherit such property, as evidenced through their Second Persona. While this chapter focused on their featured topics—religion and life—Republicans used these same techniques when advocating for many other rights. For instance, Representative Steve Russell (R-OK) used these inheritance appeals to advocate for Second Amendment rights; Representative Louie Gohmert (R-TX) used these inheritance appeals to advocate for freedom writ large by "defending" against migrants who "invaded our [southern] border"; and Representative Dana Rohrabacher (R-CA) used these inheritance-based appeals to argue on behalf of property rights in relation to patent law.[143]

These Republican congresspeople have agendas: they want to create new laws and change existing laws. Framing the founders as fathers, this discourse naturalizes the ideology of patriarchy, whiteness, and the "family" values of Christian nationalism. Throughout, these speeches use possessive appeals that frame an exclusive "us," celebrate American exceptionalism, and draw on material appeals—tours of land, monuments, documents, and page layouts—that make this exceptionalism real and inheritable. In so doing, these speeches bequeath rights and liberties, which translate into property, wealth, control, and preeminence, to the founders' metaphorical sons and those who accept the invitation of this discourse's Second Persona. This rhetoric of sovereignty reaffirms whiteness, Christian nationalism, and patriarchy as democratic governance.

Indeed, exploring how this discourse's metaphors and rhetorical techniques construct its Second and Third Personae, it becomes clear that this discourse imagines "the people" as white Christian nationalists who prioritize patriarchal control over women's freedom. Meanwhile, this discourse's Third Persona, that which is rendered un-American, is largely people of color and those who would advocate for secularism over Christianity and women's bodily autonomy over evangelical and patriarchal control. This Third Persona lurks throughout this discourse, operating as a source of fear—as that which has the potential to undo the nation. As such, the Third Persona is rendered not just un-American but capable of destroying American exceptionalism if not controlled. This coalesces as a rhetoric of sovereignty: this discourse advocates on behalf of laws, resolutions, and policies that shape US governance in ways that privilege "the people" who constitute the Second Persona while containing and controlling people who constitute the Third Persona.

Ultimately, this discourse employs fatherhood in ways that reinforce founding myths of American exceptionalism, yet this framework can offer no solutions to the problems James Madison discussed in 1826. That is, although Madison would not have put it this way, when he described the "case of the black race within our bosom, and that of the red on our borders" as baffling policy problems, he was identifying problems caused by white supremacy and colonialist Christian patriarchy.[144] As such, when US politics works within the metaphor of fatherhood and its inheritance-based reasoning, it cannot resolve the intertwined problems of racism, sexism, and colonialism because this metaphor's inheritance-based reasoning fundamentally assumes that the United States *belongs* to white men who support Christian nationalism.

Clearly, Democratic congresspeople also have agendas: they too want to create new laws and change existing laws. Attempting to expand from the founders' "rights," these speeches strategically differ from Republican speeches. Rather than focusing on possession and materiality—land, monuments, documents, and page layouts—these speeches emphasize ongoing action through time. This positions the "Founding Fathers" as leaders, focusing on what they *wanted* rather than what they created or "birthed." This frames "rights and liberties" within a logic of expansion rather than an exclusive hoarding of rights.

While this Democratic counter discourse conceptualizes US rights and liberty without the exclusivity of inheritance, it joins the Republican discourse in grounding its arguments in the myths of the founding era—framing the United States as exceptional. As such, both the Republican and Democratic discourse on rights and liberty moves from origin to telos: assuming that because the United States' founding was exceptional, its destiny will also be exceptional. Or to put it another way, its arguments assume that because the "Founding Fathers" began something great, the United States either is already great or can become great. The next chapter focuses on this exceptionalism, considering how this discourse can cement the "Founding Fathers" as secular gods in both Republican and Democratic discourse.

CHAPTER TWO

Veneration and Cynicism

JOHN ADAMS DID NOT THINK the men of European descent who composed the citizenry in the new republic were particularly special. Indeed, he fretted over their shortcomings, warning about sins such as "hubris, greed, and foolishness."[1] He concluded that "there is no special Providence for Americans... their nature is the same as that of others" and that Americans "are not a chosen people."[2]

John Jay disagreed. Writing in the "Federalist Papers No. 2," he argued that the "blessings of Providence" were specifically given to "this one connected country, to [this] one united people."[3] Thomas Jefferson seemingly agreed with Jay on the point of American exceptionalism, describing the United States as a "chosen country" and the "world's best hope" in his first inaugural address.[4]

Although real disagreements about the United States' "exceptional" nature existed during the founding era, historian Peter S. Onuf suggests that exceptionalism is now the tie that binds current US political parties together. While ideologically divided, Republicans and Democrats are not living in separate countries. There is no Red America and Blue America. Instead, the parties "depend on, draw inspiration from, and mirror one another"; they are a couple dancing to the rhythm of American exceptionalism.[5] Their rhetoric is an explicit inversion of each other's arguments. Conservatives tend to deploy "tropes of 'decline and fall,'" exaggerating "the past's perfection" as they insist on American exceptionalism.[6] Progressives tend to look to the future, claiming that the United States is a "work in progress" moving toward "a more perfect union."[7]

Progressives' and conservatives' views on exceptionalism are two sides of the same coin. Progressives see the United States as exceptionally oriented toward utopia and would thus "remake the world in their own image."[8] Conservatives, meanwhile, see the United States as exceptional and would thus like to "opt out of a dangerous world."[9] Both impulses—to expand and intervene or to retreat and protect—are built on the bedrock foundation that the United States is special, unique, exceptional. One side believes this exceptional way of life should be shared—even forcefully—with other nations and people. The other side believes exceptionalism cannot be shared; the United States is the exception and cannot become the rule. Both sides fuel their arguments "by 'getting right' with the founders," and the varied and contentious record from the founding era provides endless "grist for the polemical mills."[10]

Indeed, Onuf demonstrates that Americans' unshakable faith in US exceptionalism rests upon retellings of the founding era. He writes, "What makes Americans exceptional is not their institutions or democratic way of life or frontier experience but rather their self-conscious and self-defining embrace of American exceptionalism throughout their history."[11] Specifically, believing that the US founding "constituted an epochal moment in world history," Americans reenact and retell this founding story—especially but "not always" through "electoral politics."[12] The campaigns, voting process, inaugurations, and peaceful transfers of power all reenact the original elections that founded the US government and celebrate its founding documents, creating a "permanent revolution" and instilling an obsessive focus on the "founding" within US culture.[13]

Americans, then, think the United States is exceptional because the political and civic rituals, the educational curricula, and the reenactments of national narratives emphasize the unique elements of the founding and extol the founders' genius. This discourse, however, has a clear slippage. Sometimes the term "exceptional" is used in a normative sense—as a value judgment—where "exceptional" means "superior" or "the best." In other applications, "exceptional" is used in a descriptive sense, where "exceptional" means "contextually unique" or "unusual." This slippage results in discourses where the United States is exceptional (superior) because of the way its exceptional (unique) origins are rhetorically venerated.

For instance, consider the writing of Kim R. Holmes—the former executive vice president for the Heritage Foundation. In a 2020 essay for the foundation, Holmes defends the concept of American exceptionalism. He explicitly notes that he is focusing on "what was different and unique" about the founding and that he does not "mean 'exceptional' in a normative sense [as a value judgment], but in a descriptive sense."[14] Indeed, he writes, "There is no other country in the world that embodied the blend of classical philosophy, Christianity, and even Enlightenment ideas in the unique way America did in the founding of the republic from 1776 to 1789. It was an exceptional (meaning uncommon) mix of liberty, limited government, natural rights, and religious liberty that made the American founding unique."[15]

Holmes's essay, however, clearly demonstrates the slippage from "unique" and "uncommon" to "better" and "superior." The title of his essay is indicative: "Why American Exceptionalism Is Different from Other Countries' 'Nationalisms.'"[16] This title clearly contrasts the United States with other countries, and given the negative valance of "nationalism," anything "different" from nationalism is clearly better than nationalism. Holmes argues at length against nationalism, claiming that it would reduce the United States to the status of being a nation like any other, thus weakening "America's claim to being an exceptional nation . . . grounded in principles that are universal."[17] Holmes then explicitly moves into a normative use of "exceptional," stating that it is Americans' commitment to our founding principles—which he calls the American creed—that "makes us great and good."[18] This article's use of "exceptional" as a descriptive term that draws attention to the circumstances of the United States' founding as "unique" or "uncommon" provides cover, obscuring the normative way "exceptional" operates in this discourse as Holmes makes value claims ("great"; "good") about US principles and identity. Indeed, Holmes makes explicit value claims while stating that he uses "exceptional" in a merely "descriptive sense."[19] In so doing, he denounces "nationalism" while extolling American exceptionalism, positioning the United States as the only country that can do "nationalism" well.

Moreover, Holmes's essay for the Heritage Foundation specifically names Christianity as one of the unique aspects of the United States' founding while highlighting "religious liberty" as a key principle in US exceptionalism. Here, Holmes operates within the same logic congressional Republicans use regarding religious liberty as discussed in chapter 1. Christianity acts as a prerequisite for religious liberty: within this logic, the founders valued religious liberty only because of Christianity. As such, to maintain religious liberty, the United States must "retain" a Christian identity.

At the same time, however, Holmes disavows any racial or ethnic identity as "American." He argues that the United States cannot base its identity on ethnicity, writing, "There is no such thing as a common American ethnicity" because "in the beginning, Americans were a mixture of English, Scots-Irish, Highland Scot, German, African, Native American, French, Dutch, and other ethnicities."[20] Erasing the different ways those ethnicities mattered during the founding era and matter today, Holmes's argument joins the larger contemporary conservative movement's framing of American exceptionalism by insisting that race "does not matter" while also clearly arguing that "religion does."[21] Notably, the religion that matters is white Christianity and its "family" values. Analyzing this trend, historian Onuf notes that conservatives sweep race out of the picture while foregrounding the "moral superiority" of the United States as a "Christian nation," marking US exceptionalism in explicitly color-blind Christian terms that also signal whiteness.[22] Holmes's example is instructive in the way it highlights the key concepts and slippages at work within the contemporary rhetoric of American exceptionalism and its overlap with Christian nationalism.

As the sociologists of religion Andrew L. Whitehead and Samuel L. Perry have demonstrated and as rhetorical scholar Kristina M. Lee has recently recounted in her study of the phrase "In God We Trust," Christian nationalism is not so much a religious identity as an ideological and political framework.[23] Indeed, this framework "orients Americans' perspectives on national identity, belonging, and social hierarchies" through an "understanding of the United States as a Christian nation."[24] The influence and hierarchies of Christian nationalism are clearly demonstrated in Congress, which opens both the House and Senate chambers with a daily prayer.[25]

The framework of Christian nationalism rests on several assumptions: first and foremost that the United States was founded as a Christian nation, and subsequently that Christians—usually of a certain creed, which changes in accordance with the era—make the best politicians, and finally that "Christian values should inform public policy."[26] Moreover, Christian nationalism is largely motivated or at least mobilized by a fear of the "moral decay of society," and here "moral decay" often coincides with real or imagined threats to "patriarchal, heteronormative, nativist and white supremist values."[27]

Indeed, as historian John Fea demonstrates, "white evangelical fear" formed the basis of the Moral Majority's "political playbook" in the 1970s and 1980s and remains at the heart of contemporary manifestations of the Christian Right.[28] This political strategy, or "playbook," works by mobilizing white Christians to "win back" or "restore the culture," and as such, it is rooted in a "highly problematic interpretation of the relationship between Christianity and the American founding."[29] Assuming that the founders created a Christian nation and intended the United States to be a Christian nation, advocates for Christian nationalism largely believe they are attempting to return the nation to its original design. The political playbook, then, mobilizes "white evangelical fear" and supposedly offers a route *back* to Christian nationalism, teaching that "the best way to reclaim America would be to elect a president and members of Congress who would pass laws granting privileges" to those with a "Christian worldview."[30] In turn, these elected officials would appoint judges, including Supreme

Court justices, who would "defend religious liberty by challenging the understanding of the 'separation of church and state,'" such that prayer and Bible reading return to public schools, abortion is criminalized, and "Christian conservative values" are legally defended across the United States.[31] Ultimately, the goal is to fuse Christian morality and federal laws—and many (white) Christians feel that in pursuing this goal they are returning the United States to the founders' design.[32] With its emphasis on the founders' design, Christian nationalism often slides into an "unbiblical view of American exceptionalism," confusing the "kingdom of God with the United States of America."[33]

This chapter attends, then, to the overlapping discourses of American exceptionalism and Christian nationalism within congressional invocations of the "Founding Fathers." As detailed in the prior chapters, congresspeople typically rely on a cluster of appeals when invoking the founders as *fathers*: they create an us-other binary, use possessive pronouns (e.g., "*our* Founding Fathers"), espouse American exceptionalism, use material appeals, and develop inheritance-based arguments. While the prior chapter focused on the possessive and material appeals at play in the discourse of rights and liberty, this chapter focuses on tracing the links between the metaphor of fatherhood and veneration—an almost holy worship of the founders and American exceptionalism. In so doing, I demonstrate how this discourse reifies a rhetoric of sovereignty by delineating what constitutes the nation, who can be American, and who can govern in the name of "the people."

Focusing on veneration brings the counter discourse of cynicism into explicit relief. Cynicism expresses not just doubt but rejection. This discourse has lost faith in the "Founding Fathers" and thus in the covenant of American exceptionalism. Here, I use the terms "cynicism" and "loss of faith" in order to highlight a particular aspect of this discourse's racial realism.[34] That is, this counter discourse exhibits the hallmarks of racial realism: it is grounded in empirical observations developed from direct experiences of exclusion and oppression; and based on this epistemological standpoint, it teaches marginalized people to be skeptical of white metanarratives of progress. In this chapter, I work to demonstrate how this counter discourse reveals American exceptionalism as a myth or faith—as something many Americans *believe* in. By revealing American exceptionalism as myth, this counter discourse invites others to abandon a false faith. Identifying this counter discourse as a rhetoric of cynicism, which is best described as voicing a loss of faith, I hope to call attention to the rhetorical dimensions of faith and myth at work in this congressional discourse's racial realism. Finally, conceptualizing this counter discourse within the framework of myth and faith draws attention to how this counter discourse's fullest expression offers a new faith, one based in reality—one built on Black resistance.

Venerating Our Fathers

Senator Chuck Schumer (D-NY) routinely describes the "Founding Fathers" as "our greatest wisdom in this country" and paraphrases the founders by introducing topics with phrases such as "The Founding Fathers, in their wisdom, said . . ."[35] Moreover, Senator Schumer offers asides such as "the wisdom of the Founding Fathers shines through" when discussing current political issues.[36]

Schumer is not alone in such veneration. Indeed, it is routine on all sides of the aisle. For example, Representative Steve King (R-IA) stated, "The wisdom of our Founding Fathers just amazes me time after time."[37] Senator Steve Daines (D-MT) extolled the Senate's rules, claiming they demonstrated the founders' "wisdom."[38] Senator Mike Rounds (R-SD) described the founders' design for impeachment trials, saying, "the Founding Fathers, in their subtle brilliance . . ."[39] Senator James E. Risch (R-ID) quipped that Trump's acquittal in his first impeachment trial had "underscored again for us the genius of the Founding Fathers" for "giving us" our current government system.[40] Senator Ron Johnson (R-WI) similarly stated that he hoped everyone had a "renewed appreciation for the genius of our Founding Fathers."[41] Senator Thomas R. Carper (D-DE) opined that the Constitution had guided the United States through "choppy waters" and that "some 233 years later" the Constitution is still heralded as the "triumph and wisdom" of the "Founding Fathers."[42] Likewise, Senator James Lankford (R-OK) stated that reading the "Founding Fathers'" writings filled one with an appreciation of "their clairvoyance."[43]

This veneration extols the founders' wisdom. Attributing to them a prescient genius, politicians invoke the "Founding Fathers" while addressing contemporary political conundrums. This discourse enacts a rhetoric of sovereignty: venerating the founders maintains and reinscribes an assumption of American exceptionalism by extolling the founders as exceptionally wise and uniquely able to draft universally applicable principles of good governance.

This emphasis on wisdom, however, draws upon and activates specifically Christian associations. The Christian scriptures extol God as wise. For instance, the Old Testament's wisdom literature makes statements such as "To God belong wisdom and power; counsel and understanding are his" (Job 12:13, NIV); Jesus is described as wise in the Gospels, "and Jesus grew in wisdom and stature, and in favor with God and man" (Luke 2:52, NIV); and the New Testament epistles extol God as wise with statements such as "Oh the depth of the riches of the wisdom and knowledge of God!" (Romans 11:33, NIV).

Moreover, the Christian scriptures repeatedly describe wisdom as a precious gift God bestows upon people. For example, the Old Testament's historical literature chronicles King Solomon's wisdom as an explicit gift from God: Solomon prays to God for wisdom, and God tells Solomon that he will receive "wisdom and knowledge" so that he can govern God's people well (2 Chronicles 1:11–12, NIV; see also 1 Kings 4:29). In addition, the Old Testament's wisdom literature stipulates that "to the person who pleases him, God gives wisdom, knowledge and happiness" (Ecclesiastes 2:26, NIV). Similarly, the New Testament epistles encourage believers to ask God for wisdom, with recommendations such as "If any of you lacks wisdom, you should ask God, who gives generously to all without finding fault, and it will be given to you" (James 1:5, NIV).

These passages, however, have traditionally been translated in masculinist language to state that God bestows the gift of wisdom upon men. The verses above were quoted from the 2011 translation of the New International Version. This translation was specifically designed to "offer its readers an experience that mirrors that of the original audience" by using inclusive language when referring to humanity (e.g., "people") rather than masculinist language (e.g., "men").[44] Consider, for comparison, the way the King James Version (KJV) translates James 1:5 as "If any of you lack wisdom, let *him* ask of God, that giveth to all *men* liberally, and upbraideth not; and it shall be given *him*."[45] Similarly, the English Standard Version (ESV), which was translated in the early 2000s by prominent evangelicals, uses "man" and other masculinist terms when referring to "the whole human race."[46] The ESV renders James 1:5 as "If any of you lacks wisdom, let *him* ask God, who gives generously to all without reproach, and it will be given to *him*."[47] Following Helen Sterk, my contention here is that this masculinist language matters.[48] That is, since English translations of the Christian scriptures regularly state that God gives *men* wisdom, Christians who speak and read English come to understand that God gives *men* wisdom.

Indeed, if English-speaking cultures ever had a truly universal and inclusive understanding of terms such as "men" and "he," those meanings have certainly shifted over time. By using masculinist terms and reinforcing them in prominent newer translations, such as the ESV, these translations functionally link masculinity, wisdom, and God's anointing or blessing. Especially when coupled with broader patriarchal hierarchies, these language choices affect Christian understandings of the cosmos and men's (and women's) place within it in ways that fundamentally shape the relationship between fatherhood and wisdom within Christian cultures. For example, not only is God routinely named as a father when discussing God's wisdom (e.g., God is an "all-wise, loving Father"), but fathers are explicitly charged with representing God and God's wisdom on earth.[49] For instance, Ken Leaman wrote in an article for Young Adults of Worth—a Christian organization focused on retaining children as Christians into adulthood—that "the role of father includes imparting Godly wisdom to their children.... Our earthly father is to represent our Heavenly Father."[50]

Read within this socioreligious context, the political veneration of the "Founding Fathers" as *wise* activates a number of related associations. First, it situates the founders as divinely blessed, since—within this framework—wisdom is a direct blessing from God. Essentially, the founders' wisdom is proof of their blessedness. Second, it reinforces their authority. Their (blessed) wisdom is a sign of their God-given authority to care for and protect their family—the nation. And third, it associates them with God, conferring a godlike status upon the founders. Indeed, phrases such as "the Founding Fathers, in their wisdom..." are blasphemously close to the common liturgical phrase "God, in his wisdom..." (Luke 11:49, NIV).

In their congressional speeches, contemporary politicians from across the political spectrum routinely venerate the founders as wise fathers. Activating a number of socioreligious associations, this discourse affirms the general concept of American exceptionalism, enshrining the "Founding Fathers" as divinely blessed, even godlike, and thus reaffirming their ongoing sovereignty—as fathers—over the American family.

Celebrating the United States

A significant portion of congressional discourse focuses on celebrating the United States. Indeed, congresspeople routinely engage in epideictic speeches that praise the United States and uphold US values such as "freedom." For instance, new senators ceremonially introduce themselves to the Senate, and there is a plethora of ceremonial celebrations, such as Bald Eagle Day, Constitution Day, and National Bible Week, not to mention the national holidays. Analyzing a representative portion of this discourse, I focus here on the links between the founders' metaphorical fatherhood, American exceptionalism, and how these founding myths are wielded as a rhetoric of sovereignty.

During the early months of the 2016 campaign, Senator Gary Peters (D-MI) made his introductory speech as a new senator from Michigan. His speech opens by stating that "since our Nation's founding, Michigan has been at the frontier of America, helping build a stronger and more secure country."[51] Senator Peters continues by describing how the "very first Congress" affirmed the "Northwest Ordinance" that "created" the "midwestern region from which the Michigan Territory would be born."[52] He continues to describe the "pioneers" that settled in Michigan—including "the Peters family" who moved to Michigan in the early 1840s.[53] After a lengthy speech describing Michigan's resources, infrastructure, institutions of higher education, and economy, Peters begins his conclusion by linking his lineage not just to Michigan's early "pioneers" but to the "Founding Fathers." He states, "On the Senate floor, we are standing on the shoulders of giants. This includes our Nation's Founding Fathers and more recent predecessors."[54] He then closes with the statement, "Together, we will continue to build a State and a country that embody the opportunity, the possibility, and the promise that has made our country a shining beacon for so many around the globe."[55]

Senator Peters's speech is ceremonial in nature. He specifically celebrates Michigan while situating Michigan and the United States more broadly as a great nation with a bright future. This celebration is grounded in a mythological rendering of the nation's founding—complete with its First Congress, pioneers, and frontier. Moreover, Peters's ethos is developed out of his lineage as he traces his bloodline back to those early pioneers and more metaphorically traces his current role as a senator back to the "Founding Fathers." His conclusion is overt in its American exceptionalism, positioning the United States as a "shining beacon" on the world's stage. Yet here, Peters looks ahead to Michigan and the United States' future—to the nation "we will continue to build."[56] The pairing of past and future, of origin and telos, or destiny, is clear. The United States' exceptional origins, its republican government, and colonial conquest of the "frontier" has set the country up for an exceptional destiny, and the "Founding Fathers" serve as the foundation—the giants—upon which the rest of the United States stands.

This logic—the move from origins to telos and the lineage traced back to the founders—undergirds most of the celebratory discourse within the *Congressional Record*. For example, every year in the days before June 20th, members of the House and Senate submit resolutions or make speeches designating June 20th as American Eagle Day. This tradition goes back to 1982, when President Ronald Reagan issued a proclamation designating June 20, 1982, as National Bald Eagle Day and designating the entire year of 1982 as the Bicentennial Year of the American Bald Eagle.[57] Reagan's proclamation officially commemorated the June 20, 1782, decision to make the American bald eagle the national symbol and the national bird. During the recent election cycles, Senator Lamar Alexander (R-TN) and a bipartisan coalition submitted almost verbatim resolutions designating June 20 as American Eagle Day.[58] The rationales offered to support these celebratory resolutions are instructive.

The resolutions begin with the reminder that "the bald eagle was chosen as the central image of the Great Seal of the United States on June 20, 1782, by the Founding Fathers at the Congress of the Confederation" and continue to explain that the "bald eagle is unique only to North America and cannot be found naturally in any other part of the world, which was one of the primary reasons the Founding Fathers selected the bald eagle to symbolize the Government of the United States."[59] Similarly, Representative David P. Roe (R-TN) offered almost verbatim speeches in 2015 and 2019 as part of American Eagle Day's celebrations in the House. In both these speeches, he says, "On June 20, 1782, the eagle was designated as the national emblem of the United States by the Founding Fathers at the Second Continental Congress" and then continues, stating, "The bald eagle is an inspiring symbol of the spirit of freedom and democracy in the United States. Since the founding of the Nation, the image, meaning, and symbolism of the eagle has played a significant role in art, music, history, commerce, literature, architecture, and culture of the United States. The bald eagle's habitat only exists in North America."[60]

This celebratory discourse focuses on origins, noting that even before the Unites States became the United States the founders had chosen the bald eagle as the nation's symbol. This also establishes a lineage, linking the bald eagle's importance back to the founders. Finally, this discourse emphasizes how unique—or exceptional—the

United States is, noting that North America is the bald eagle's only habitat while conspicuously ignoring Canada and Mexico. This discourse further ties the idea of exceptionalism to the founders, directly stating that the "Founding Fathers" chose the bald eagle primarily because it was unique to this land; although, again, the bald eagle's range includes Canada and Mexico.

Similarly, consider a trio of speeches given in the Senate on September 18, 2019, in celebration of Constitution Day. The Constitution was signed by thirty-nine of the fifty-five delegates to the Constitutional Convention in Philadelphia on September 17, 1787. Constitution Day was designated as a holiday in 2004 through an amendment by Senator Robert Byrd (D-WV) as part of an omnibus spending bill, and it is typically celebrated annually on September 17. On Constitution Day, all publicly funded educational institutions, federal agencies, and the like are required to provide educational programming regarding the Constitution. Speaking on September 18, 2019, Senators Joni Ernst (R-IA), Steve Daines (R-MT), and James Lankford (R-OK) all commemorated the prior day in their celebrations of the Constitution.

For example, Senator Joni Ernst (R-IA) began by stating that it is typical "to exchange gifts on anniversaries, but yesterday we celebrated the anniversary of a truly remarkable gift given to each of us as Americans: the Constitution."[61] She continues,

> On September 17, 1787, our Founding Fathers concluded the Constitutional Convention by proposing a new form of government based upon inalienable rights and self-determination of the American People. The Founders of our great Nation devoted incredible foresight to the very structure on which our country is built, and with the goal of protecting our rights as citizens for generations to come.[62]

Similarly, Senator Steve Daines (R-MT) celebrated Constitution Day by stating,

> Two hundred thirty-two years ago, our Founding Fathers gathered at Independence Hall in Philadelphia and signed a document that

remains the supreme law of the land today. In those two hundred thirty-two years, the United States has become the most powerful, the most prosperous Nation in the history of the world, and that success has come as a result of the framework set by our Constitution. The genius of the Framers was their determination to maximize the freedom of the individual while recognizing the need for a central government limited in size by our Constitution.[63]

Likewise, Senator James Lankford (R-OK) stated,

On September 17, 1787, this great experiment was finalized to try to form what they considered a more perfect Union, and the birth of our Constitution happened. This was a radical experiment in self-government, and most of the rest of the world at the time stared at those whom we now call our Founding Fathers and thought, that will never work.[64]

These speeches focus on the past, on a specific moment of origin: September 17, 1787. Senator Daines (R-MT) calls attention to this origin moment by situating it in space—Independence Hall, Philadelphia—and situating it in time by repeating the phrase "two hundred thirty-two years." Senator Ernst (R-IA) focuses on this origin moment by framing the Constitution as a material item, a "gift" bestowed on us by the "Founding Fathers." This activates the inheritance framework so frequently used in congressional discourse. Senator Lankford (R-OK) personifies this sense of inheritance and lineage by describing the Constitution as birthed—by the fathers—on September 17, 1787.

These celebrations of Constitution Day engage in the typical veneration of the "Founding Fathers," positioning them as exceptionally wise. Senator Ernst (R-IA) states that the founders had "incredible foresight"; Senator Daines (R-MT) applies the word "genius" to the founders; and Senator Lankford (R-OK) suggests they were so brilliant the rest of the world could not even conceive of how their plan might work.

Grounded in this moment of origin and drawing a lineage back to the founders' fatherly wisdom, these speeches invoke American exceptionalism. Senators Ernst (R-IA) and Lankford (R-OK) both emphasize principles of republican and democratic governance (self-determination, inalienable rights) as utterly unique to the US context—describing it as a "new form of government" and a "great experiment" so "radical" other countries balked at the notion. Senator Daines (R-OK) likewise emphasizes these principles (e.g., "freedom of the individual") but pushes further to state that, because of the Constitution, the United States has become "the most powerful, the most prosperous Nation in the history of the world."

This celebratory discourse moves from origin to destiny based on the "Founding Fathers'" lineage: their prescient wisdom created a mold for society, and thus society is shaped in their exceptional—glorious—image. This discourse is routine in the *Congressional Record*. It is seen throughout speeches commemorating days such as Bald Eagle Day and Constitution Day; speeches of introduction or retirement; speeches eulogizing a former congressperson or a prominent constituent; speeches welcoming a chamber back into session; and so on. This celebratory discourse is not just patriotic. It not only celebrates the United States; it celebrates the United States as exceptional—unique and superior to other nations—and its evidence for this claim is the founders' wisdom and lineage. It is not just that the "Founding Fathers" were wise; it is that the United States is their child, birthed with the Constitution. As long as Americans are their children—heirs who receive their gifts through time—Americans share their exceptional nature. Ultimately then, this celebratory discourse identifies who can be American: only those who can identify as the "Founding Fathers'" children—only true heirs.

Keeping the Covenant

Covenants in the Christian scriptures are sacred promises—most often between God and a chosen representative, such as Abraham or King David, or a chosen people, such as the Israelites. Covenants typically follow an if-then formula. A covenant's if-statement offers the terms or conditions of the agreement, and the then-statement stipulates the promised blessing or curse. For example, within the Old Testament, God's covenant with the Israelites (Leviticus 26 and Deuteronomy 28) can be summarized as "If you walk faithfully with Me, [then] I will reward you by blessing you and your land, but if you walk unfaithfully [then] I will punish you by cursing you and your land."[65]

Puritan leader John Winthrop famously invoked the Israelite covenant for the colonists in his 1630 sermon "A Model of Christian Charity." Imagining the Massachusetts Bay Colony as the "new Israel," Winthrop claimed their settlement would "be as a citty upon a hill" (*sic*).[66] Taking up this role as the "new Israel," Puritans in the "New World" embraced a covenantal existence, believing that *if* they walked faithfully with God, *then* God would bless them and "their" land. Invoking this covenant throughout their sermons, American Puritans adopted a three-part sermon sequence now known as the jeremiad. Jeremiads first affirm how good life has historically been within the covenant, then reveal a crisis—condemning a violation of the covenant—and finally imagine a utopian future through the restoration of covenantal living.[67] This three-part sequence moves from a pristine past, to an immediate crisis, to a millennial future—in which the congregation's reaffirmed covenantal living has ushered in heaven on earth.

Over time, this sermon genre became quite thoroughly secularized within white political discourse and is now known as the white American jeremiad.[68] Although secularized, it retains its covenantal if-then logic, its three-part structure, and its sense of a moral framework.[69] That is, white "reformers of the early American Republic" transferred this sacred discourse to more national and social applications, and US politicians have been widely using secular versions of the white American jeremiad, borrowing its "moral underpinnings" to assert what is right and what is right for the United States.[70] Most famously Ronald Reagan used this secularized jeremiad in his "Reaganomics" speeches, swapping out the Christian God for the "invisible hand" of market capitalism, which would supposedly reward hardworking (moral) Americans.[71]

Analyzing contemporary political expressions of American exceptionalism, Jason Edwards demonstrates that political discourse is often jeremiadic, arguing that the founders operate as "god-like figures" throughout this discourse.[72] In short, the American covenant of exceptionalism has been secularized: it is now largely between the "Founding Fathers" and their heirs rather than the Christian God and his people. Covenantal logic, then, undergirds the political veneration of the founders. The founders operate throughout this discourse as gods who will bless their children if the children keep their commands—primarily represented by the Constitution.

Yet this secularized covenant of American exceptionalism is fused with the appeals of Christian nationalism. Indeed, understanding Christian nationalism as an ideology rather than a religion per se, I read this congressional discourse as both drawing upon and reifying the sense of "national identity, belonging, and social hierarchies" that exist when the United States is conceptualized as a Christian nation.[73] As such, congressional discourse routinely makes blatant use of Christianity and espouses policies championed by Christian leaders. For example, Senator Sheldon Whitehouse (D-RI) repeatedly quoted from Pope Francis's *Laudato Si'* encyclical letter, exhorting his fellow senators to heed the pope's warning and to find "the courage to stand up against the power of these selfish forces and do what is right for our people and our planet."[74] This speech rails against climate change, urging the Senate to take action and making its appeals in explicitly Christian language. Senator Whitehouse not only uses Pope Francis's encyclical, but he likens the senators who side with the fossil fuel industry to Pharisees, saying, "Jesus himself, the Lamb of God, lost his temper twice, the Bible tells us; once at Pharisees and once at the traders and money changers in the temple. He went after them with a lash, actually. Are we to take their side now? Must we, the Senate, serve Caesar in every single thing? Is there no light left here at all?"[75]

Here, Whitehouse uses a number of explicitly Christian references. He not only names Jesus but names him as the Lamb of God, recounts a gospel story with detail and precision, and uses two phrases, "serve Caesar" and "no light left here at all," that are direct biblical allusions. The first is to the contrast Jesus makes between serving God and serving Caesar (Matthew 22:15–22), and the second is to the repeated biblical metaphors that liken Jesus and God more broadly to light (Luke 1:79, John 1:5; John 8:12; John 12:46; 1 John 1–2).

Senator Whitehouse's explicit use of biblical appeals are directly tied to American exceptionalism and his invocation of the "Founding Fathers." He states, "This responsibility, this call from Pope Francis matters particularly for America, the indispensable and the exceptional nation. Years ago, Daniel Webster described the work of our Founding Fathers as having 'set the world an example.' From John Winthrop to Ronald Reagan, we have called ourselves a city on a hill, set high for the world to witness, to emulate."[76]

Whitehouse not only names the United States as an "indispensable" and "exceptional nation," but he frames the "Founding Fathers" as having achieved their goal: they "set the world an example." Whitehouse then leverages that identity—a city on a hill—in an attempt to shame his colleagues into once again becoming the exemplary nation. This is covenantal, jeremiadic logic. Put simply, Whitehouse's speech argues that once the United States was a city on a hill, but now it has abandoned the covenant through greed and climate disruption. This crisis is rendered in explicitly Christian language: US senators have become Pharisees, forsaking their role as the chosen people. Yet Whitehouse promises that the United States can reclaim its exceptional place by returning to the covenant, becoming the world leader on climate change.

There is a sort of breathless, seamless move in this discourse between the "Founding Fathers" as the gods of a secular American covenant of exceptionalism and the Christian nationalism that at least nominally names Jesus as Lord. Indeed, this discourse seems to conflate the United States and the kingdom of God, using Christian appeals to further an American identity as an exceptional nation. That is, by doing what Pope Francis and—as rendered in this discourse—what Jesus want, Whitehouse declares the United States can reclaim its rightful place on the world's stage. Christianity is the means; exceptionalism is the end.

This reveals a mediating factor in the origins-telos dynamic traced throughout this chapter. The founders serve as secular gods who created or birthed the country and thus prescribe its destiny—but the route from origin to destiny is often through Christian nationalism. For example, speaking at the beginning of the 2016 presidential campaign, Representative Robert Dold (R-IL) presented a one-minute oration in the House chamber. Quoted in its entirety here, this brief speech is titled "Persecution of Christians."[77]

> I rise today to address the glaring issue of the persecution of Christians around the globe.
>
> Our Nation was founded on the principles of religious liberty and tolerance, and the United States continues to promote these ideals. We must remain steadfast in our efforts to help individuals who are persecuted simply due to their faith. Everyone around the globe, Mr. Speaker, should be free to live a life of faith, to worship as they choose, without fear of persecution from a ruthless regime. This basic freedom, which was enshrined by our Founding Fathers, must not only be promoted here, but also around the world.
>
> As a shining city upon a hill with the eyes of the world upon us, it is our Nation's duty to be a leader in the fight against the persecution of Christians. As ISIS continues to attack Christians in the Middle East, we must continue to show that our Nation will stand up and defend those who cannot defend themselves.[78]

Despite the numerous types of religious persecution taking place in the world, Representative Dold makes his speech specifically about Christians and Christianity. The title and opening statement, "I rise today to address the glaring issue of the persecution of Christians," situate Dold's concern as explicitly and exclusively pertaining to Christianity. Dold then invokes the nation's founding, mythologizing the nation's origin and the principle of religious liberty. Here, Dold invokes the "Founding Fathers," situating them as the creators of US religious liberty and as having originated America's exceptionalism, insinuating that the founders wanted the United States to be an example to all other nations. Dold then directly uses the language of exceptionalism which is fused with a Christian metaphor (a light on a hill), stating that the United States is "a shining city upon a hill with the eyes of the world upon us," and thus the country must be "a leader in the fight against the persecution of Christians." Preserving Christians and Christianity is how this speech imagines the United States maintaining its exceptional destiny. That is, preserving Christians and Christianity is how this speech imagines the United States moving from its origins as a world leader in religious liberty to its telos as a world leader in religious liberty. Throughout, this speech privileges those with a Christian worldview, attempting to steer legislation in a way that would reinforce those privileges. This is the rhetoric of Christian nationalism.

In another instance, Senator Deb Fischer (R-NE) spoke in support of President Trump's nominee, Brian Buescher, for the US District Court for the District of Nebraska. During Buescher's confirmation hearing, Democrats such as Senator Mazie Hirono (D-HI) questioned Buescher's ability to enforce "equal protection of the law for LGBT people" since Buescher is a member of the Knights of Columbus, a Catholic fraternal organization which has "a long record of opposing equal protection of the law for LGBT people."[79] Responding to this line of questioning, Senator Fischer characterized it as tearing "at the fabric of our core American values—the freedom to worship and pray as we choose."[80] She then argues that the Senate has a chance "to send a clear message that we share our Founding Fathers' contempt for religious tests for public office by confirming Brian Buescher to the Federal Bench."[81] She continues, stating, "I think it is important to reiterate that reverence for our Constitution and our laws is part of what it means to be an American," and then she paraphrases Abraham Lincoln, claiming that Americans "should transfer reverence for our Founders to reverence to the laws that they created."[82] Finally, she concludes by stating that only by respecting "our Constitution" could we "honor our past" and "protect the future generations of this great Nation."[83] Here, Senator Fischer explicitly uses the Religious Right's "playbook," advocating for and installing judges who "defend religious liberty" by overturning the past few decades of jurisprudence when it comes to the "separation of church and state."[84] That is, Fischer advocates for Buescher's judicial appointment using the language of "religious liberty" even as she helps install a federal judge whose appeal is in his inability to separate his religion from his rulings.

In her speech, Senator Fischer makes clear use of the three-part jeremiadic structure: invoking the "Founding Fathers," Fischer grounds US origins in a secular covenant that valued religious liberty; she describes the present as a time of crisis in which the "fabric of our core American values" is being torn asunder; and then she points the way toward the country's covenantal destiny as a "great Nation." Fischer frames this way forward as a return to the *secular* covenant, a return to religious liberty, but she urges her fellow senators to confirm a judicial nominee who explicitly identifies as Christian and who politically supports "family" values—where "family" is code for both whiteness and heteronormativity. In this speech, the path from origin to destiny is through Christian nationalism: the support of Christian political agents and their politics of "family" values.

Occasionally—compared to the larger witness of the *Congressional Record*—some congressional politicians downplay the veneration of the "Founding Fathers" within a framework of heightened Christian nationalism. In these instances, the founders are venerated as the country's wise fathers, but the covenant of American exceptionalism is explicitly framed as Christian—not secularized. Thus, the founders appear as fathers and not as gods, which is a significant change in tone from the usual veneration afforded to the founders.

Consider, for example, the speech Representative Virginia Foxx (R-NC) offered in the House on September 17, 2019, in commemoration of Constitution Day. Representative Foxx begins her speech by stating that "when our country was founded, the idea of a democratic republic was not foreign; it was nonexistent."[85] She then announces that "our Constitution truly is a *miracle*," continuing that "aside from its genius, its history helps us appreciate the *blessing* it is."[86] She then quotes at length from a book, *Seven Miracles That Saved America*, to provide "three reasons to believe God had a hand in the crafting of the Constitution."[87] Foxx reads these three reasons: (1) the timing in which the Constitution was written, (2) the "miraculous compromise" wherein the founders came to agreement, and (3) the "4,400 Miraculous Words" of the Constitution itself.[88] For this last reason, the document's brevity and yet enduring relevance is presented as evidence that, like the Bible, God had a hand in its crafting. Foxx ends her speech—still quoting—by stating that the Constitution has made the United States a "shining light on the hill" and that it provides "inspiration for peoples all over the Earth," and by finally concluding with the question "Is that not a miracle?"[89]

In this speech, Representative Foxx moves through the customary mythologizing of US origins, extolling the founders' "genius" and quite clearly stating that their wisdom in writing the Constitution was miraculously handed down to them by the God of the Christian scriptures. This demonstrates the callousness of white Christian nationalism as Foxx presents the Constitution—which condones the slave trade and created the three-fifths rule—as if God miraculously crafted it.

Yet in Foxx's speech, the "Founding Fathers" are relatively demoted compared to other congressional speeches. That is, there is little room for the veneration of the founders in this speech's Christian nationalism. Beyond extolling the founders' genius, this speech focuses primarily on attributing the Constitution to God. This downplays the secular aspect of US covenantal exceptionalism, emphatically presenting the United States as a Christian nation. Within this speech's framework, the United States was created by God; Christianity is the United States' origin and destiny.

Similarly, consider the speeches presented on November 20, 2019, in celebration of National Bible Week. National Bible Week originated in 1941 when President Franklin Delano Roosevelt "declared the week of Thanksgiving to be National Bible Week."[90] Like the House and Senate's daily prayers, National Bible Week demonstrates the clear and ongoing influence of Christian nationalism within Congress.[91] For the 2019 celebration of National Bible Week, Representative Doug Lamborn (R-CO) was granted sixty minutes in the House, which he filled by scheduling a number of speakers who offered a sequence of short speeches. Representative Lamborn opened the hour with a short speech, and then in the House's traditional manner, he provided transitions from one speaker to the next. For example, after Representative Brian Babin's (R-TX) speech, which noted how "fitting" it is to "bring attention to the very book that was so influential in the founding of our nation" and was "perhaps the most accessible book to our Founding Fathers,"[92] Representative Lamborn transitioned, stating, "Mr. Speaker, I thank the gentleman from Texas [Babin] for sharing his heart with us tonight" and then stating, "I yield to the gentleman from Pennsylvania (Mr. Thompson [R-PA]), as we go across the country and hear from folks all over this great country of ours."[93] In the middle of this sequence, Representative Lamborn made his own short speech, and he closed the hour with a final statement.

This celebration of National Bible Week is peppered with references to American exceptionalism. The speeches routinely refer to the United States as a "great country" and a "great nation," and they state that Americans are "truly blessed" to live in the United States.[94] These speeches primarily ground their covenantal exceptionalism on the Bible and the Christian God, demoting the Constitution and the "Founding Fathers" into secondary figures in this covenant of Christian nationalism.

For example, in his opening, Representative Lamborn states that "this is the week set aside to recognize the Bible as a foundational building block of Western civilization, the Judeo-Christian heritage, and the legacy that motivated and shaped the founding of the United States."[95] Likewise, Representative Glenn Grothman (R-WI) argues that the Bible is important because "our forefathers" were reading it when they "wrote our Constitution, when they wrote our Declaration of Independence" and as they "designed our wonderful country."[96] In his own speech, Lamborn recounts that "Our Founding Fathers understood how important it was for the American people to have Bibles," telling the story of how Congress "authorized the first known English language Bible to be printed in America" by passing a "congressional resolution."[97] Here, he chides his contemporary colleagues, stating, "I'm not sure how many votes this would get if we brought this today. I know I would support it."[98] In his conclusion, Representative Lamborn returns to the theme of American exceptionalism, stating that "civilizations have risen and fallen, generations have come and gone" but that the United States is still standing—and still celebrating "the enduring Word of God."[99]

These speeches essentially revert to a more Puritan formulation of the covenant of American exceptionalism, attributing this exceptionalism directly to God. They maintain some veneration of the founders as men who channeled God's blessings for this country, however, foregrounding the founders' role within this Christian-nationalist rendition of the covenant of American exceptionalism. In both the more secular and the more Christian-nationalist versions of this covenant, Christianity continues to be the means through which the United States achieves its glorious destiny. That is, the secular version is not very secular. Moreover, both versions of this covenant feature the same possessive, inheritance-based logic that suffuses so much of the congressional record: these are *our* fathers, and the Constitution is a legacy they bequeathed to *us*.

When reflecting on the United States' past or celebrating specific aspects of US identity, congressional politicians routinely venerate the "Founding Fathers," centering the covenant of American exceptionalism on their godlike or God-ordained fatherhood. In so doing, this discourse directly incorporates Christian nationalism into its rhetoric of sovereignty. This discourse follows the Christian Right's playbook, courting conservative Christians as a voting bloc. Yet as evangelical historian John Fea writes, by depending on "political influence" in order to supposedly "restore the nation" to Christian morals, conservative Christians not only rely on a selective amnesia through which they collectively remember the founders and the founding era, but they confuse "the kingdom of God with the United States of America."[100] Indeed, as Fea writes, "Evangelicals claim to follow a Savior who relinquished worldly power—even to the point of giving his life," and yet they continually "place their hope in political candidates," enacting and reifying Christian nationalism. Fusing American exceptionalism and Christian nationalism, this congressional discourse governs the United States. It enacts a rhetoric of sovereignty—a way to speak that establishes not just a version of the United States but the symbols and identities that constitute "the people" and good governance.

Losing Faith: Racially Realistic Cynicism

The covenant of American exceptionalism and its fusion of Christian nationalism is not monolithic within Congress. Instead, this discourse is contested by the rhetoric of cynicism, which calls the entire covenant of American exceptionalism into question as it offers a dose of racial realism.

Cynicism voices a sort of "tragic alienation" from something once imagined as great or good. Or to put it another way, cynicism encompasses a loss of "faith" in something or someone.[101] This is different from simply admitting that something or someone is flawed. For instance, while the rare Republican occasionally stated during the recent election cycles that the founders had made some mistakes during their lifetimes, these passing asides never entered into cynicism, never distanced themselves from the myth of the founders as fathers, never voiced a loss of faith in the founders or the covenant of American exceptionalism that finds its roots in the idealized collective memory—or mythology—of the founders.

Expressing such realistic cynicism is politically risky. The metaphor of fatherhood establishes a sense of American lineage and positions the founders as the gods or dignitaries of the covenant of American exceptionalism, establishing the US identity to the extent that even questioning the paternalization of this nation is risky. To lose faith in the founders is akin to being unpatriotic and can be construed as a loss of faith in the United States itself.

Despite the risk, members of the Congressional Black Caucus and other Democrats occasionally give voice to such cynicism, expressing it in one of two ways. First, one might express a loss of faith in how visionary the founders actually were. This is the less risky option of the two. It presents the founders as incomplete: they were generally good men who tried, but they ultimately left the country unfinished.

For example, consider Representative Robin Kelly (D-IL) as she spoke during the 2016 election cycle. A member of the Congressional Black Caucus, Representative Kelly formally addressed the Speaker of the House—as is the tradition—but she clearly intended her words for the American people, saying, "Mr. Speaker, in this hour, the Congressional Black Caucus will have a conversation with America about the issue of race relations in this country."[102] Representative Kelly continues by noting that "this isn't a new topic of discussion" and then confesses, "To be honest, I really wish there were no need and no appetite remaining in America so as to have to address this topic."[103] Here, already, the tones of cynicism are present: Representative Kelly identifies the topic of "race relations" as an old topic, one that presents an ongoing "need" in the United States. She presents little by way of faith that the nation is overcoming this problem. Indeed, in this framework, there is a distinct lack of faith in any originating greatness and a lack of faith that Americans are assured an exceptional destiny. Instead, the problem is old and ongoing.

Continuing, Representative Kelly states,

> It is amazing that the same nation that saw pilgrims journey to our shores on the Mayflower and that same nation that saw Founding Father Ben Franklin make groundbreaking discoveries in electric science is the same nation that was able to land a man on the moon and harness the electromagnetic spectrum for our mobile devices. We still wrestle with the same problem that confronted Ben Franklin and the Founding Fathers so long ago: the issue of race relations in America.[104]

Here, Representative Kelly seemingly recounts the mythology of US origins, naming the pilgrims and Ben Franklin's electricity experiments, and while she lauds the United States for its technological progress, instead of extolling US greatness this historicizing points to a clear flaw in the design. Indeed, Kelly marvels at what the United

States has achieved so far—she is *amazed* at US progress given its clear problem, which she moderately names as "race relations." There is a cynicism here. In this speech, the founders are not gods who guarantee the covenant of American exceptionalism. They are men who faced a problem (race relations) and left it unsolved.

In a fairly similar manner, Representative Brenda L. Lawrence (D-MI) spoke in support of removing the deadline for the ratification of the Equal Rights Amendment (ERA). A member of the Congressional Black Caucus, she concluded her speech by quoting Shirley Chisholm—one of the founding thirteen members of the Congressional Black Caucus—noting that Chisholm was "the first African American woman in Congress."[105] Quoting Chisholm, she states, "The time is clearly now to put this House on record for the fullest expression of that equality of opportunity which our Founding Fathers professed. They professed it, but they did not assure it to their daughters, as they tried to do for their sons."[106] Representative Lawrence then immediately repeats this sentiment in slightly modified terms, stating, "The time is clearly now to put this House on record for the fullest expression of that equality of opportunity which our Founding Fathers *possessed*. They *possessed* it, but they did not assure it. We try as they tried to do for their sons."[107] This speech presents the founders as fallible. Dabbling in materialism, Lawrence changes Chisholm's "professed" to "possessed." But here, this materialism reveals that the founders *owned* "equality of opportunity" and yet could not bequeath it even to their sons. Indeed, the founders failed twice: first, they failed to assure this inheritance to their sons; and second, they failed by not even attempting to make equality a reality for their daughters.

As atypical as this discourse appears when compared to the rampant veneration of the founders throughout the *Congressional Record*, this first expression of cynicism is mild when compared to the second. Indeed, in the first, the founders are demoted from gods back to men—men who were *not* extraordinarily blessed by God. In the second expression of cynicism, however, the founders are seen as visionary and the country they created is indeed great, but only great for some, and that greatness depends upon the oppression of others. In the second expression of cynicism, the founders are not gods—but they might be devils.

This argument is bold, and Black Democrats are cautious as they voice this cynicism in Congress. Consider, for example, how Representative Hakeem S. Jeffries (D-NY) described the federal government in a speech that was part of an hour time slot dedicated to members of the Congressional Black Caucus in the House. Representative Jeffries directly addressed the American people, stating, "This is a most distinguished venue from which to speak to the American people, an appropriate one, I would add, given the House's constitutional relationship to the people of America, this, of course, being the only institution that was envisioned by the Founding Fathers as one in which the people serving in the institution would be directly elected by the people."[108]

He goes on to explain how the "Senate's Members" in the "original constitutional version" were elected by state legislatures and that the presidency "to this day, is a vehicle through which the individual is selected by the Electoral College."[109] He then emphasizes the House, stating, "So this is the people's House, the institution most intimately connected to the people of America and the place where we should speak truth to power."[110]

While Representative Jeffries avoids maligning the founders, his speech hopes to reveal to the American public that the federal government was not—and is not—designed democratically. He repeatedly emphasizes that the House is the only representative body and clearly states that it is the only representative body by the founders' design. Jeffries' speech reveals that the federal government was designed for hierarchy, was designed to subordinate "the people's" voice.

More pointedly—and yet at a remove—in the year of the four-hundredth anniversary of when enslaved Africans were first brought to the United States, Representative Barbara Lee (D-CA) had an essay by Nikole Hannah-Jones from "The 1619 Project" read into the House record. Representative Lee is the "highest ranking African American woman in Democratic Leadership," serving as co-chair of the Policy and Steering Committee, and the former chair of the Congressional Black Caucus (111th Congress).[111] Yet she provides no speech or statement of her own, simply submitting Hannah-Jones's essay for the record.

Hannah-Jones's essay clearly states that as Thomas Jefferson penned the words of the Declaration of Independence, writing "that all men are created equal," an enslaved teenage boy named Robert Hemings waited in the room, serving "at his master's beck and call," and that Hemings would "enjoy none of those rights and liberties" of which Jefferson wrote.[112] Continuing, Hannah-Jones notes that by 1776 Britain was increasingly "conflicted over its role" in slavery, and Londoners were attempting to "abolish the slave trade."[113] This would have "upended the economy of the colonies," dismantling the "wealth and prominence" that enabled the "Founding Fathers" to "believe they could successfully break off from one of the mightiest empires in the world."[114] Here, Hannah-Jones directly links the American Revolution to slavery, stating that the founders were able to imagine and succeed in this revolution because of "the dizzying profits generated by chattel slavery."[115] Noting that "ten of this nation's first twelve presidents were enslavers," Hannah-Jones suggests that this nation was founded "not as a democracy but as a slavocracy."[116]

Embracing a realistic cynicism, Representative Lee endorsed Hannah-Jones's account of the United States' founding. The founders are bold and visionary in this rendering, but they are also greedy and inhumane. There can be no faith in these men; they are no gods. Instead, there is a tragic alienation from the founders, a loss of faith. These men created something—the United States—that is based in and designed for oppression.

There is, however, a different sort of faith circulating within this discourse. For example, early in her essay, Hannah-Jones describes how Crispus Attucks—a "fugitive from slavery"—was the "very first person to die for this country in the American Revolution."[117] Working from this fact, Hannah-Jones stipulates that Black Americans "are this nation's true 'founding fathers.'"[118] Here, Hannah-Jones's writing puts "Founding Fathers" within quote marks, marking the phrase with irony even as she momentarily displaces the usual host of white men from this position. Toward the conclusion of her essay, Hannah-Jones returns to this theme, stating that "no one cherishes freedom more than those who have not had it" and noting that "black Americans, more than any other group embrace democratic ideals."[119] Here, she notes that despite having an "unemployment rate" that is "nearly twice that of white Americans," Black Americans "are still the most likely of all groups to say this nation should take in refugees."[120] She concludes, then, that "the truth is that as much democracy as this nation has" is due to "black resistance," and she then writes, "our founding fathers may not have actually believed in the ideals they espoused, but black people did."[121]

This discourse traces a different lineage: one originating in the revolutionary blood of the enslaved and fugitive Crispus Attucks and flowing through the resistance of Black Americans and their commitment to freedom. Within this rendering, the "Founding Fathers" are charlatans and hypocrites. They founded a hierarchical, caste-bound country, and every ounce of democracy and freedom this country enjoys is due not to their vision but to Black resistance. The faith circulating within this essay is not faith in the "Founding Fathers," Americans' lineage as their children, or Christian nationalism. This faith rests on Black people, and Hannah-Jones draws a direct *American* lineage for herself in her essay's closing words, tracing her Americanness back to the Black people who founded America.[122] In so doing, Hannah-Jones doubles down on core values of freedom and equality but resituates them, cynically demonstrating that they cannot be traced back to the founders but are discovered instead in the lineage of the enslaved. While refraining from adding her own words, Representative Lee endorsed this argument, underscoring both its realistic cynicism and its faith by entering it into the *Congressional Record*.

Black congresspeople and other Democrats have good reason for demonstrating caution as they voice this realistic cynicism, or loss of faith in the founders. They are lampooned by Republicans, who use these expressions of cynicism to accuse "the left" of not believing in the Christian-nationalist covenant of American exceptionalism—and by extension of being un-American.

For example, consider the first speech from Senator Rick Scott (R-FL) before the Senate—a speech he titled his "Maiden Speech" rather than using less gendered phrasing such as a "Speech of Introduction."[123] The speech begins with brief stories of his childhood—his adoptive father's tours in WWII and his mother taking him to church—and then even briefer accounts of his own service in the Navy, and his marriage and subsequent family. The speech turns away from the biographical as Senator Scott states, "I now thank God every day for my mom and for this country," and continues, "unfortunately the left has worked hard over the last fifty years to discredit the values of the America I was raised with—the values of the America I want my grandsons to grow up with."[124] He briefly admits that the United States is not without its troubles, stating, "We all acknowledge that Americans, our country, and our institutions have flaws," but then doubles down, saying, "but the left has worked to discredit our Founders. . . . The left thinks it is OK that our schools don't teach about the Founding Fathers or free markets. They want you to think America was never great."[125] He concludes his "Maiden Speech" by vowing to "fight" for American exceptionalism, stating, "I ran for public office to fight for the country I was raised in because that is the country our children and our grandchildren deserve. They deserve what my mom gave me—a free country with unlimited potential for every citizen. I hope everyone will join me in this fight."[126]

In this speech, Senator Scott admits but then brushes aside any concerns that the founders or the United States—as represented by his reminiscence of the 1950s—might be less than ideal for some Americans. Moreover, he equates cynicism toward the founders with disbelief in American exceptionalism. This makes sense within the covenantal, jeremiadic logic governing American exceptionalism: regardless of whether the founders are gods who maintain a secular covenant or are lynchpins within God's covenant of American exceptionalism, the covenant and its jeremiadic logic moves from origin to destiny. Therefore, if the origins are unexceptional, the destiny will be as well. Losing faith in the "Founding Fathers," then, undoes the entire covenant—unless, for example, one is willing to relocate that covenant to Black founders as Nikole Hannah-Jones did, a move Senator Scott seems unprepared to make.

Conclusion

The *Congressional Record* is littered with the veneration of the founders. This is clearly the dominant discourse, and it manifests in both passing asides that celebrate the "Founding Fathers" and in speeches dedicated to celebrating the United States. The vast majority of (white) congresspeople venerate the founders, extolling their wisdom and exalting their creations—both the Constitution and the country more broadly.

My analysis of this venerating discourse reveals the covenantal, jeremiadic, and Christian-nationalist nature of this imagined relationship between the founders and the contemporary United States. Whether the founders operate as secularized gods or whether they operate as dignitaries within a seemingly Christian covenant, the country's greatness is assured—destined—but only if Americans are true to their imagined Christian origins. Or to put it another way, US greatness is assured, but only for true Americans . . . who by inference are white, patriarchal, and support "family" values of Christian nationalism. This emphasis on Christianity demonstrates a profound collective amnesia, especially in light of many of the founders' pronounced religious skepticism. Indeed, Thomas Jefferson's skepticism was so well known during the founding era that some Americans buried their Bibles when he became president, fearing he would take them away.[127]

It is my contention that these Christian-nationalist appeals are often designed to rally a Christian-identifying voting bloc. Indeed, while some Democrats make these sorts of appeals—for example, Senator Sheldon Whitehouse (D-RI) quoted extensively from Pope Francis—it is Republican congresspeople who weave these Christian appeals into their celebrations of Constitution Day and who spearhead events like the commemoration of National Bible Week.

What is unspoken in these Christian appeals is their implicit patriarchy and whiteness. That is, venerating the "Founding Fathers" elevates both whiteness and masculinity as uniquely blessed by God during the founding era or as godlike in itself; yet the supremacy of whiteness and masculinity cannot be openly celebrated within US politics. That is, most politicians know that it sounds bad to say white men are more divinely blessed than others. Christian values, however, can be celebrated aloud, and "Christian values" carries with it an implied whiteness and masculinity in the American context—despite the realities that Black people are the most churched demographic in the United States and that women outnumber men in Christian churches.[128]

Indeed, it is no accident that white Christians are among "the strongest supporters of Confederate symbolism (e.g., monuments) and of economic and social policies that oppress Black people."[129] Historically, the Christian church helped institutionalize race and white supremacy in the colonies. As historian Rebecca Goetz demonstrates, Virginian colonists "conceptualized Christianity and heathenism as hereditary" and thus as *races*, imagining that only white colonists could be Christians and that "in reproductive terms" all enslaved Black people could not be Christian and would always be slaves.[130] Scholars such as Deborah Gray White, James H. Cone, and Robert Jones then trace the American church's white supremacy: from pro-slavery arguments before and during the Civil War, to Lost Cause arguments after the Civil War, to lynching rhetoric during Reconstruction and through the Civil Rights Movement, to the contemporary evangelical "culture wars."[131] This social, religious, and historical context has generated a fused "white-Christian-American identity," where Christianity is almost synonymous with being a good American and being white.[132] By touting Christianity and "family" values, congresspeople operate in a discourse of inferential racism, using Christianity as code for white and mobilizing a voting bloc through a playbook that targets "white evangelical fear" of moral decline—where moral decline overlaps with the weakening of "patriarchal, heteronormative, nativist and white supremacist values."[133]

Understanding how the metaphor of fatherhood works in US politics explains the contemporary crises and demonstrates the necessity of other ways to conceptualize the founders in public memory. Imagining the founders as this nation's fathers not only paternalizes the nation but sets up a logic of inheritance. This rhetoric of sovereignty produces purity tests for who can be "American" that privilege white men who tout "family" values—and the women who support them. This not only reinforces structural inequalities; it leads to violence and even terrorism as white men supposedly defend their inheritance.

In light of this structural inequality and violence, members of the Congressional Black Caucus offer a counter discourse of racially realistic cynicism. This reimagines the founders in public memory—and thus reimagines US structures, identity, and sovereignty, undoing the inheritance logic of American exceptionalism. Despite the risky nature of voicing such cynicism, members of the Congressional Black Caucus lead the way, asking Americans to lose faith in the "Founding Fathers." This counter discourse has significant power, working to resist inheritance logic even when it escalates into the rhetoric of defense, as the next chapter demonstrates.

CHAPTER THREE

Checks and Balances

———

THE PHRASE "CHECKS AND BALANCES" is routinely bandied about in US politics. Despite its contemporary usage, the phrase itself is not part of the United States' founding documents. The phrase is associated with the political treatise *The Spirit of Laws* by Charles-Louis de Secondat, Baron de Montesquieu. Originally published in French in 1748 and then republished in English in 1750, *The Spirit of Laws* was controversial enough that the Roman Catholic Church added it to its list of prohibited books, the *Index Librorum Prohibitorum*. Although the Catholic Church did not appreciate its sentiments, many of the US founders found Montesquieu's work quite useful for their own purposes.

The idea of "checks and balances" works in concert with the "separation of powers." At heart, these two concepts combine to imagine a government in which the powers of governing are separated among different branches (e.g., legislative, executive, and judicial) and in which these branches can "check and balance" each other, ensuring no branch can impose tyranny over the others. For instance, in *The Spirit of Laws*, Montesquieu imagined a legislature with two houses that could "check one another by the mutual privilege of rejecting" one another's decisions, and together those houses would restrain an executive power—which in turn could restrain the legislative.[1] Separation of powers and checks and balances can apply not only to branches of government but also to levels of government. Dividing power among levels (e.g., national, state, and local) is known as Federalism.[2]

The founders had two primary influences that steered them toward Federalism, the separation of powers, and the ability for governmental branches and levels to "check" one another. Reading the Enlightenment works of Montesquieu, Harrington, Locke, and Blackstone provided one part of this foundation, along with the histories of Greek democracies and the Roman Republic. Indeed, many ancient Greek city-states featured a separation of powers, which Aristotle described as a "mixed" government in *Politics*.[3] Likewise, the Roman Republic separated powers among the Senate, Consuls, and Assemblies, and the Roman historian Polybius explained how this system used what we now refer to as "checks and balances."[4]

The founders were also influenced by observing the Iroquois Confederacy. The Iroquois Confederacy was founded in approximately 1142, placing it among the world's oldest participatory democracies and making it one of the very few that have persisted from antiquity into the contemporary era.[5] The Iroquois Confederacy joined six nations: the Kanienkehaka (also known as the Mohawks), the Onondaga, the Cayuga, the Oneida, the Seneca, and the Tuscarora—who joined the confederation considerably later in 1722. The Iroquois Constitution features many of the elements adopted in the US Constitution. It restricts members from holding more than one office within the Confederacy, delineates who has the power to declare war, explains how to remove leaders, designates two legislative branches, and balances power between the Iroquois Confederacy and the tribal nations.[6] Thus, the Iroquois Confederacy specifically modeled a separation of powers, Federalism, and checks and balances. The founders were acquainted with the Iroquois Confederacy and clearly looked to "Native governments for inspiration."[7]

Even as the founders drew inspiration from Native governments, however, they also generally considered "Native people as inferior."[8] For instance, in a 1751 letter to James Parker, Benjamin Franklin wrote that the Iroquois Confederacy was a model for the type of federalist union he imagined among the colonies, while also insulting the Iroquois. He wrote, "It would be a very strange Thing, if six Nations of ignorant Savages should be capable of forming a Scheme for such an Union . . . and yet that a like Union should be impracticable for ten or a Dozen English Colonies."[9]

After a rather failed attempt in the 1777 Articles of Confederation, the former English colonies cohered into such a union through the US Constitution.[10] Like the Iroquois Confederacy and Montesquieu's imaginary government, the US Constitution provides several "checks" that balance power among its branches and levels. Most famously, there are two legislative branches of Congress, and neither can pass legislation without the other. Similarly, the president can veto legislation—and Congress can overrule a veto through a two-thirds majority vote in both branches. Writing in the "Federalist Papers No. 51 (1788)," James Madison described the decision to distribute power in multiple "offices" where "each may be a check on the other" as offering "auxiliary precautions" against tyranny.[11] Although tyranny is now associated primarily with autocratic rulers and dictatorships, the founders' distrust "of tyrannies extended to popular majorities."[12]

Thus, as constitutional experts Steven G. Calabresi and Michael J. Gerhardt explain, the Senate was designed to frustrate direct democracy, ensuring the country could not be steered by the majority-will of the people.[13] This was achieved through a number of stipulations in Article I, Section 3 of the Constitution. First, senators were originally selected by their "respective State legislatures," not by the people.[14] Second, the Senate is not representative. Regardless of the number of people living in a state, every state receives two senators. This empowers less populace states, ensuring that they can protect and further their own interests against the will of more populace states—especially since the House cannot pass any legislation without the Senate's approval. Third, unlike the House's two-year appointments, senators have six-year appointments. Since senators are not constantly facing re-election campaigns, they can vote in ways that displease their state without fearing reprisal through an imminent election challenge.

Fourth, the minimum age for senators was set at thirty, while House representatives can serve starting at age twenty-five. This age requirement was designed "to increase the likelihood that senators would be better educated" and more mature during their service—making them more "disposed than their House counterparts to take the long view on important issues."[15] Moreover, the Senate can act independently of the House in four ways: it can "advise and consent to presidential nominations"; it can ratify treaties; it can convict and remove "high-ranking officials for misconduct"; and it can approve constitutional amendments.[16] The House, meanwhile, can act independently only by impeaching a federal official—and this has no tangible effect unless the Senate votes to convict and remove that official.

When the states ratified the Seventeenth Amendment in 1913, senators became selected through popular election, making them answerable to the people of their state. The lengthy term of service still provides some insulation, however, protecting senators from imminent electoral reprisals. But more significantly, the Senate is still unrepresentative: it does not reflect the population of the United States, enabling senators who represent a minority of people to frustrate the majority of people. Again, this is not a flaw in constitutional design; this is the design. The Senate is meant to be a check against the "tyranny" of the people who determine the representatives in the House.[17] Speaking in 2019, Senator Chuck Grassley (R-IA) recalled this design, noting that the "Founding Fathers" intended for "the Senate to be a check on the House of Representatives" lest the United States be ruled—and here he quotes from James Madison—by "the impulse of sudden and violent passions."[18]

The trope of "checks and balances" and especially the role of the Senate within US governance operate as a containment strategy. Namely, the US government is designed to *contain* tyranny, where tyranny can be imagined as an autocratic ruler, a foreign threat, or as the will of the masses. Or to put it more simply, the US government is designed to contain and domesticate presidents, foreign influence, and "the people." As such, US governance traffics in the rhetoric of containment.

Containment rhetoric works to "tame the threat of alternative views" by disciplining and confining such threats.[19] This is achieved by framing the "alternative views" as "other" and as "outside" the "dominant values and structures of US culture."[20] For instance, when the US House voted to impeach President Bill Clinton in 1998 on "strict party lines," Republicans framed his affair and the fact that he lied under oath as so far outside the norms of US morality that he was no longer one of "us."[21] He was "other" and a "threat" to US politics. Here, Republicans worked to "contain" the threat, disciplining Clinton and restricting Democrats' power more broadly.

As discussed by rhetorical scholars such as Karrin Vasby Anderson, Lisa Flores, and Kristan Poirot, politicians in the United States have relied on the rhetoric of containment to shape the "nation's identity and practice since colonial times."[22] Indeed, containment rhetoric is on display in both Benjamin Franklin's slur as he referred to Native people as "ignorant Savages" and Senator Grassley's description of the House (and thus "the people") as being ruled by "sudden and violent passions." In both instances, these statesmen are saying "not-us" or "other," and seeking to confine—to stop, to halt, to reduce and minimize—the role these disparate "others" can have within the United States.

At its core, then, containment rhetoric distinguishes between "us" and "them," or more precisely "us" and "other."[23] This is primarily accomplished in two ways. The first is a fairly straightforward demarcation of "us" and "other" that typically characterizes "us" as "civilized" and "other" as "barbarian" or "uncivilized."[24] Here, the rhetoric of American exceptionalism usually informs the notion of "us" as "civilized," making the national identity unparalleled in its sense of culture. For instance, when colonizing Indigenous lands, early Americans imagined themselves as a divinely instituted civilized community with a mandate to contain "barbarism."[25] As political scientist David Campbell recounts, this containment operated in three primary ways: (1) the colonies enacted "Puritan doctrines of civility" to contain the "internal barbarian"; (2) they developed "frontier structures" to contain Native Americans, keeping them out of colonized areas; and (3) they developed "colonial slave codes" that contained those racialized as "barbarians" within colonized areas while profiting from their labor.[26] Campbell concludes that this history inscribes "fear of the Other" into "US identity" and demonstrates how the rhetoric of containment is the go-to discourse through which US politicians combat that fear—with real, violent consequences for those deemed as "other."[27]

Indeed, the United States' history demonstrates how creative US legislators have been when it comes to containing the "fear of the Other," which is repeatedly read onto Black people, Native Americans, immigrants of color, women, and LGBTQ+ people.[28] Consider the "jurisprudence" clause in the Fourteenth Amendment, which—post–Civil War—denied most Native Americans citizenship, or the Expatriation Act of 1907 under which "US-born women lost their citizenship if they married foreign men."[29] Categorizing "others" as barbaric, foreign, and threatening—as quintessentially "not-us"—the rhetoric of containment fundamentally shapes US governance, often violently delineating "the people" and enacting a rhetoric of sovereignty.

Beyond the fairly clear-cut demarcations of us/other and civilized/barbarian, the second way in which the rhetoric of containment typically surfaces is through sexist, heterosexist, and racist appellations. This second aspect builds on the first. It depends on the us-other dichotomy and its civilized-barbarian assumptions but operates by layering sexist, heterosexist, and racist metaphors, stereotypes, and accusations onto the "other."

For instance, the rhetoric of containment long thwarted women's suffrage in the United States. As rhetorician Karlyn Kohrs Campbell recounts, this rhetoric sought to "contain" women to the "private sphere," often by accusing women who spoke to "promiscuous" audiences—audiences comprised of both women and men—of being "unwomanly, aggressive, and cold."[30] Similarly, when Women's Liberation activists attempted to pass the Equal Rights Amendment in the 1970s, their efforts were contained in US media, which, as feminist critic Susan J. Douglas explains, castigated them with sexist descriptions such as "ugly, humorless, disorderly man-haters in desperate need of some Nair."[31] Indeed, women in US politics continue to face this rhetoric of containment, with even high-ranking female politicians such as Hillary Clinton and Michelle Obama facing harsh sexist slurs such as "bitch" and much worse—including racist slurs for Obama.[32] These metaphors, stereotypes, and accusations work by mobilizing the hierarchies of sexism, heterosexism, and racism against those deemed as "other." To call Hillary Clinton or Michelle Obama a "bitch" is to constrain or attempt to constrain their political subjectivity: to use sexism to draw a line between "us" the civilized people and the "others" (the "bitches"). Such a demarcation needs no further explanation. Within a sexist society, it is—in and of itself—a clear indication of who can rightfully wield political power and who absolutely cannot be entrusted with political power.

Both aspects of containment rhetoric—the fairly straightforward distinctions between "us" and "other" (and civilized/uncivilized) and the slipperier metaphors, stereotypes, and accusations that typically draw on sexist, heterosexist, and racist assumptions—work to "tame a potential threat to hegemonic culture" by reinforcing the "status quo" and containing "resistance."[33] And here it is important to note that liberal politicians, social movements, and progressive activists often wield this rhetoric alongside conservatives. For instance, Betty Friedan, the "mother" of the so-called Second Wave of feminism, famously named lesbians the "lavender menace" in the 1970s.[34] As rhetorical critic Kristan Poirot demonstrates, Friedan's heterosexist epithet attempted to eradicate one of feminism's supposedly "foremost internal threats" and thus make a version of feminism more palatable to US mainstream culture.[35] As this example demonstrates, both liberals and conservatives in the US political landscape can use the rhetoric of containment: it is a widely available "hegemonic response" to "acts of resistance," whether that resistance comes from the so-called Right or Left.[36] Prompted by a "perceived threat" and born from the "desire of control," the rhetoric of containment sets clear "parameters" that work to limit and control those designated as "other." And while "heteronormativity, patriarchy, xenophobia, ableism, and classism" typically inform who is designated as "other," no political party has a monopoly on the rhetoric of containment in the United States.[37]

Yet as rhetoricians Lisa A. Flores and L. Rae Gomez argue, containment rhetorics are "constitutive," meaning that they make "race" and "gender" by marshaling the clear-cut delineations of us/other. For instance, the contrast of "we, the people" and Middle Easterners *makes* race as it maps "us" and "other," "civilized" and "uncivilized," "secure" and "threat" onto bodies that are categorized as white people and people of color.

In a similar way, the much slipperier aspect of containment rhetoric mobilized through metaphors, tropes, and stereotypes makes "race." For example, consider rhetoricians Lisa A. Flores's and Mary Ann Villarreal's case study analyzing the ways in which media coverage marked the "raced bodies of Black and non-Black people of color" through the repeated trope of "ignorant" when narrativizing illegal voting in 2017 and 2019. That is, the coverage of would-be Texan voters such as Rosa Maria Ortega and Crystal Mason emphasized their *ignorance* when they illegally voted in 2017 and 2019, respectively. Ortega was a permanent resident and Mason was a convicted felon; both statuses disqualify these women of color from suffrage in Texas. However sympathetic some of this media coverage was, it drew upon the racist tropes or stereotypes that link whiteness to intellectual superiority and bodies of color—especially women of color—to narratives of "backwardness and inferiority."[38]

That is, "race" is a "virtually pure construct, with none but the most superficial biological stratum," and "gender" is likewise an elaborate, culturally specific construction mapped onto bodies that are always already categorized according to social expectations for childbearing and childrearing.[39] To put it another way, social categories such as "race" and "gender" are not naturally occurring, universal, static distinctions. Rather, race and gender "exist" because of the way societies are organized socially, economically, and legally, among other structures—such as religion. Or to put it more succinctly, categories such as "race" and "gender" exist because we make them and police their boundaries. The rhetoric of containment, then, is one of the most significant ways in which race and gender are constituted in US society, and it is one of the clearest examples of how US politics police these boundaries—always pushing some people back into their so-called place.

This chapter explores how the rhetoric of containment operates within contemporary politicians' invocations of the "Founding Fathers" as they make arguments that hinge on the concept of "checks and balances." Within the recent election cycles, senators and representatives railed for "checks and balances" on everything from offshore drilling to judicial nominations, but the topics of (1) Second Amendment rights, (2) war powers, and (3) impeachment were especially prominent. Analyzing this discourse, I demonstrate how Republicans and Democrats use the founders as authority figures to lay claim to power. Here, the founders operate as conduits for power—but this power is one of exclusion and containment. That is, Congress receives its power to contain "others" from the "Founding Fathers"; moreover, the right-ordering of power—the principles of containment and exclusion within US governance—is likewise achieved through the founders' fatherly wisdom. The metaphor of fatherhood both provides the power for containment and organizes the principles or hierarchies of containment. As such, this discourse draws on the long-standing associations within hegemonic masculinity between fatherhood, authority, and wisdom—and the assumptions of whiteness that undergird the associations between fathers and goodness.

At its root, the congressional rhetoric of "checks and balances" operates within an inheritance-based ideology: the power to *contain* descends from the fathers. The discourse of "checks and balances," however, escalates inheritance into defense and restoration. That is, by containing "others," politicians seemingly defend "the people" and restore the nation. And in this congressional discourse, both the obvious demarcations of us/other and civilized/uncivilized and the subtler or slipperier sexist and racist metaphors, stereotypes, and accusations circulate—always framing "others" in both sexist and racist allusions that, by contrast, situate the United States in masculinist, white-supremacist, and tacitly Christian identities.

The Second Amendment

Entering his final year in the executive office, President Obama signed a sequence of gun-related executive orders. Republican representatives in the House responded with a flurry of fervent speeches regarding "the issue of gun control and Americans' Second Amendment rights."[40] Analyzing these Second Amendment speeches, I demonstrate how this discourse escalates from inheritance-based logic to defense-oriented rhetoric—and how this discourse attempts to constrain the executive branch, enacting a rhetoric of sovereignty.

The Second Amendment itself is quite brief. "A well regulated Militia, being necessary to the security of a free State, the right of the people to keep and bear Arms, shall not be infringed."[41] Born out of Anti-Federalists' suspicions and fears, the Bill of Rights explicitly circumscribes the federal government. The Second Amendment addresses the fear that the federal government—which, constitutionally, has control of the military—would use the military to oppress the states. During the founding era, the states organized their own militias and periodically gathered white male citizens for militia trainings. The states did not provide weapons, however. White male citizens brought their own weapons to militia maneuvers, and those weapons were then typically "registered on government rolls."[42] During the founding era, Black people—whether enslaved or free—were typically "prohibited from possessing firearms."[43]

When the Bill of Rights was ratified in 1791, the federal government's standing army was small and equipped with basically the same weapons that white male citizens typically used on their property and thus within their state militias. As such, the Anti-Federalists believed a state militia could likely defeat the federal government's "forces in battle" if the federal government used its army to invade a state.[44] Thus, while the Second Amendment does nothing to circumscribe the federal government's control of the military, it mollified the Anti-Federalists by ensuring the states could marshal their armed militias to fend off the federal army if needed.

After the Seventeenth Amendment decoupled federal senators from their state's legislatures, the Senate bowed to popular opinion and brought state militias under federal control through the 1916 National Defense Act, in the midst of World War I.[45] Relatedly, the US military has grown immensely since the founding era, and firearms have become more deadly. As such, the US military is not only much larger than the states' original militias, but it is also much better equipped than standard US citizens. These changes largely negate the protection that the Second Amendment offers states: state militias—now known as the National Guard—answer to the president, and no one would imagine that they could fend off the US military. Since most people in the United States no longer fear that "the nation's armed forces" will invade and overthrow their state's sovereignty, however, the protections originally offered by the Second Amendment now seem largely unnecessary.[46]

For most of US history, then, the Second Amendment legally pertained to the states' increasingly obsolete right to form a militia. The Supreme Court rulings in *District of Columbia v. Heller* (2008) and *McDonald v. City of Chicago* (2010), however, argued that the Second Amendment ensured *individuals'* right "to have arms for their own defense" within their homes, in addition to ensuring the "right of the states to maintain a militia."[47] As such, constitutional law now interprets the Second Amendment as ensuring that the "government may not ban the possession of handguns by civilians in their homes," although there are caveats regarding mental illness and felons, and the lower courts often disagree on issues such as carrying firearms in "sensitive places" (e.g., schools and churches), the commercial sale of firearms, the concealed carry of firearms, and civilians' access to military-grade firearms.[48]

Obama's gun-related executive orders in January 2016 focused on tightening background checks, narrowing "who can sell guns without a federal license," and more vigorously enforcing existing federal policies.[49] These executive orders expanded the ones Obama had signed in 2013 following the Sandy Hook massacre.

Executive orders are not described in the Constitution; instead, the Constitution merely states in Article II, Section 1, "The executive Power shall be vested in a President of the United States of America."[50] Every president, however—starting with George Washington—has issued executive orders to manage the operations of the federal government and effect policy changes among federal officials and agencies.[51] In short, executive orders are a primary way in which presidents wield the executive power constitutionally vested in them. These executive orders can "have the force and effect of law," creating a contentious overlap with Congress—which is constitutionally tasked with making federal laws. Despite this contention, Congress has rarely countered an executive order in recent decades even though it can legislatively revoke and modify such orders—or inhibit an executive order by defunding it.[52] Instead, when executive orders are revoked, modified, or superseded, it is typically done by a new president who can easily supplant an existing executive order by signing a new one.

When Obama rolled out gun-related executive orders in January 2016, he teared up on national television, discussing the recent school massacres and noting that over one hundred thousand people had died in the United States as a result of gun violence that decade. He also called on Congress to enact new legislation.[53] Responding to Obama's executive orders, Representatives Barry Loudermilk (R-GA), Steve Russell (R-OK), Lynn Westmoreland (R-GA), Earl "Buddy" Carter (R-GA), and John Abney Culberson (R-TX) invoked the "Founding Fathers" to "check" President Obama's power. Analyzing these speeches, I demonstrate how this discourse escalates the logic of inheritance into the logic of defense as it contains executive power by framing Obama as "other" through sexist and racist metaphors, tropes, and accusations.

Essentially, these speeches up the ante: rather than treasuring an heirloom, they imagine defending a home—or land. As such, they tend to skip much of the geographical tours, the descriptions of monuments, and the discussions of documents and their page layouts common in Republicans' speeches regarding "rights and liberties." Instead, these speeches first situate the speaker as an authority figure while belittling opponents; second, they discuss materiality directly through homes, land, and borders; and third, they create a verbal defense through argumentation.

Throughout, this discourse appeals to the "Founding Fathers," using the metaphor of fatherhood not just to undergird inheritance-based logic but to further draw upon the associations between fatherhood, masculinity, wisdom, and righteous aggression to frame "us" and contain "other." Ultimately, these speeches invoke the "Founding Fathers" to situate both Republican politicians and US gun owners as the United States' first and last defense against tyranny—and to situate President Obama and liberals more broadly as traitors who make the United States vulnerable to attack. This is a rhetoric of containment. It contains the right to govern through fear-soaked accounts of the "threat" that "others" present to US sovereignty.

Authority and Belittling

Within this discourse, Republican politicians build their ethos by overtly naming their authority and expertise. For instance, Representative Barry Loudermilk (R-GA) substantiated his argument that "guns don't kill people. People kill people," by saying, "I have been around guns all my life and I have yet to have a gun jump up and just arbitrarily start shooting anyone."[54] This quip is unnecessary—one need not be around guns throughout one's life to know they do not "jump up and just arbitrarily start shooting" people. Yet it builds his ethos as a gun enthusiast. Similarly, Representative Steve Russell (R-OK) claimed to be an authority, stating, "As the only Member of Congress who owns a firearms manufacturing business, I know about what I speak."[55] Rather than recognizing how this might create a conflict of interest, Russell touts his business as a claim to authority and expertise. Citing more formal authority, Representative John Abney Culberson (R-TX) began his speech by stating that he is the "chairman of the Commerce, Justice, Science, and Related Agencies Appropriations Subcommittee," and Loudermilk additionally touted himself as "a member of the Committee on Homeland Security."[56]

Even as these statements position the speaker as an authority on gun-related matters, these speeches actively belittle President Obama. Although, the language here is often obtuse as these speeches skirt the House rules of decorum against "impugning" the president's motives (which is known as "engaging in personalities toward the president" and receives a reprimand from the Speaker of the House).[57] For instance, Representative Lynn Westmoreland (R-GA) invoked the founders to mock President Obama. After extolling the Second Amendment as "plain and simple" and describing himself as "a man who likes to keep it simple," Westmoreland then opined, "Unfortunately, I think our Founding Fathers spoke too plainly for certain people and certain presidents to understand."[58] He continues by ironically noting how often "that President" reminds "us that he taught constitutional law" and concluding that Obama "disregards the Constitution so regularly."[59] Here, Westmoreland groups himself and the "Founding Fathers" together as "plain and simple" men, creating a juxtaposition with President Obama—whom he describes as elitist and overly intellectual. Given the ways elitism and intellectualism are often feminized in US society, Westmoreland's jibe has a gendered aspect to it, especially since he contrasts this intellectualism with "plain and simple" men like the "Founding Fathers."

The specter of "uppity" also circulates in this discourse. Accusations of "uppity" are racist: they are mobilized primarily against Black people and to a lesser extent non-Black people of color as a way of indicating that said person has attempted to infringe upon white space, status, or property. Indeed, the concept of "uppity" is a racist manifestation of the term "presumptuous."[60] In the post–Civil War and Jim Crow eras, it reified the "power dynamics of subordination and domination between Black and Whites" and the ideology "of White supremacy."[61] In more contemporary eras, the sentiment of "uppity" is invoked to hallow white people's "resentment toward Blacks who hold high-status positions of power and thus *do not know their place* in a society dominated by Whites."[62] When Westmoreland snidely remarks that President Obama keeps reminding Congress that he taught constitutional law and when Westmoreland lampoons Obama as so elite he cannot understand the founders' "plain and simple" language, Westmoreland's speech activates the racist stereotype of "uppity."

In a similar vein, Representative Earl "Buddy" Carter (R-GA) described Obama as having signed these executive orders because "things [didn't] work out his way" and added that these executive orders demonstrate Obama's "complete lack of leadership."[63] Here, Obama is portrayed not as an intellectual elite but as a child throwing a fit after not getting his way. Given the links between leadership and masculinity, by impugning Obama's leadership, this speech undermines his masculinity. Likewise, given the emasculation of Black men as childish—consider the racist epithet of "boy" as used against adult Black men—the description of Obama as a childish despot throwing a temper tantrum activates racist tropes.[64]

Next, after noting that humans have an "inherent" survival instinct that necessitates the use of guns for self-defense, Representative Russell remarks that the "President is certainly welcome to choose not to defend himself."[65] This insinuates that Obama is out of touch with everyday humans, and casts Obama as not *man* enough to defend himself—again, reinforcing the sexist and racist emasculation of Black men.[66] Then, Russell calls for serious and sober-minded deliberation, noting that "serious people decline to trivialize any right expressly addressed in the Bill of Rights," and concludes by stating that "no President's tears will ever shake us from the defense of [the] Constitution."[67] Again, these statements situate Obama as overly emotional and not a serious or rational person—both of which undermine Obama's masculinity and activate racist stereotypes that equate whiteness with rationality and Blackness with creaturely emotionality. By touting the speaker's authority and belittling President Obama, this discourse assumes and reinforces a sexist and racist hierarchy that links masculinity, guns, authority, whiteness, and leadership as superior to femininity and Blackness. Meanwhile, both femininity and Blackness are linked to an array of subordinated qualities, such as an uppity or false intellectualism, emotions, childlikeness, triviality, and pacifism.

Property, Land, and the United States

When extolling "rights and liberties," as discussed in chapter 1, Republican politicians often made appeals that were rooted in abstract associations of materiality. They discussed monuments and page layouts in order to imagine "freedom" as a tangible, real, inheritable sort of thing. Some of this abstract materiality infuses this Second Amendment discourse as Republicans discuss the "right to bear arms." For instance, Loudermilk notes that the word "liberty" is engraved "at the base of the rostrum."[68] Likewise, Russell notes that the "Founding Fathers" had such esteem for "individual" gun rights that they placed this right "at number two."[69] And both Loudermilk and Russell name-drop figures such as Montesquieu, William Blackstone, and James Madison, and Russell additionally mentions *The Federalist Papers*.[70] Compared to the speeches on religious liberty and the "right to life," however, these are passing references.

Instead of dwelling on monuments and documents, these speeches move much more concretely to discuss property and land. For instance, Russell opens his speech by focusing on property, telling stories of white women who defended their homes against would-be robbers.[71] He tells of Sarah McKinley, a young widow with an infant in her arms who killed an intruder with her husband's shotgun, and of Arlene Orms, a widow who was eighty-eight when she shot at a home invader—prompting him to flee. Clothing the home in images of white feminine innocence and vulnerability, Russell connects guns to the masculine self-defense of property, which includes women. Indeed, guns stand in for men: they take the place of these widows' deceased husbands.

Loudermilk, meanwhile, parroted Trump's 2016 campaign talking points, connecting the threat of gun violence not to individual property but to the United States as a country—and a land. After noting that "guns don't kill people. People kill people," Loudermilk then immediately states, "Bad people that use guns come into this country, and often those guns are smuggled in through the southern border."[72]

He follows this by stating that many of these people "are intent to do ill to people in this Nation."[73] Then, Loudermilk argues that refugees in US resettlement programs want to "conduct terrorist attacks against this Nation."[74] Here, Loudermilk complains that President Obama has refused to properly staff the Border Patrol with "boots on the ground" and has not staffed the FBI to monitor all resettled refugees, but instead—through an executive order—Obama is going to have the Bureau of Alcohol, Tobacco, Firearms and Explosives "investigate American citizens."[75] These remarks assume a clear hierarchy: the United States, US citizens, and white people are imagined as good and inherently superior to other lands, non-US citizens, and people of color—whom Loudermilk further characterizes as bad, violent, and malicious. Indeed, he frames the United States and (white) Americans as under attack and then pivots, suggesting that Obama is actually assisting this attack by investigating US citizens (the good guys) rather than shoring up the United States' defenses.

Russell makes this nationalist us-other dichotomy even clearer in a lengthy speech. He paraphrases President Obama, who noted that gun deaths in the United States are on the rise and "the worst among developed nations."[76] Russell then disputes Obama's claims, but when he does so, he changes the terminology. Rather than discussing "developed or undeveloped" nations as Obama had, Russell refers to "civilized or uncivilized nations." Here, Russell's containment rhetoric draws on white-supremacist notions of class and masculinity popularized during the Progressive Era. As historian Gail Bederman demonstrates, this framework directly posits the "white race" and the United States as "civilized" while sweeping other nations and people of color into the dustheap of history as "barbarian" or "uncivilized" and therefore unable to evolve into the type of men who will lead humanity into the future.[77] By describing the United States as "civilized" and other nations as "uncivilized," Russell not only reinscribes these masculinist, white-supremacist associations but directly imagines the United States and white people as being above gun violence. By his logic, homicides are an ugly, "uncivilized" thing that happens over there among bad people. Indeed, Russell states that "the United States" ranks not at the top but in the "bottom half of homicides worldwide among civilized or uncivilized nations."[78] Moreover, Russell directly notes that in 2014 "only eight percent" of gun deaths in the United States (15,000 deaths) were homicides—the other deaths (184,756 deaths) were accidents or suicides. Rather than considering how this situation might be improved through legislation regarding safety measures for guns or providing broad mental-health access, Russell uses these statistics to demonstrate that the United States is "civilized": according to Russell, the United States does not have significant *homicidal* gun violence and thus does not need executive orders to reduce gun violence.

These speeches juxtapose the United States and other countries, clearly building on the assumptions of American exceptionalism and white-supremacist associations to characterize the United States as good and other countries as bad. The argumentation focuses on the United States as a nation and visualizes US borders—both literally at the southern border and more abstractly at immigration points. The nation imagined in these speeches is not only "good" and "civilized" but clearly threatened by "bad people" from *other* countries—who are then imagined as Latinx migrants or smugglers, or as Arab terrorists. Again, this is the rhetoric of containment. Drawing on the "Founding Fathers" to imagine the United States as an exceptional—and exceptionally civilized—nation, this discourse seeks to contain racialized others and those, like Obama, who would institute gun-safety laws. Yet as this containment rhetoric emphasizes borders, it operates within a logic of defense: like a fortress under siege, the United States must defend its borders.

Verbal Defense and Confrontational Language

Even as these speeches discuss physical defense—borders and guns—they also feature explicit verbal defenses. That is, using a masculinized style, these speeches feature prolonged argumentation and direct confrontation.[79] For example, Representative Russell begins a lengthy sequence of rebuttals by appealing to the "Founding Fathers." First, he names what he imagines his opponents would say, claiming that "gun control advocates" often "turn to the false assertion that the

Second Amendment was never intended for individuals."[80] Then—without quoting any of the founders—he counters this assertion by insisting that James Madison and the other "Founding Fathers" would have agreed with William Blackstone that guns were an important aspect of one's individual "self-preservation and defense."[81] Having begun with the founders, Russell moves sequentially through a number of rebuttals. He begins each rebuttal by naming an argument and then countering it. For instance, he states, "Okay. Fine, you say. But there is no reason why people need military style firearms," before arguing that the "framers of the Constitution" would disagree with that statement. Similarly, he asks, "Well, what about that gun show loophole?" and "Well, what about Internet sales?" and "What about the terrorist watch list?" In this way, Russell raises and rebuts a wide variety of arguments.

Likewise, both Representative Carter and Representative Loudermilk provided rebuttals in their speeches to counter the idea of providing support for mental illness. Carter agrees with his imagined opponents that efforts should be taken to "address mental illness in this country" but then counterargues, working to contain the executive branch, stating that "directing millions of dollars in new investment for mental health care is not the role of the president. That is the role for Congress."[82] Similarly, Loudermilk claims to "applaud" Obama's proposal to fund "$500 million toward mental health care" but then counterargues that such spending is inappropriate as long as the United States has soldiers suffering from PTSD—and here he accuses Obama and the Department of Veterans Affairs of abandoning US soldiers.[83]

Beyond these rebuttals, these speeches are directly confrontational, again, without violating House decorum by impugning the president's motives. For example, Representative Carter (R-GA) concludes his speech by asking both Democrats and Republicans "to stand up for this institution [Congress] and protect" the nation "our Founding Fathers fought and died for."[84] Similarly, Representative Westmoreland (R-GA) describes Obama as trampling on the Constitution and then calls his colleagues into action, saying, "I think it is time that we brought attention to some of these illegal actions" that "some presidents" create.[85] He concludes by stating, "I think it is time for us not only to make the citizens aware, but to make this whole world aware of what has been going on and what we are going to do to stop it." Likewise, Representative Loudermilk (R-GA) makes the confrontational argument that while Obama claims to be making the United States safer through these executive orders, he is "making America more dangerous because he continues to ignore what the will of the people is."[86] Continuing this confrontational tone, Representative Russell (R-OK) closes his speech with fighting words. After describing Obama's administration as "abrogating" the Bill of Rights and thus losing "the moral right to govern the Republic," Representative Russell warns that "America's gun owners will not go gently into these utopian woods."[87] This confrontational—even threatening—discourse and this argumentative style enact the type of defense for which these speeches advocate. This rhetoric exacerbates the us-other dichotomy working throughout this containment rhetoric: "us" and "other" are not only differentiated and juxtaposed, but they are enemies engaged in battle.

Checking Obama and Containing Liberals

These speeches discuss guns directly, and they metaphorically use guns to represent the United States and freedom. This nationalizes the topic: by defending guns, these representatives defend the United States itself. Likewise, gun owners and advocates come to represent the defense of not just guns but of the United States and liberty. By nationalizing this policy issue, this discourse situates itself as defending the United States against Obama. Indeed, by calling for "checks" against Obama, these speeches frame Obama and liberals more generally as the true problem. These speeches imagine the United States as under attack from "uncivilized" outsiders, but within this discourse's logic, such an attack is possible only because of Obama's weak leadership—which is characterized in sexist and racist terms.

Yet this discourse accuses Obama of tyranny. For instance, Representative Carter notes that "If our Founding Fathers wanted an executive fiat government, they would have created one" and concludes that this country is "not controlled by one man, but by many."[88] Representative Russell notes that Congress will "stand in the way of any executive who will not uphold the Constitution of the United States."[89] Representative Westmoreland describes Obama as ruling by "oral decree."[90] Representative Loudermilk invokes the wisdom of "our Founding Fathers" and then quotes Montesquieu to say that if "the legislative and the executive power is vested in one person" then "there can be no liberty."[91] Finally, Representative Culberson directly explains how he has "checked" Obama, stating, "The Department of Justice and the Department of Alcohol, Tobacco, Firearms and Explosives have already been put on notice, that if they attempt to interfere with our Second Amendment rights, I have the authority, as chairman, to block their ability to move money within the agency."[92] Here, Culberson asserts that his ability to "check" an "out of control executive" through the "power of the purse" is an "authority entrusted" to him by the "Founding Fathers."[93]

These speeches escalate inheritance into defense. Building on the bedrock of US containment rhetoric, this discourse uses nationalist appeals soaked in masculinist white supremacy. These speeches frame the United States as a material reality—property, land, borders—in need of protection. Indeed, these speeches invoke the "other" as a kind of boogeyman, imagining people of color (both Latinx and Middle Easterners) infiltrating US borders with malicious intent. Defending the United States then becomes a two-part operation. The first is physical, and here guns, border agents, and FBI agents are imagined as a defense against racialized invaders. The second is argumentative: through their own rebuttals and confrontational speech, these Republican congresspeople defend not just gun rights but the United States. These speeches target Obama, claiming that the United States needs defense because a weak (feminine, racialized) president has weakened its borders and undermined its liberty—by ruling despotically. While the ideas of a weak president and a despotic president seem incompatible, these speeches fuse them through sexist and racist allusions that belittle Obama into a childlike status such that his tyranny is that of a child throwing a tantrum. Simultaneously, these speeches belittle Obama by denigrating his leadership and by drawing attention to his (feminine) emotions—his tears—and suggesting he uses emotions manipulatively—like a femme fatale—to undermine US rights.

Drawing on the covenant of American exceptionalism and the longstanding norms of containment rhetoric in US political discourse, this congressional discourse links a masculinist, white-supremacist defense to the "Founding Fathers." It suggests that the founders imagined a day like this and thus built defensive tools—such as guns and checks and balances—into this nation's design. These speeches routinely invoke the "Founding Fathers" as both indefatigable champions of gun owners' individual rights and as genius architects of "checks and balances." Within this discourse, then, the "Founding Fathers" authorize Republican congresspeople as they defend against the president. Ultimately, this Republican discourse moves from inheritance to defending that inheritance. Yet this defense is decidedly masculinist and depends upon and reinforces white-supremacist binaries—us/other, white/not-white, good/bad, civilized/uncivilized, citizen/noncitizen—that have long been used to contain "others" in the United States.

War Powers

Both Republican and Democratic congresspeople call for checks and balances when presidents take military action overseas in ways that seem indistinguishable from war actions. Article I, Section 8 of the Constitution lists Congress's powers, stipulating, "Congress shall have Power . . . To declare War, grant Letters of Marque and Reprisal, and make Rules concerning Captures on Land and Water."[94] In Article II, Section 2, however, the Constitution describes the executive branch, stating, "The President shall be Commander in Chief of the Army and Navy of the United States."[95] These two clauses—known as the Declare War Clause and the Commander in Chief Clause—split military oversight between Congress and the president in unclear ways.

The Commander in Chief Clause ensures that a "democratically accountable" civilian oversees the military and that when Congress "authorizes military operations" the president is in charge of those operations.[96] Moreover, during the debates in Philadelphia, James Madison argued that giving Congress "the power to declare war" would not inhibit the president from repelling "sudden attacks."[97] Seemingly, then, the president derives power from the Commander in Chief Clause to act independently of Congress—at least to defend colonized land and property.

The Declare War Clause, however, grants Congress the exclusive power to declare war. This had broad implications during the nation's founding era. Early presidents sought Congress's approval before engaging in military conflicts such as the War of 1812 as well as "lesser" conflicts such as the quasi-war with France (1798), the "conflicts with the Barbary States of Tripoli and Algiers," and "conflicts with Native American Tribes on the Western frontier."[98]

Contemporary presidents act far more independently. They use military action in retaliation or to repel attacks not just on US soil but on US citizens abroad or consulates and other territories. Similarly, presidents use military force at will when arguing that it does not "amount to war."[99] For example, President George H. W. Bush deployed troops to Saudi Arabia while keeping the troops out of combat roles, and President Bill Clinton deployed so-called peacekeeping troops to Bosnia. Similarly, President Obama claimed his "bombing campaign in Libya in 2011" did not amount to war and thus did not "require Congress's authorization."[100] More broadly, contemporary presidents argue that "using force against non-state actors such as terrorist organizations does not amount to war."[101]

Even when Congress authorizes military use, there is significant debate regarding the extent of that authorization. For instance, after Congress authorized military activity in Vietnam through the 1964 Gulf of Tonkin Resolution, Presidents Johnson and Nixon expanded the "scale and scope" of that conflict "dramatically beyond what Congress could have anticipated."[102] Similarly, after 9/11, Congress enacted the Authorization for Use of Military Force (AUMF), intending "to authorize the use of military force against" those directly "responsible for the September 11 attacks."[103] Presidents Bush, Obama, and Trump all subsequently "interpreted its broad language" to authorize a wide array of military strikes and operations in countries and against groups and individuals that had "little or no connection to 9/11."[104]

In general, Congress splits along party divisions when supporting or tacitly condoning contemporary presidents' expanded use of their commander-in-chief authority. During the 2020 campaign, however, both Republicans and Democrats vocally disagreed with the Trump administration's policies. In what follows, then, I analyze representative examples of Republicans' and Democrats' congressional speeches calling for checks and balances regarding war. There were many such speeches; thus, I focus on the more substantive ones and those that advanced congressional resolutions or were part of executive sessions in Congress. As such, I analyze Senators Mike Lee's (R-UT) and Bernie Sanders's (I-VT) speeches regarding Trump's 2019 veto of Congress's resolution to end military actions against Yemen; Senator Rand Paul's (R-KY) speeches regarding the provision of weapons to Middle Eastern countries; and Senators Chuck Schumer's (D-NY) and Richard J. Durbin's (D-IL) speeches regarding the 2020 strike against Qasem Soleimani in Iran—and Iran's retaliation. Notably, the Senate is governed by different rules of decorum than the House; senators have more leeway in directly insulting the president, the vice president, and administration officials, although their language regarding other senators and the states is tightly governed.[105]

This War Powers discourse relies on many of the same tactics used in the Second Amendment discourse analyzed above. Working to contain Trump and other countries, it belittles, it rebuts and confronts, and it mobilizes an us-other binary between the United States and countries where predominantly people of color live. Unlike the Second Amendment discourse, however, it does not posit the speaker as an authority figure and, ultimately, does not operate through defense but restoration. This discourse is pervaded by a sense of loss—Congress, and the Senate specifically, has lost its power to "contain" and thus lost its rightful *place* of power. Thus situated, this discourse relies on masculine appeals rooted in the "Founding Fathers," envisioning a *restoration* of the Senate's inheritance—their power to contain.

Restoring Masculine Power to Congress

This discourse belittles without feminizing the president. Indeed, the president cannot be presented as weak because this discourse imagines that he holds all the power—power that rightfully belongs to Congress. For example, Senator Rand Paul (R-KY) repeatedly stated that the policy of selling weaponry to Middle Eastern countries—especially Bahrain and Qatar—"makes no sense" because they use it to arm terrorists. He posed rhetorical questions such as, "Why in the world?" and "What kind of bizarre world do we live in?"[106] Later, he sarcastically lampooned the Trump administration—without naming Trump—saying, "The administration wants to give nuclear technology to Saudi Arabia. That is genius."[107] Likewise, Senator Chuck Schumer (D-NY), taking advantage of the comparatively lax Senate rules regarding imprecations of the president, described Trump's foreign policies as "riddled by chaotic, uninformed, erratic, and impulsive decision-making."[108] Schumer continued to describe Trump as "bumbling," "rudderless," and "egotistical."[109] He concluded one of his many speeches on this topic by stating that "all of the tweeting and all of the bravado is no substitute for strategic thinking and long-term foreign policy goals."[110] Similarly, Senator Richard J. Durbin (D-IL) described Iran's retaliatory bombing of two military bases after the strike against known terrorist Soleimani as "entirely predictable" to everyone except President Trump and Secretary Pompeo.[111] These belittling insults lack the feminized and racist components that characterized the belittling of Obama over gun-control policies. That is, as a white man, Trump is not the target of racist metaphors, associations, or stereotypes—but he also avoids being the target of sexist, feminized attacks. He is not presented as weak. This discourse accuses Trump of using his power irresponsibly and without sound judgment but does not position him as weak and feminine.

Moreover, this discourse makes no personal claims to authority. These senators do not name their official titles, discuss their backgrounds, or claim expertise on the topic. Predicated on the idea that Congress has lost power, these speeches cannot juxtapose strong senators and a weak and feminized president. Instead, they call—repeatedly—for Congress to *collectively* reclaim its (masculinized) power. For instance, Senator Lee (R-UT) asked Congress to "take a stand"; Senator Sanders (I-VT) noted that Congress had "abdicated its constitutional role" and asked his colleagues to reassert Congress's "constitutional authority"; Senator Paul (R-KY) asked the Senate to vote for "restoring Congress's proper role as a check on Executive power"; Senator Durbin (D-IL) asked senators to "step up"; and Senator Schumer (D-NY) argued that Congress must "assert our authority over matters of war and peace."[112] This "step up" and "take a stand" language is vaguely masculine as it metaphorically invokes the concepts of a boxing match or schoolyard brawl. Doubling down on these masculine appeals, Senators Sanders, Schumer, and Durbin all explicitly invoke the traditionally masculine quality of courage. For instance, Schumer noted that every White House adviser with "strength and courage" had left rather than submit to Trump's policy decisions.[113] Likewise, Sanders concluded his speech by stating, "I hope very much that the Members of this body summon up their courage and vote to override Trump's veto," and Durbin stated, "It is time for Members of this important body to show some courage."[114]

Beyond these masculine associations, these speeches advance their arguments through the traditionally masculine style of refutation and explicit confrontation.[115] For example, Senator Lee (R-UT) dedicated an entire section of his speech to rebuttals, offering four lengthy rebuttals back-to-back and overtly introducing them with statements such as "contrary to the claims of some of our critics . . ." and "still others say . . ."[116] Senator Paul (R-KY) introduced his bill to "quit arming terrorists" with the confrontational statement, "You say: Well, certainly you are not serious. Yes, I am serious. We send arms to terrorists."[117] Similarly, Senator Durbin (D-IL) argued that "some have had the audacity" to suggest the strike against Soleimani was authorized by the 2002 AUMF and then confrontationally stated, "Let me be clear. I cannot imagine that anyone—anyone—who took either of those votes nearly 20 years ago—and I was here at that time—thought that they were approving a war with Iran two decades later. I certainly didn't."[118] These rebuttals and confrontations directly position this discourse as part of a fight. The senators are combative. They are not just talking about war; they are enacting a verbal war.

Here, Durbin (D-IL) specifically attempted to shame Republican senators by feminizing them, insinuating that they have not been man enough to enter the fight. He asked, "Will my Republican colleagues finally show some backbone?" and stated that "the Republican leadership [in the Senate] should not roll over and play the role of lapdog when it comes to such a serious, life-and-death matter."[119] While both statements impugn Republicans for not fighting, the "lapdog" reference specifically feminizes Republicans by equating them with small domestic animals that are seen as frivolous and associated almost exclusively with women.

Drawing on the classic us-other and civilized-uncivilized differentiations in containment rhetoric, this discourse describes the countries, rulers, and people of Saudi Arabia, Bahrain, Qatar, Iran, and Iraq as backward and hostile. For example, Senators Lee (R-UT) and Sanders (I-VT) offer a litany of human rights abuses committed by Saudi Arabia, and Sanders specifically notes—without explanation—that Saudi Arabia "treats women not as second-class citizens but as third-class citizens."[120] Likewise, Senator Paul (R-KY) describes "the Middle East" as a "powder keg" and a "hot cauldron" that could "boil over" at any minute.[121] These old-timey metaphors—neither cauldrons nor powder kegs are contemporarily used—situate the Middle East as backward and out of touch with modern sensibilities. Moreover, Paul (R-KY) and Schumer (D-NY) state, respectively, that these countries "hate our country" and "hate the United States."[122] This discourse works to contain the Middle East, drawing on and reinforcing an us-other binary that characterizes the United States as good, civilized, and righteous, and Middle Eastern countries as bad, backward, and villainous.

The countries of Israel and Yemen are the exceptions to this rule. Senator Paul repeatedly refers to Israel as an endangered ally, and Senators Lee, Sanders, and Paul all characterize Yemen as a victim of Saudi violence. This emphasizes a loss of (masculinized) power and the necessity of reclaiming that power. For instance, Sanders notes that "our weapons are being used to kill women and children" in Yemen.[123] This shames the United States in a specifically gendered way: relying on the premise that (white) men have the ability and responsibility to protect women and children, this statement frames the United States as masculine and thus shames the United States for having not just failed but inverted its (white) masculine responsibility. Sanders concludes this speech by noting that with this vote the Senate has the opportunity to say "that the people of Yemen need humanitarian aid, not more bombs" and to tell "Saudi Arabia we will not follow their lead."[124] Here, Sanders argues that this vote could restore the Senate's (masculine) role by reclaiming the right to lead rather than following Saudi leadership and by providing protection and food to feminized victims. This draws upon paternalism and white saviorism to imagine a restoration of the Senate and US power by protecting women of color in countries imagined as backward.[125]

Moreover, senators call upon their colleagues to protect "American blood and treasure," in the words of Senator Lee (R-KY).[126] Here, senators argue that by allowing a president to commit the United States to ongoing hostilities in the Middle East and to sell weapons to Middle Eastern countries, they endanger "American soil," again, in the words of Senator Lee.[127] These senators are concerned with the amount of tax monies the United States might spend on future hostilities in the Middle East and with the number of soldiers who might be wounded or killed in future hostilities. This is especially true of Senator Lee, who uses a variation of the dramatic phrase "American blood and treasure" three times with an additional fourth reference to "American blood" in a single speech.[128] These senators chastise their congressional colleagues, arguing that if their colleagues believe these hostilities are warranted, they should pursue congressional approval for this military engagement rather than letting the president usurp congressional power. For instance, Senator Durbin (D-IL) taunts his colleagues to "step up and face [their] constituents and record [their] votes accordingly" if they want to commit US taxes and soldiers to these hostilities.[129] Again, this carries a fairly masculinized appeal, essentially asking senators to "man up" by facing their constituents.

Ultimately, this discourse assumes that Congress already has power and only needs to "step up" in order to restore their authority. This invokes the "Founding Fathers" while relying on a subtle geographic metaphor. For instance, Senator Schumer (D-NY) describes an "exquisite balance" that "the Founding Fathers put into *place* between the Congress and Presidency."[130] Likewise, Senator Lee (R-UT) states that "the Founding Fathers *placed* this power in the legislative branch."[131] This imagines congressional power as a material thing—as something inalienable to Congress because it was bestowed by the founders. Indeed, Senator Lee reiterates that "Congress and Congress alone may declare war," and Senator Paul (R-KY) reminds his colleagues that the "Founding Fathers were wary of granting any President too much power" and that the Constitution grants the "power to declare war" to "Congress and not to the President."[132] Thus, Paul concludes by directly asking his colleagues to "restore" Congress's power and the "separation of powers that is necessary to preserve our great Republic."[133]

This congressional discourse from Democrats, Republicans, and Independents mobilizes a number of masculinized and white-supremacist appeals as it operates through a logic of loss and restoration. It mourns the loss of what it claims is Congress's rightful place of power and the loss of what it imagines as the United States' rightful place as a moral superpower in a global theater. These "rightful places" are constructed through masculine appeals—and a hefty dose of white supremacy and white saviorism. This power, however, is the power to contain. Specifically in this discourse, it is the power to contain the president and the power to contain "backward" countries. Ultimately, this discourse assumes that such containment power is always already theirs. It is a place—bequeathed by the fathers—and the Senate can reoccupy it if only they are courageous enough, strong enough, *man* enough.

Impeachment

The Constitution discusses impeachment in relation to the legislative, executive, and judicial branches. Describing Congress in Article I, Section 2, it famously stipulates that the US House has "the sole Power of Impeachment."[134] The House has used this power to impeach several federal judges, one senator, and three presidents—Andrew Johnson (1868), Bill Clinton (1998), and Donald Trump (2019 and 2021). Later, Article I, Section 3 explains that the Senate has "the sole Power to try all Impeachments."[135] They have convicted only a handful of judges. During presidential impeachment trials, Article I, Section 3 further stipulates that the chief justice of the Supreme Court must preside and that a president can be convicted by at least a "two thirds" vote of the present senators. When discussing the executive branch in Article II, Section 4, the Constitution addresses impeachment, stating, "The President, Vice President and all civil Officers of the United States, shall be removed from Office on Impeachment for, and Conviction of, Treason, Bribery, or other high Crimes and Misdemeanors."[136] This clause provides explicit guidance, enumerating impeachable offenses. The phrase "high Crimes and Misdemeanors" is considerably vaguer than treason and bribery, however. Article II also prevents the president from pardoning someone who has been impeached. Finally, when discussing the judicial branch in Article III, Section 2, the Constitution stipulates that "the Trial of all Crimes, except in Cases of Impeachment; shall be by Jury."[137] This singles out impeachment cases, ensuring that they are not brought before federal judges or considered by the people of a jury.

Generally speaking, impeachment was designed to empower the legislative branch, enabling Congress—not "the people"—to check federal officials' abuse of power. In practice, the threat of impeachment with its associated scandal prompts most presidents to remove any disgraced officials (e.g., cabinet members) before the House convenes to impeach. Likewise, after an insurmountable scandal, most "civil officers of the United States" choose—as Nixon did—to "resign rather than endure an impeachment."[138]

The rarity of the impeachment process has heightened the confusion surrounding the phrase "high Crimes and Misdemeanors": with only a few cases, there is little precedent to establish the phrase's purview. The phrase itself is "unique to the impeachment context," and the Constitution offers it without explanation.[139] On the surface, it would seem to exclude "incompetence" and "general unfitness for office" from impeachable offenses, but as constitutional experts Neil J. Kinkopf and Keith E. Whittington note, the "line between general unfitness and abuse of office can be blurry."[140]

Indeed, Kinkopf and Whittington demonstrate this blurriness with a sequence of questions. For instance, can mistakes constitute grounds for impeachment and conviction, or must an official have "bad intentions?"[141] Similarly, does impeachment and conviction apply when an official commits disgraceful acts or degrades the United States' honor, or is it only justified by criminal acts? Moreover, can "private misdeeds justify impeachment," or must the act in question be "connected to the conduct of the office that individual holds?"[142]

There is no consensus on these matters. Instead, as Gerald Ford noted while still a member of the House, an impeachable offense is "whatever a majority of the House" considers it to be, and a convictable offense is whatever "two-thirds of the members of the Senate" can be persuaded "is so serious" that it justifies "removing an individual from office."[143]

On December 18, 2019, during the 2020 election cycle, the House passed two articles of impeachment, known as H. Res. 755. This resolution impeached Trump for (1) abusing the power of his office for personal political gain by attempting to influence Ukrainian officials to investigate Joe Biden and for (2) obstructing Congress's investigation of that abuse of power. An almost entirely party-line vote passed this resolution with a considerable majority in the House. On February 5, 2020, the Senate voted to acquit Trump.

The Senate vote was likewise cast along party lines, with only Senator Mitt Romney (R-UT) crossing over: he was the only Republican to vote to convict Trump in 2020, becoming the first senator to vote to convict a president of her or his own party. In Trump's second impeachment trial, six other Republican senators—Richard Burr (NC), Bill Cassidy (LA), Susan Collins (ME), Lisa Murkowski (AK), Ben Sasse (NE), and Pat Toomey (PA)—joined Mitt Romney in (again) crossing party lines, voting to convict Trump of the article of impeachment for the incitement of insurrection brought by the House on January 13, 2021. Since an impeachment conviction requires a two-thirds majority (at least sixty votes), however, the Senate acquitted Trump for a second time on February 13, 2021—after Biden's inauguration—with only fifty-seven senators voting to convict.

During the first impeachment and its trial (September 24, 2019– February 5, 2020), Republicans and Democrats constantly invoked the "Founding Fathers," forming arguments that centered around the principle of containment as expressed through the trope of checks and balances. The second impeachment proceedings were much briefer—and extended beyond the campaign time frame. As such, I attend here to the congressional speeches during Trump's first impeachment proceedings. Throughout this discourse, Democrats largely framed their actions as a check upon executive power and as a constitutional duty—as something that must be done. Here, their discourse is mixed: sometimes they operate through inheritance logic in which their duty is handed down by the "Founding Fathers" and sometimes they attempt to sidestep inheritance while relying on the covenant of American exceptionalism and the mythos of the founding era to argue on behalf of a timely intervention. Republicans, meanwhile, frame their actions almost entirely through inheritance's defense-based logic—arguing that they are "checking" the House, and Democrats more widely, and thus defending "the people."

As such, rather than the restoration-based discourse on display in War Powers arguments, this impeachment rhetoric largely returns to defense-oriented arguments. Rather than juxtaposing the United States and countries populated primarily by people of color, however, the us-other binary animating this defense rhetoric revolves around political parties. Indeed, drawing on the trope of "checks and balances" and invoking the founders as fathers, Democrats attempted to constrain Republicans and vice versa throughout this impeachment discourse. Both parties framed the other party as "other" and as outside the bounds of decency for US politics, enacting a rhetoric of sovereignty as they attempted to undermine the other party's right to rule in the name of "the people."

Democrats' Impeachment Rhetoric, 2019–2020

In 2019 and 2020 congressional Democrats insisted that impeachment was a necessary check upon executive overreach. For example, below is Representative Robin Kelly's (D-IL) entire speech, delivered to explain her vote to impeach Trump on December 18, 2019.

> Madam Speaker, today is a solemn day in America, a day that none of us hoped for when we came to Congress, but the events of today are something that each of us swore that we were prepared to execute in *defense* of the Constitution of the United States against all enemies, foreign and domestic. This is the oath that binds the men and women of the 116th Congress, as *our* democracy implores we defend *her*. A clear and present *threat* to American democracy is what brings us here. The architect, a President who asked that a foreign nation interfere in our election: this was *our* Founding Fathers' greatest fear.
>
> I cast this solemn vote for the many individuals in my district who entrusted me to be their voice in Congress. They entrusted me to uphold our Constitution for them. I vote "yes" for Sarah in Chicago, Doug in Kankakee, Diane in Flossmoor; "yes" for Kathy in Momence, Kathryn in Crete, and Jimmy in Park Forest. The facts are simple. The path forward is clear. Impeachment is not an option, it is an *obligation*, because no one is above the law.[144]

This speech employs a serious tone and emphasizes a sense of duty and obligation necessitated by the president's actions and the founders' design for democracy. Kelly's speech subtly frames Democrats' impeachment efforts in patriarchal stereotypes, casting "our democracy" as a woman who "implores we defend her" and thus situating Democrats' leadership in a traditionally masculine role as protector. Moreover, by framing Trump's request that Ukrainian officials investigate Biden as foreign interference in an election, this discourse appeals to the founders, stipulating that Trump's actions were "our Founding Fathers' greatest fear." Using possessive pronouns, this discourse ratchets up the importance of the moment, heightening the sense of danger and therefore the need for protection. At the same time, Trump—the "architect" who asked a "foreign nation [to] interfere in *our* election"—is situated outside of this speech's "we."[145] This speech constructs an us-other binary in which Trump is clearly "other"; he exists outside "us" and has no claim to "our" democracy nor the lineage of "our Founding Fathers." In addition, this discourse stipulates that no one can be "above the law," marking the "Founding Fathers'" design as absolute.

These appeals permeated much of Democrats' impeachment discourse. For instance, Senator Chuck Schumer (D-NY) stated, "Our Founding Fathers feared foreign interference in our elections and considered it one of the greatest threats facing our fledgling Republic."[146] Representative Carolyn B. Maloney (D-NY) stated, "Our Founding Fathers established a system of checks and balances that spread out power between the branches of government. They decided that no one would be a king, that no one is above the law, including the President."[147] Representative Gregory W. Meeks (D-NY) stated, "This Nation's Founding Fathers fought to end unaccountable rule. We did not free ourselves from a King to turn the President into a monarch."[148] Representative Gwen Moore (D-WI) argued that Trump's behavior was "the exact thing our Founding Fathers feared" and closed by quoting the King James's masculinized version of Mark 8:36, charging her colleagues to consider "what shall it profit a man to gain the whole world only to lose his own soul."[149] Representative Suzanne Bonamici (D-OR) stated, "No one is above the law, and the President must be held accountable for his actions" before endorsing an impeachment proceeding she described as "designed by our Founding Fathers to uphold our values and maintain the checks and balances that are essential to a functioning democracy."[150] Representative James R. Langevin (D-RI) stated that a "system of three coequal branches of government" provides "the checks and balances necessary to ensure the people's voices are heard; and that no one is above the law" before describing the House majority's vote to impeach as "using the powers the Founding Fathers enshrined in the Constitution to address a President who has violated his oath of office."[151] Rather than belittle Trump, this discourse frames Trump as coveting too much power, as trying to be king rather than president. Using possessive pronouns, it frames US democracy as grand but jeopardized, arguing that Congress must assume the role of protector to defend this republic from Trump's greedy and aggressive leadership.

Leaning into a masculinized role as protector, Democratic leaders in the Senate belittled their Republican colleagues—essentially calling them weak for refusing to hear from witnesses during the Senate trial. Much like the Senate Democrats' discourse on War Powers, this impeachment discourse asks Republicans to "take a stand," face their constituents, and generally man up. For instance, Senator Chuck Schumer (D-NY) noted that only four Republicans would need to join Democrats in order to form a majority and thus subpoena witnesses and documents, stating, "Four Republicans could do what the Founding Fathers wanted us to do: hold a fair trial with all the facts," and then concluded, "Every single one of us in this Senate will have to take a stand. How do my Republican friends want the American people, their constituents, and history to remember them? We shall see."[152] This discourse employs masculinist appeals, shaming Republicans for not acting like honorable sons.

Much of Democrats' impeachment rhetoric, then, invoked the "Founding Fathers," subtly leaning into traditional gender roles and masculinist appeals that operate within a defense-based framework—and its undergirding inheritance-based reasoning. This is especially true of Democrats' shorter impeachment-related speeches, suggesting that these appeals are particularly accessible arguments within Congress when seeking to constrain the other political party.

This inheritance-defense logic was not totalizing in Democrats' discussions of impeachment, the Constitution, and their role as public servants, however. Especially when speaking at greater length, Democrats' impeachment rhetoric sometimes hinted at cynicism, suggesting the "Founding Fathers" were not genius architects who built a republic that must be preserved and defended but good men who drafted an unfinished design—one that requires ongoing intervention.

For example, Representative Juan Vargas (D-CA) began with the usual invocation of the "Founding Fathers," cited Trump's actions as an "abuse of power," and called for "checks" against that abuse of power.[153] To conclude, however, Vargas stated, "The Founding Fathers wrote the Constitution, but it is our actions in high office that give those great words meaning and power."[154] Here, Vargas largely rejects inheritance logic. What the founders wrote—the Constitution—has no meaning or power. It is not a thing, not a reality in and of itself. Instead, public servants create its meaning and create the US Republic through their ongoing actions.

Senator Cory Booker (D-NJ) more overtly took up a cynical framework by stating that the "Founding Fathers" and their "founding documents" represent an "imperfect genius."[155] He then recounts how the Articles of Confederation largely failed to "confederate" the thirteen states, and thus the Constitution was later drafted in an attempt to fix problems the Articles of Confederation had left unsolved. He argues, "With the benefit of hindsight, it is easy to view the development of our Nation as preordained, inevitable—as if it were an expected march toward the greatness we now collectively hail, that this was somehow a perfectly plotted path toward a more perfect union. But it wasn't."[156]

While dabbling in American exceptionalism, Booker also hints at cynicism, arguing throughout this lengthy speech that the founders themselves had to try and try again, and that they set in motion a government system that requires ongoing intervention: we must try and try again.

Similarly, Senator Thomas R. Carper (D-DE) begins a lengthy speech by highlighting the ways in which the founders had seemingly "irreconcilable" differences and how they debated over the "new form of government," ultimately compromising by creating a system with "checks and balances."[157] This early portion of the speech explicitly enshrines the covenant of American exceptionalism, especially celebrating the founders for their willingness to debate and compromise. Carper introduces a hint of cynicism, however, stating,

> Our Constitution, agreed to in 1787, sought to establish "a more perfect Union"—not a perfect union, "a more perfect Union." The hard work toward a more perfect union did not end when Delaware became the first State to ratify the Constitution on December 7, 1787. In truth, it had only just begun. We went on as a nation to enact the Bill of Rights, abolish slavery, give women the right to vote, and much, much more. Throughout our history, each generation of Americans has sought to improve our government and our country because, after all, we are not perfect.[158]

He then quotes William Jennings Bryan, who stated, "Destiny is not a matter of chance. It is a matter of choice," to stipulate that "we do not leave our destiny to chance. We make it a matter of choice. And we choose to make this a more perfect union, a reflection that the hard work begun in Philadelphia in 1787 is never—never—truly complete."[159] Directly arguing that the founders' work was never completed, Carper suggests the founders left an unfinished project behind. Moreover, by recounting a history of changes (e.g., the Bill of Rights, abolishing slavery, suffrage), Carper rejects the idea that the founders bequeathed a pristine republic that ought to be preserved; instead, he advocates for ongoing change and intervention.

Carper then invokes the "Founding Fathers," closing his speech by quoting Benjamin Franklin's answer to the question of what type of government the United States would have, stating, "A republic, if you can keep it," and then concluding, "I intend to keep it."[160] Here, Carper directly engages inheritance-based logic, mixing it into his argument. Within the larger impeachment context and the immediate context of his prior arguments, however, the emphasis is not on the founders' genius creation. The emphasis is instead on ongoing actions—such as convicting Trump's impeachment—that Carper argues are necessary interventions as the United States continually builds "a more perfect union."

Democrats' impeachment rhetoric, then, highlights a tension. Much of this discourse uses the "Founding Fathers" in subtle masculinist appeals that rely on inheritance and its escalated defense-based logic to constrain Trump and Republicans more broadly. Yet this discourse is mixed with cynicism that argues for ongoing change and imagines the United States not as a pristine creation of the fathers' genius but as an ongoing project.

Republicans' Impeachment Rhetoric, 2019–2020

Democrats framed their arguments largely in terms of protecting the United States by constraining an aggressive and overbearing president; likewise, Republicans framed their impeachment discourse as defending the United States by constraining a partisan majority. The rampant possessive pronouns throughout this discourse creates an us-other binary that operates in partisan terms, imagining Democrats as "other," as illegitimate heirs due to their "partisanship."

For instance, Representative Michael Guest (R-MS) argued that while the "Founding Fathers understood" what was "important," the "House majority has chosen impeachment instead."[161] He continues, arguing that "the majority is prioritizing a partisan political process over substantive policy issues that would strengthen our country."[162] Likewise, Representative Denver Riggleman (R-VA) argued that the "Founding Fathers" who called Virginia home would not "be pleased to see Congress subverting the will of democracy by holding an impeachment vote because the majority party simply cannot accept the 2016 election."[163] Similarly, Representative Gregory Murphy (R-NC) quotes Alexander Hamilton, arguing that "our Founding Fathers" warned us "about the danger of mob rule."[164] He then complains that "the majority can exert its influence regardless of justice" and concludes with an appeal that juxtaposes Christians and Democrats, stating, "Our country needs prayer, and not this disruptive partisanship."[165] In the same manner, Representative Lance Gooden (R-TX) argues that Democrats are going to "get away with" impeaching the president "simply because they have the votes."[166] He then characterizes the 230–197 House vote to impeach Trump on the article of "abuse of power" as a "thin partisan majority."[167] Additionally, Representative Tim Walberg (R-MI) invokes "our Founding Fathers" to argue that "sadly, the majority has reduced this serious constitutional action to a purely partisan tactic."[168]

Having characterized Trump's first impeachment as partisan, Republicans in both the House and Senate then argued that partisan politics undermine US democracy by attempting to reverse the 2016 election and preempt the 2020 election. For example, Representative Gooden (R-TX) turned from his indictment of impeachment by "a thin partisan majority" to stipulate that impeachment should not "be used when an election is just around the corner."[169] Similarly, Representative Vern Buchanan (R-FL) argued that abusing "the impeachment process" subverted the votes of "63 million Americans" and then concluded, "Elections are the heart of our democracy. Our Founding Fathers devised a simple way to remove a President if you disagree with him. It is called an election, and we have one coming up in less than a year. Madam Speaker, let's let the people decide this next November."[170]

Likewise, Representative Chris Stewart (R-UT) argued that this impeachment "erodes our Republic" and that "our Founding Fathers" got impeachment right by setting the bar at "high crimes and misdemeanors" and ensuring that everything else had to be settled "at the ballot box," where the "American people decide."[171]

In the Senate, this discourse explicitly invokes "checks and balances," focusing on the Senate "checking," or containing, the House. For example, Senator Mitch McConnell (R-KY) argued, "The Founding Fathers who crafted and ratified our Constitution knew that our Nation might sometimes fall prey to the kind of dangerous factualism and partisanship that has consumed—literally consumed the House of Representatives. The Framers set up the Senate specifically to act as a check against the short-termism and the runaway passions to which the House of Representatives might fall victim."[172]

He continued to belittle the House, describing it as operating under "animal reflexes" and stating, "The Senate's time is at hand. It is time for this proud body to honor our founding purpose."[173] In a similar manner, Senator Mike Lee (R-UT) described Federalism in a lengthy speech, concluding that the House's vote to impeach represented the type of "partisan derangement that worried our Founding Fathers" and that "the Senate exists exactly for moments like this."[174] Likewise, Senator Steve Daines (R-MT) argued that "our Founding Fathers" had the "wisdom to establish a two-thirds Senate vote" for conviction and that the Senate was protecting "the will of the American people who elected the President" against a "purely partisan threat" coming from the House.[175]

The House, however, is the only representative federal body; neither the Senate nor the Electoral College are representative of "the people." As such, Republicans' claims that the House threatens US democracy and that Senate Republicans have a duty to protect the preeminence of presidential elections are rather disingenuous. Indeed, President Trump was elected in 2016 despite receiving nearly three million fewer votes than Hillary Clinton. As such, while Republicans rightly note that the Senate was designed to "check" the House—and thus US majorities—there is some duplicity at work in suggesting that presidential elections offer the best *representation* of the will of "the people."

During these impeachment proceedings, Trump sent a public letter to House Speaker Nancy Pelosi. The letter encapsulates the themes echoed throughout Republicans' broader impeachment discourse, and many Republican politicians read the following portion of the letter into the *Congressional Record*.

> By proceeding with your invalid impeachment, you are violating your oaths of office, you are breaking your allegiance to the Constitution, and you are declaring open war on American Democracy. You dare to invoke the Founding Fathers in pursuit of this election-nullification scheme—yet your spiteful actions display unfettered contempt for America's founding and your egregious conduct threatens to destroy that which our Founders pledged their very lives to build. Even worse than offending the Founding Fathers, you are offending Americans of faith by continually saying "I pray for the President," when you know this statement is not true, unless it is

meant in a negative sense. It is a terrible thing you are doing, but you will have to live with it, not I!¹⁷⁶

This letter and its repeated reading in Congress highlight the key themes of Republicans' impeachment discourse. First, the letter frames impeachment as an attack, in Trump's words, on "American Democracy." Second, it invokes "*our* Founding Fathers" while directly denying Pelosi's right to invoke the founders. Here, it operates in a clear us-other binary in which Pelosi and the House Democrats are "other," are illegitimate heirs who have no claim to the "Founding Fathers." Third, it frames impeachment as an attack on US voters by arguing that impeachment is a "election-nullification scheme" even though the House is more representative than the Electoral College. Fourth, it welds together Christianity and Republicanism by insinuating that Pelosi is a false Christian in addition to being an illegitimate heir to the "Founding Fathers'" legacy—marking her as "other" on two accounts. Finally, this discourse frames the founders' legacy in explicitly material terms: Trump wrote and Republican congresspeople repeated that Pelosi was threatening to "*destroy* that which our Founders pledged their very lives to *build*."¹⁷⁷ Here, the founders' legacy is positioned as a thing—as something that can be inherited and defended.

Indeed, Republicans' impeachment discourse rests on a materialism that activates inheritance-based reasoning as it calls Republicans to defend against Democrats. For example, Representative Greg Walden (R-OR) claimed that "the anti-Trump crowd has *weaponized* impeachment and converted it into a partisan *tool*."¹⁷⁸ Likewise, Senator James E. Risch (R-ID) described the impeachment as a "stunning *attack*" and a "purely political *attack*" before situating impeachment as a material thing by describing it as a "sacred *item*" that the "Founding Fathers *gave us*."¹⁷⁹ He continues to say that "it was not intended to be used as a political *bludgeon*" and that the United States' "separate but equal" government underscores "the genius of the Founding Fathers *giving* us three branches of government" that can check each other.¹⁸⁰ Similarly, Representative Robert B. Aderholt (R-AL) stated that the House was "abusing one of the most powerful *tools* that has been *entrusted* to Congress in the Constitution by our Founding Fathers."[181] This discourse draws upon materiality to imagine impeachment as a thing and imagine that both impeachment and the US government have been given or entrusted to the current Congress by the "Founding Fathers." Throughout, this discourse enacts a rhetoric of sovereignty, arguing that Democrats cannot legitimately rule in the name of "the people" because they are not true heirs.

Conclusion

When invoking the "Founding Fathers" to argue for "checks and balances," congressional politicians escalate from the rhetoric of inheritance to restoration or defense in order to constrain others. Drawing on the associations among fatherhood, wisdom, and righteous aggression, these arguments consistently rely on masculinist and often white-supremacist appeals that reinforce us-other binaries. The bipartisan speeches regarding War Powers contrasted the United States with Middle Eastern countries, arguing for a restoration of congressional power. In both the Second Amendment and impeachment discourses, however, the binaries ultimately framed the opposing political party as a threat to the United States. This was directly stated in Republicans' impeachment rhetoric, was clearly insinuated in much of Democrats' impeachment rhetoric, and was more circuitously conceived in Republicans' Second Amendment rhetoric—where Obama and liberals were accused of weakening the United States and thus becoming responsible for the imagined violence carried out by racialized immigrants and Middle Easterners.

At the root of this discourse is the assumption that the "Founding Fathers" bequeathed not just land and liberties but power and authority—and that "others" are attacking "our" rightful seat of power and must be contained. Both Republicans and Democrats claim to be the "us" in this us-other binary. More chillingly, both parties construct this binary through masculinist appeals, white-supremacist assumptions, and the occasional use of Christian language. Lurking within the congressional discourse of "checks and balances," then, is the assumption that white men with Christian nationalist ideologies are the true US heirs: they inherit the founders' power, and they rightfully wield that power to defend their own interests. Within this framework, all "others" are rendered suspicious if not an outright threat. The rhetoric of sovereignty and the rhetoric of containment clearly overlap, limiting who counts as "us" and therefore who can govern, even as it constructs large portions of the US population as "other."

Yet even within this dominant ideology and its readily available assumptions and appeals, there exists a counter discourse. By positioning the founders as men who learned to compromise and who governed through trial and error, rather than as idealized geniuses, politicians such as Representative Juan Vargas (D-CA), Senator Cory Booker (D-NJ), and Senator Thomas R. Carper (D-DE) articulate an alternative ideology. In this framework, power is not inherited, restored, or defended, but rather politicians are public servants who intervene by broadening enfranchisement (e.g., voting rights) and by containing only corrupt officials who have abused their power. This offers a clear alternative to the narrow confines of inheritance-based logic. Without denigrating the founders, it generally rejects the metaphor of fatherhood—rejects the premise of inheritance and its escalating rhetoric of restoration and defense when it comes to US democracy.

Moreover, this demonstrates how cynicism—a loss of faith in the founders' wisdom—operates within Congress as a counter discourse or a way around the metaphor of fatherhood and the hierarchies of its inheritance-based reasoning. Yet cynicism is a risky discourse for Democratic congresspeople, and they often capitulate into a revised covenant of American exceptionalism. Indeed, as discussed in the next chapter, both Democrats and Republicans largely agree that the "Founding Fathers" bequeathed a legacy that determines what constitutes good governance on a daily basis in Congress.

CHAPTER FOUR

Debate and Bipartisanship

THE ELECTORAL COLLEGE WAS DESIGNED for a government without parties. Article II, Section 1 of the Constitution dictates that each state receives the number of electors equal to its number of senators and representatives. Within this original design, electors were expected to deliberate (putting brakes on the popular vote), and then each elector was expected to vote for the two men he thought would make a good president—one of whom had to be a candidate from outside the elector's own state.[1] The candidate with the majority of electoral votes became president, and the man with the next highest number of votes became vice president. If the votes were tied, the House decided through a one-state, one-vote election.

With this system newly in place, George Washington was unanimously elected as the first US president in 1789, winning a vote from all sixty-nine electors in the nascent Electoral College. With thirty-four votes, John Adams became his vice president. Their election provided a regional balance between the North and South as Adams came from Massachusetts and Washington from Virginia.[2]

Although Washington staunchly resisted partisan politicking, the founders and early senators and representatives had other ideas. From the earliest days, these politicians coalesced into the Federalists (spearheaded largely by Hamilton) and the Anti-Federalists (spearheaded largely by Jefferson and Madison); indeed, Jefferson and Madison were quite publicly supported by a party known as the Democratic-Republican Party.[3] As such, although Washington famously implored his colleagues in his 1796 Farewell Address, warning them "against the baneful effects of the spirit of party," his plea was essentially too little, too late.[4]

Only four years later, the 1800 election saw party pairings for president and vice president: John Adams and Charles Cotesworth Pinckney ran together as Federalists, and Thomas Jefferson and Aaron Burr as Democratic-Republicans. The Federalist electors realized that if they all cast both their votes for Adams and Cotesworth, it would tie the election—potentially sending the election to the House—and thus, they refrained from a party-line vote. The Democratic-Republican electors, however, "were not so sagacious."[5] Casting a heretofore unprecedented party-line vote, these electors voted "for their party's champions," creating a majority tie, with Jefferson and Burr receiving seventy-three votes each.[6] This sent the election to the House, which then had to choose the president from among the five top-ranking candidates. At the time, there were sixteen states and the one-state, one-vote rule gave the less-populous states an outsized role in this election. This brought the House into a deadlock; they voted thirty-six times before Delaware's Representative Bayard, an ardent Federalist, switched his vote to Jefferson to stave off an impending crisis as the governors of Pennsylvania and Virginia—both Jeffersonians—threatened to "call out their state militias" and march against the Capitol.[7]

In light of this near crisis, senators drafted what is now the Constitution's Twelfth Amendment, and the states ratified it before the presidential election in 1804. The Twelfth Amendment limits the House vote to the top three candidates, narrowing the pool in hopes of avoiding another dead heat. This played a significant role in the 1824 election, favoring John Quincy Adams and staving off Andrew Jackson's presidency for another four years. The Twelfth Amendment's other structural change, however, has shaped every election since 1804 by caving to the party system. The Twelfth Amendment changes the way electors vote: one vote is now for the president and the other is for the vice president. This ensures that electors can vote for a presidential candidate and his or her running mate without triggering a "tied vote" and sending the election to the House.

By enabling electors to cast their votes for a "party ticket" rather than choosing two separate candidates for president, the Twelfth Amendment tacitly condoned political parties. In concert with this amendment, states began maximizing their power within the Electoral College by consolidating their votes. Rather than having "the people" or state legislators select the electors, states moved to a system in which the candidate who won that state's popular vote selects its electors. This creates a party-line, winner-take-all approach that was in effect in every state but South Carolina by 1836.[8] Today, forty-eight states and the District of Columbia (which was awarded three electoral votes by the Twenty-Third Amendment) follow this party-line, winner-take-all approach, allotting all electoral votes to the majority candidate from that state.[9] Nebraska and Maine are the outliers—binding their electors to vote for the majority winner of the congressional district to which they are allotted, and thus typically splitting their state's electoral votes.

These two changes—the ability to cast a party-line vote and the requirement that almost all electors cast party-line votes for their state's majority winner—have accelerated partisanship at the national level by erasing the vast majority of states' minority votes from the presidential election. Swing states such as Michigan, Florida, and Ohio erase nearly half their votes through this party-line, winner-take-all approach within the Electoral College. Moreover, this system erases Black votes in Southern states such as Mississippi (whose population is thirty-eight percent Black), Louisiana (whose population is thirty-three percent Black), Alabama (whose population is twenty-seven percent Black), and South Carolina (whose population is twenty-six percent Black).[10] Since the 1960s, over eighty percent of Black people have voted for Democratic candidates in each presidential election, and yet the winner-take-all system erases these votes in Southern states, which have consistently seen majority wins for Republican candidates—again, since the 1960s.[11]

The Electoral College's current erasure of Black votes in Southern states hearkens back to a regional factionalism that was written into the Electoral College's original design. By tying the number of a state's electors to that state's number of representatives and senators, the Electoral College repeated the three-fifths rule that shaped the House's composition. Article I, Section 2 of the Constitution stipulates that the House will be "apportioned" based on states' "Number of free Persons, including those bound to Service for a Term of Years, and excluding Indians not taxed, [and] three fifths of all other Persons." Black enslaved people were these euphemistically termed "all other Persons." In addition to legally fractionalizing Black people's personhood—a precedent cited in the *Dred Scott* ruling and countless other discriminatory policies—the Constitution's three-fifths clause gave Southern states additional representatives and electors beyond their apportioned number of "free Persons."

Essentially, Southern voters commanded an outsized representation in the House and Electoral College since they had representatives and electors apportioned—at a rate of three-fifths—for a large population that could not vote.[12] With this compromise in place, Southern voters soon established a majority within the federal government. By 1812, Southern voters had acquired a House majority of 76 out of 143 representatives.[13] If unable to count three-fifths of non-voting, enslaved people toward their apportionment, they would have only had a minority of 59 representatives.[14] Indeed, Jefferson likely would have lost the 1800 election and Andrew Jackson certainly would have lost the 1828 election without Southern states' additional electors.[15] The three-fifths rule was undone by the Thirteenth and Fourteenth Amendments, but the Electoral College's allowance for a party system and states' winner-take-all policies functionally maintains this inequity, resulting in a system where Black people in Southern states count toward apportionment but their votes do not count in presidential elections.

From the very beginning, then, the founders were embroiled in regional factionalism, and the federal government caved to partisan politicking after only fifteen years—redesigning the Electoral College to suit parties rather than thwart them. Yet congressional politicians regularly invoke the "Founding Fathers" to call for debate or rally bipartisan support on policy issues. Enshrining the founders as nonpartisan geniuses who excelled at compromise, US political discourse engages in American exceptionalism through a sort of selective amnesia.

Studying the gaps and silences in collective memory, rhetorician Kristen Hoerl traces the effects of what she terms "selective amnesia."[16] Following Hoerl, I situate selective amnesia as the inversion or counterpart of collective memory. Collective memory is not naturally occurring.[17] Instead, collective memory is made: it is a choice—and a political choice at that—to commemorate some figures, events, and places with US currency, public monuments, school curricula, public architecture, museums, heritage sites, and so on. For every choice made to select some figure, event, or place, there are other figures, events, and places that are *not* selected. That is, as rhetorical theorist Bradford Vivian would put it, for every contribution to collective memory there is a forgetting.[18] For example, as demonstrated by Kristen Hoerl, and then Andre E. Johnson and Anthony J. Stone Jr., US public discourse enshrines a specific memory of Martin Luther King Jr. while forgetting his later critiques of structural inequality and largely ignoring or negating the work of other Black rights activists such as Malcolm X and Stokely Carmichael.[19] Hoerl's concept of "selective amnesia" draws attention to the gaps, the omissions, the untold histories, the absent monuments, the unnamed activists, and the *silences* that permeate US public discourse and make collective memory.

These omissions are telling. Collective memory is contested but largely coherent. While never monolithic or univocal, collective memory generally provides a community with a particular sense of the past. This offers the community a collective identity and outlines a slate of values that guide the community toward a shared future. Indeed, as rhetorician Barbara Biesecker put it, collective memory tells "us something specific about who we are as a people" and about "who we may become."[20] Yet to achieve a generally coherent collective memory—and its ensuing collective identity and shared future—requires that a community's erasures or "forgettings" are likewise coherent. That is, a community must repeatedly make the same types of erasures and omissions in order to present a generally coherent collective memory. Or to put it another way, in order to achieve collective memory, there must be a pattern to the silences.

Focusing on a pattern of omissions or silences brings the concept of selective amnesia back to Philip Wander's conceptualization of the Third Persona. The Third Persona is a negated audience—those who are largely silenced, erased, or omitted by a discourse. For example, consider again the way in which the Constitution (Article I, Section 2) stipulates that the House will be "apportioned" according to each state's "Number of free Persons, including those bound to Service for a Term of Years, and excluding Indians not taxed, [and] three fifths of all other Persons." This brief euphemistic phrase, "all other Persons," is a negation, a silencing or glossing-over that marks enslaved Black people as the Constitution's Third Persona. Yet as Wander notes, this negation is not only achieved in discourse; it is likewise enacted "in history."[21] Indeed, the ways in which Black people might have voted between the founding era and the Civil Rights Act of 1964 and the consequences thereof are lost to time. Those votes never happened: not only was an audience negated, but a whole history was. Moreover, the negation of "all other Persons" skips over chattel slavery, the Atlantic slave trade, the agricultural economy based on enslaved labor, and other relevant histories and realities during the founding era. Which is to say, even as the Constitution contributes to collective memory, it enacts a selective amnesia—a forgetting of how "all other Persons" arrived in what was becoming the United States, and their roles within and contributions to the United States of America. To put it bluntly, collective memory has consequences—and those consequences can become more apparent when one attends to selective amnesia.

Some of these national negations and forgettings are intentional. For instance, as rhetorical critic Ryan Neville-Shepard recounts, the white-supremacist "Southern Strategy" as wielded by GOP politicians like Barry Goldwater in the 1960s and GOP political consultants such as Lee Atwater in the 1980s was certainly intentional.[22] Indeed, Lee Atwater "apologized for his 'naked cruelty'" on his deathbed, and yet his repentance could not undo the damage he knowingly caused.[23] The consequences of collective memory and its corollary, selective amnesia, are not always intentional or knowingly done, however. To paraphrase a portion of a liturgical Christian prayer, there are both sins of commission and omission—sins caused by what one has done and sins caused by what one has left undone. Or to put it in more secular terms, when it comes to collective memory and selective amnesia, the idiom "what you don't know can't hurt you" is blatantly false: what you don't know can hurt you—and it can certainly hurt others.

Yet, once something has been erased from collective memory, its later omissions and the consequences of those omissions become less intentional—less a matter of choice than a matter of culture. As Neville-Shepard points out, rhetorical theorist Kenneth Burke named this sort of agency a "trained incapacity," stating that one's "very abilities can function as a blindness."[24] Elaborating, Burke noted that in such a scenario, one need not refuse "to face reality," but rather one's "past training" can cause "them to misjudge their present situation."[25] Essentially, whole communities can be trained to ignore, negate, and omit that which stares them in the face—to the point that they cannot see reality. This does not equate ignorance with innocence. Indeed, my weekly recitations of the liturgical prayer paraphrased above, have led me to a moral perspective in which omissions—the things "left undone" by ignorance as well as apathy—are still sins. Rather than connoting innocence, this concept contextualizes a significant portion of US politics. What those living in the United States and those governing the United States do not know about US history matters. The history that is negated or erased from US collective memory has tangible negative consequences for the Third Persona—who is likewise erased or negated by the discourse of US collective memory.

As such, this chapter focuses on the effects of collective memory's silences—focuses on what is forgotten about the founding era's partisanship as US congressional discourse invokes the "Founding Fathers." And here, I build upon Kristen Hoerl's and Ryan Neville-Shepard's theorizations and applications of "selective amnesia" by explicitly delineating how the rhetoric of containment functions within collective memory's silences and negations.[26] Containment rhetoric, as discussed in chapter 3, posits us-other binaries through direct contrasts and through metaphors, tropes, and the like in order to contain the threat of difference—thereby excluding "others" from power and political sovereignty.[27] Analyzing the effusive celebrations of "bipartisanship" in congressional discourse—and the chastisements or accusations of partisanship—this chapter demonstrates how the collective memory of the founders and its selective amnesia work to contain both rival political parties and those historically negated by US political sovereignty. That is, wielded by both Democrats and Republicans, the invoked collective memory of the founders as bipartisan leaders works to discipline the other party—while continuing to negate those who have long been left out of or constrained within the US social contract.

Analyzing congressional appeals to bipartisanship, this chapter focuses on the way congressional politicians use collective memory and selective amnesia to enshrine debate and bipartisanship as an idealized form of government. Noting the ways in which these appeals to collective memory work to constrain the Third Persona, this chapter further demonstrates the disingenuous consequences at play within such idealizations of bipartisan governance. That is, when bipartisanship—in and of itself—is heralded as the mark of a good policy, then any policy without bipartisan support can be denounced as bad governance or even an attack on the founders' vision for democracy and, thus, the United States itself.

Bipartisanship as Ideal Governance

The rhetoric of bipartisanship relies on the logic of inheritance. The ideal of bipartisanship derives its power—its status as the ideal—from its apparent link to the founders. For example, in January 2016, the 2016 election cycle had been underway for nearly six months, and Obama was entering his final months in the White House. Prior to Obama's State of the Union address, Senator John Cornyn (R-TX) spoke on the Senate floor. Cornyn's speech reflected on Obama's performance as president, looked forward to his final months, and—engaging in campaign rhetoric—emphatically stated that the United States needed "a new president" who would enact a different type of governance than Obama had.[28] Senator Cornyn opened his speech by reminding his audience of Obama's first speech in a joint session during 2009, stating,

> It was a hopeful speech. It was an optimistic speech—one that appealed to the better angels of Republicans and Democrats and the whole Nation alike. He said we needed to pull together and boldly confront the challenges we face, but somewhere along the way he seems to have forgotten the benefit of finding common ground where folks can agree. It seems we have seen the Obama administration more involved in dividing the American people when facing opposition and then preferring to go it alone rather than to work with Congress under the constitutional scheme created by our Founding Fathers.[29]

Cornyn's speech makes clear assumptions of what constitutes good governance: "finding common ground" amidst disagreement, and collaboration among the constitutional branches—meaning, a president who works "with Congress." Moreover, Cornyn links this vision of good governance to the "Founding Fathers," invoking the founders as the *creators* of "our" good governance.

The *Constitutional Record* is teeming with similar invocations and idealizations of good governance that rely on inheritance logic, invoking the founders in order to establish the apparent goodness of bipartisanship. For example, after a crude-oil energy bill known as H.R. 702 acquired the votes to pass the House, Representative Michael Conaway (R-TX) made a short speech, stating, "I want to brag on the House," and then celebrated how this bill "went through the process" to achieve an "old-fashioned deal" and receive a "big bipartisan vote."[30] He concluded by saying that "the House of Representatives functioned the way that the Founding Fathers intended it to."[31] Similarly, speaking about an appropriations bill, Senator Ron Wyden (D-OR) stated, "It would be fair to say that we have spirited debates in the Senate, and fiscal battles that play out in this Chamber take place at virtually every new cycle and certainly with every election. That is as it should be. That ensures that we have vigorous debate about important issues the Founding Fathers wanted this Senate to be part of."[32] These speeches celebrate debate and bipartisan dealmaking as hallmarks or evidence that Congress is following the "Founding Fathers'" design. Or to put it another way, by doing what the founders wanted, Congress acts with the "Founding Fathers'" blessing.

As these examples demonstrate, congressional politicians routinely draw upon a collective memory of the founders that situates them as great debaters, collaborators, and compromisers. Forgotten in these accounts are the vicious arguments, literal duels, and stark partisanship that marked the founding era.[33] Yet the ideal of bipartisan debate and "old-fashioned" dealmaking is so entrenched that both congressional Republicans and Democrats use it to critique each other. That is, within this invocation of the "Founding Fathers" and their collective memory, anything that can be construed or negated as *not* bipartisan can be constrained as "other" and un-American.

For instance, Representative Alcee Lamar Hastings (D-FL) argued against a trade policy, concluding his speech by complaining that the Republican majority had pushed this legislation forward without allowing Democrats to contribute to or debate the bill. He stated,

> Legislation as important as the ones at hand deserve an open and transparent process where Members of both parties and both Houses of Congress may debate and offer amendments as they please. This process, envisioned and designed by our Founding Fathers to serve as a safeguard to democracy, continues to be eroded by the majority's insistence on grouping multiple, unrelated bills together under one rule and limiting the number of

amendments that can be made in order, as well as the time available for debate.[34]

Here, debate and bipartisan contributions are unquestionably good because, as Hastings stipulates, this is the process "envisioned and designed by our Founding Fathers." As such, Representative Hastings critiques Republicans because they have limited debate and minority contributions in the House. Representative Louise McIntosh Slaughter (D-NY) made the same critique when Republicans in the House issued its forty-fifth "closed rule" in a single session. As Representative Slaughter explains, "Under a closed rule, no amendments are allowed on the House floor, which limits debate and silences half of the American people who are represented by the minority of the House."[35] She continues by describing the majority Republican House as a "regime," lambasts the regular use of closed rules, and then concludes by invoking the founders, stating, "For this body to function as the Founding Fathers intended, we need debate and we need openness."[36] Insisting that debate and bipartisan contributions are the lifeblood of democracy, these representatives link debate and bipartisanship to the "Founding Fathers" and thereby uphold them as the gold standard for US governance. This reasoning presumes an inheritance-based logic that rests on a collective memory of the founders as being above party politics. Although riddled with omissions, this collective memory is leveraged as current politicians prove their legitimacy to govern—prove they are legitimate heirs—by eschewing and bemoaning partisanship.

Not only is debate and bipartisanship idealized as the epitome of democratic governance within congressional discourse, but politicians routinely use bipartisanship as a stamp of approval for contemporary policies. For example, as the 2020 election approached, Senator Chuck Schumer (D-NY) made numerous speeches calling for additional cyber defenses to prevent foreign election interference. These speeches were nearly indistinguishable, and I have excerpted only a subset below, demonstrating how Schumer made these appeals by (1) stating that it was not a partisan issue, (2) claiming there was bipartisan support for such legislation, (3) lambasting Senate Leader Mitch McConnell (R-KY) for not bringing the issue to the floor despite its bipartisan support, and (4) invoking the "Founding Fathers."

Here, it becomes clear how this collective memory, selective amnesia, and the Third Persona operate in order to contain or attempt to contain the "other" in US rhetorics of sovereignty. That is, Schumer leverages the collective memory of the founders as nonpartisan—omitting their stark partisanship—in a way that renders McConnell and other Republicans as "other" and seeks to contain their ability to govern. For instance, on June 10, 2019, Schumer stated, "We have to make sure our election systems are resilient and our cyber defenses are up to date. There is nothing partisan about that.... So why, when there is bipartisan legislation, is Leader McConnell just sitting on his hands and refusing to bring it up?"[37] Returning to this topic eight days later, Schumer stated, "We hope that Leader McConnell will stop stonewalling the need to improve the security of our elections.... Preventing foreign countries from interfering in our elections is not a Democratic or a Republican issue; it is an American issue. It is the very thing George Washington and so many of the other Founding Fathers warned us against over 200 years ago. There is no need for this to be partisan."[38] Speaking again in July, Schumer stated, "Everybody, regardless of party—Democratic, Republican, liberal, or conservative—should be against [foreign election interference]. This is one of the things the Founding Fathers were most afraid of."[39] A few days later, Schumer again argued, "Election security goes into McConnell's legislative graveyard, even though it should be the most nonpartisan of issues."[40] In December of 2019, Schumer spoke at length, stating,

> The annual Defense bill, which passed the Senate months ago, remains in conference, in part, because Leader McConnell and Senate Republicans refuse to include important election security legislation. There is bipartisan legislation on this issue—the DETER Act and DASKA—that would trigger sanctions on any government that tried to interfere with American elections. I don't care what your

party is—Democratic, Republican, or any other, no good American wants Russia or any foreign power to be able to interfere in our elections. It is one of the things the Founding Fathers were most worried about. How can our Republican leaders sit blithely by, as the danger is real and as a bipartisan group is trying to prevent Russia from interfering and doing what we can to stop it. He is holding up the NDAA bill, in part, because of this provision. Why the Republican leader and the Republican committee chairs are blocking this legislation is beyond me.[41]

Schumer's speeches came on the heels of the special counsel investigation in which Robert Mueller investigated Russian interference and potential collaborations between Russian operatives and Trump's 2016 campaign. In light of the investigation and President Trump's public relationship with Russian president Vladimir Putin, the legislation Schumer championed was extremely partisan—even if the reforms, such as paper ballots, were commonsensical and had bipartisan support.

Schumer's arguments, however, assume that bipartisanship is—or ought to be—a trump card, marking the reforms as automatically good. Likewise, Schumer links this legislation to the founders, making an a priori argument that if the "Founding Fathers" were worried about foreign interference, we should be even more concerned about it. With these two arguments in place, Schumer nationalizes this policy issue, creating a litmus test for a "good American" as he states that "no good American wants Russia or any foreign power to be able to interfere in our elections."[42] At face value, this statement appears commonsensical; however, this litmus test is embedded in a persuasive speech regarding a highly divisive topic. Schumer is attempting to persuade and to paint the opposition as *bad* Americans.

To craft this effect, Schumer relies on the apparent goodness of bipartisanship and the "Founding Fathers'" collective memory. The Third Persona in this speech is a "bad American": one who allows foreign interference and who thwarts bipartisan governance. Schumer's speech explicitly seeks to constrain then Senate Leader Mitch Mc-

Connell's ability to govern by associating him with "bad Americans"—both for seemingly allowing foreign interference and for blocking bipartisan legislation.

Finally, given the apparent goodness of debate and bipartisanship, congressional politicians use appeals to nonpartisanship not just to bless particular policies—such as election reforms—but to bolster their own authority. This discourse turns on the juxtaposition of the First and Third Personae as speakers wield the collective memory of the founders as nonpartisan leaders in order to claim power and constrain their opposition, the negated Third Persona, from that power.

For example, when speaking about the potential of military action in Iran, Senator Richard Durbin (D-IL) issued the classic "separation of powers" appeals—as discussed in the prior chapter—and then invoked nonpartisanship to increase his own authority in the Senate. Durbin stated,

> The Constitution is clear. Article I, Section 8 says that the power to declare war is the explicit power of the US Congress, and it should be.... Our Founding Fathers were wise in making sure this awesome power did not rest with a King-like or Queen-like figure but with the people's elected representatives. I have made this same argument in the House and in the Senate during my career, regardless of who sat in the White House, a Republican or a Democrat.[43]

Here, Durbin bolsters his argument by claiming to be nonpartisan on this issue. He claims to check presidents' power regardless of whether they are Republicans or Democrats, and this claim bolsters his authority. Essentially, he argues that he cannot be dismissed as partisan because his record is explicitly nonpartisan. At the same time, this speech negates or domesticates the opposition, which in this instance was Republicans who were supporting then President Trump's aggressive statements regarding Iran. This speech constrains their power by rendering them "other": Durbin's speech paints them as partisan and therefore unfit to govern.

Congressional politicians' idealization of debate and bipartisanship relies on the collective memory of the founders as fair men who valued debate and supported the best policies without partisanship—this is a collective memory riddled with selective amnesia. Remembering the founders as nonpartisan, congressional politicians use inheritance logic (1) to bless congressional rules that encourage debate and bipartisan contributions, (2) to bless legislation that has bipartisan support, and (3) to assert their own moral authority by demonstrating a nonpartisan record. At the same time, this discourse constrains the opposition by negating them as the Third Persona—as "bad Americans," unfit to govern because of their partisanship.

Bipartisan Appeals as Rhetoric of Constraint

Most congressional appeals that invoke the collective memory of the "Founding Fathers" as nonpartisan engage in the rhetoric of constraint to some degree; however, for some of this discourse, constraint seems to be the entire point. Returning to Senator Cornyn's (R-TX) 2016 speech regarding President Obama clearly demonstrates how congressional politicians constrain the other party by leveraging the founders' reputations as nonpartisan dealmakers against that party.

In his opening statement, Cornyn describes the US government as constitutionally requiring the president and Congress to work together, stating that this was the "scheme created by our Founding Fathers."[44] Then, reflecting on the prior seven years and leaning into the Senate's leeway for engaging in personalities toward the president, Cornyn describes Obama's "method of governing" as being "able to tell people: Well, I [Obama] have gotten my way and I haven't had to do the hard work of working with people of different points of view to find the areas where we agree."[45] Cornyn continues, describing Obama as "impatient" and then offering two hypothetical characterizations, stating, "Maybe he doesn't believe in consensus building. Maybe he just doesn't like his job very much."[46] Here, Cornyn defines the "job" of president as being able to build consensus through a "legislative process" in order to "actually get important things done."[47]

Cornyn then contrasts Obama with President Lyndon B. Johnson, stating that Obama is the "antithesis" of Johnson, who "knew how to get things done" by "rolling up his sleeves and working with Congress and people with different points of view" instead of just "jamming" his policies "down the throat of the minority party."[48] Here, Cornyn specifically identifies "ObamaCare" legislation, noting that it passed with only "Democratic votes" and that this was "not a way to build durable or sustainable policy."[49] Finally, Cornyn argues that what he describes as Obama's "go-it-alone strategy" is responsible for polarizing the United States, stating, "The way this President has chosen to govern" is "responsible for the polarization we see among the American people when it comes to politics and some of the sorts of craziness of our current political process . . . I think he is actually largely responsible for that—maybe not entirely, but largely."[50] Throughout this speech, Cornyn describes Obama as hopelessly indifferent to bipartisan support and, thus, as responsible for the heightened levels of partisanship seen in the US 2016 campaign cycle.

This speech clearly works to constrain Obama's legacy and character. The specter of racist stereotypes lurks within this containment rhetoric: Obama is characterized as lazy or unwilling "to do the hard work," he is imagined as childlike ("impatient" and only concerned with getting his way), and he is portrayed as uppity—jamming his agenda down the "throat of the minority party." More broadly, Cornyn constrains the contemporary Democratic party. Indeed, while Cornyn offered a (white) masculinized commendation to Democratic president Lyndon B. Johnson for "rolling up his sleeves" to "get things done," Cornyn has no such praise for any current Democrat. Instead, Obama is constrained as unfit for leadership—too impatient, too insular, too partisan, and by comparison with Johnson, not white and manly enough—and the Democratic party is seen as hopelessly partisan, falling in line with Obama's seeming penchant for partisanship and misguided policies. Here, Republicans' lack of support for Obama's policies is Cornyn's evidence that the policies are misguided. The fact that no Republican voted for "ObamaCare" is all the evidence Cornyn needs to situate "ObamaCare" as bad for the United States.

Republican congressional politicians made a similar move during Trump's first impeachment trial. For example, Representative Ted Yoho

(R-FL) stipulated that "our Founding Fathers" had warned the nation against "excessively partisan politicians" who would "overturn an election simply because the President is a member of the opposing party."[51] Similarly, Senator Kevin Cramer (R-ND) ignored Senator Mitt Romney's (R-UT) vote, focusing instead on the House. Cramer argued that "an impeachment inquiry which has only partisan support" was explicitly the type of "partisan derangement that worried our Founding Fathers."[52] Notice here the work of the Third Persona: Senator Cramer's speech frames "us" as the "Founding Fathers'" nonpartisan heirs and constrains the House's Democratic representatives as "other"—deranged in their partisanship. Yet these speeches' "evidence" or "proof" that divides "us" from the deranged "others" is the lack of bipartisan support. That is, Republican politicians' unwillingness to support impeachment is their evidence that impeachment is unwarranted and that Democrats are partisan.

This argument rests on inheritance logic that links bipartisanship to the founders. First, this logic situates bipartisan support as an ultimate good; second, it situates bipartisan support as evidence that a specific policy or congressional resolution is good; and finally, it frames a lack of bipartisan support as evidence that a policy or congressional resolution is bad—is un-American. This argumentation, of course, assumes or asserts that the speaker's own party is primarily swayed by the nation's best interests rather than internal partisan politics.

When in the minority, Democrats make fairly similar arguments. For example, in December 2019, Democratic senators objected to the confirmation of Lawrence VanDyke to the Ninth Circuit Court of Appeals, which has jurisdiction over Montana and other western states.[53] Speaking the day prior to VanDyke's confirmation, the Democratic senator Jon Tester from Montana reflected on the founders' design for the federal judiciary. He stated that "the Founding Fathers were incredibly visionary" in their decision to "insulate" the "federal judiciary" from "political influence," noting that the founders gave "senators the most solemn of responsibilities" by tasking them with "evaluating judicial nominees on their independence, their fairness, their temperament, and their judgment."[54] Tester then pivots to denounce

Republicans, saying, "Unfortunately, these days, the Republican majority seems to have thrown qualifications out the window. Instead they give out lifetime appointments to the court like candy. This doesn't prevent partisanship from influencing our judicial system; it ensures partisanship."[55] Here, Tester explicitly accuses Republican senators of violating the founders' design by corrupting the judicial branch through partisan appointments that result in partisan judges.

Tester additionally attempts to constrain Republicans, accusing them of violating democracy by going against the will of the people of Montana. Tester explains that VanDyke lost an election to the Montana Supreme Court and that the Trump administration has bypassed "the people" by appointing VanDyke to the Ninth Circuit Court of Appeals. Tester concludes by urging his Republican colleagues in the Senate to oppose VanDyke's nomination, but he does so with a barbed comment, stating, "I know it is too much to hope that the Senate will act with as much common sense as the folks in Montana do, but I do expect us to have the decency to respect the will of Montana voters and reject Mr. VanDyke for a seat on the Ninth Circuit Court of Appeals."[56] Tester's barbed appeal was largely ineffective, and fifty-one Republican senators voted to confirm, appointing VanDyke to the court.[57]

Just as congressional politicians use their record of nonpartisanship to augment their own credibility, bolstering the appeal of their First Persona, they also seek to contain others through accusations of partisanship that can make other politicians appear untrustworthy. For example, during Trump's first impeachment trial, Senators Bill Cassidy (R-LA) and James E. Risch (R-ID) submitted a question calling attention to Senator Zoe Lofgren (D-CA), who was on the record stating during Clinton's impeachment trial that Republicans were attempting to undo the 1996 election and were turning impeachment toward a "partisan use," which she then claimed was "a phenomena much feared by the Founding Fathers."[58] White House counsel Pat Cipollone played a video recording in his closing argument of Lofgren making that statement, and Republican senators Cassidy and Risch followed up by having the statement reread and asking, "What is different now?"[59] Lofgren's statement from 1999 explicitly accused Republicans of partisanship and advanced the same arguments that Republicans were using to defend Trump in 2019.

By highlighting Lofgren's statement, White House counsel Cipollone and Senators Cassidy and Risch doubled down on their accusations of Democrats' partisanship. Indeed, their excerpt from Lofgren's statement in 1999 certainly makes Democrats appear willing to voice any argument that is convenient—even directly gainsaying their own arguments whenever it serves their partisan goals. This portrays Democrats as unprincipled, suggesting their only concern is a partisan win. Here again, these arguments draw on a collective memory riddled with selective amnesia, clearly framing partisanship as a direct violation of the "Founding Fathers'" design—a point Lofgren made herself in 1999, which only further condemns her in 2019, constraining her ability to govern and Democrats' governance more broadly.

Similarly, when Republicans contradict themselves or seem to contradict themselves, Democrats are quick to point it out, likewise constraining Republicans as unprincipled partisans. For instance, Article I, Section 9 of the Constitution establishes that Congress controls the national budget, deciding how tax monies are spent. Until 1921, Congress itself drafted the budget. Then the 1921 Budget and Accounting Act moved "many of the preliminary budget-setting functions to the President and the Executive Branch," requiring the president to "submit a proposed annual budget"; this budget is then amended by congressional committees.[60] Finally, Congress votes on the budget and submits the budget as a bill (or bills) for the president to sign. In 2019, President Trump's budget draft requested $5.7 billion to build "234 miles of steel wall" at the southern border. Congress declined to allocate this money, providing only $1.375 billion for "55 miles of fencing."[61] After signing the budget bill, President Trump declared a national emergency on the southern border, which enabled him to "divert $3.6 billion from military construction projects to the wall."[62] Trump supplemented this with $2.5 billion from a "counternarcotics program" and "$600 million from a Treasury Department asset forfeiture fund," bringing the total—including the $1.375 allotted by Congress—

to approximately $8 billion in funding for a wall between Mexico and the United States.[63] Senator Chuck Schumer (D-NY) described Trump's actions as stealing "from our military to build the border wall."[64] More pointedly, Schumer accused Republican senators of partisanship, especially noting that this partisanship had led Republicans to contradict themselves.

Here, Schumer undermines Republicans' credibility, suggesting their defense of the Constitution and objections to (Democratic) presidential overreach are merely partisan politicking.[65] He explicitly asked, "Where are our Republican colleagues?" and then continued by stating, "I am sure if the shoe were on the other foot and a Democrat were President and declared an emergency to reappropriate funds, my Republican colleagues would be up in arms. . . . When President Obama did far less, they were screaming bloody murder. But now they are remarkably silent."[66] Schumer's statements tacitly invite Republicans to join Democrats in objecting to Trump's national emergency declaration. Functionally, however, this speech is designed to shame and constrain Republicans as "bad Americans" and therefore unfit for governance. Schumer accomplishes this by suggesting that congressional Republicans have no actual concern for the Constitution's integrity or for presidential overreach. Here, Schumer describes presidential overreach as "the No. 1 fear of the Founding Fathers," further delegitimizing Republicans by arguing that their partisanship has led them to disregard the "Founding Fathers'" primary concern.

Disingenuous Appeals

When congressional politicians invoke the "Founding Fathers" to appeal for bipartisanship, their appeals are largely disingenuous. Their appeals are accompanied by barbed comments—even insults—and often focus on constraining the other party rather than recognizing the other party's right to co-governance. These appeals largely work to paint the other party as partisan rather than inviting members of the other party to join a particular effort. There are two different types of disingenuous bipartisan appeals at work, however.

First, a party can go through the motions of inviting the other party to join an effort. For instance, Senator Chuck Schumer (D-NY) regularly made these types of half-hearted invitations, as exemplified by his speeches inviting Republicans to support election cybersecurity bills and to object to Trump's 2019 national emergency declaration. Similarly, Senator Richard Durbin (D-IL) invited Republicans to join his efforts to prevent war in Iran and protect the "separation of powers."[67] Likewise, Senator Jon Tester (D-MT) invited Republicans to oppose Lawrence VanDyke's confirmation.[68] These appeals are disingenuous not because bipartisanship is actually unwanted—goodness knows the Democrats in these examples badly wanted Republicans' votes. Instead, these appeals become disingenuous by constraining the other party as "other," even while tacitly inviting bipartisan cooperation. Essentially, the invitation is made in bad faith: assuming that bipartisanship is not a possibility, these speeches seek to constrain—they shame and insult the other party—even as they frame their own party as open to bipartisan negotiations, thus signaling their own governance as virtuous.

For instance, Senator Schumer (D-NY) concluded his speech regarding Trump's national emergency declaration by stating, "So it is about time our Senate Republicans stand up for the rule of law, stand up for our Constitution, and stand up to the President when he is wrong. . . . Senate Republicans will have that opportunity this week, likely tomorrow, and the American people will clearly be able to see whose side each Republican is on—the people's side, the Constitution's side, or the President's side."[69] Here, Schumer effectively throws down a gauntlet. He directly challenges Republican senators in masculinized language (e.g., "stand up for our Constitution") and wields "the people" as a threat, implying that US voters will negatively judge Republicans. Threats, challenges, and shaming rhetoric are largely ineffective ways to build political coalitions and bipartisan collaborations—but they effectively create us-other binaries and work to constrain the "other's" ability to govern.

This first type of disingenuous bipartisan appeal seems to want bipartisan collaboration but also seems entirely resigned to not having it—or at least, not having enough bipartisanship to form a majority on a given political issue. Rather than attempting to build bipartisan collaborations, this disingenuous rhetoric speaks a rhetoric of sovereignty, seeking to publicly shame members of the other party as cowards who bow to partisan pressures rather than fulfill the founders' design for good governance. Indeed, assuming from the outset that such collaboration is impossible, these appeals largely seek to embarrass the other party—often through masculinized appeals that challenge the other party to "take a stand" and "face the American people."

The first type of disingenuous bipartisanship, then, wants bipartisan support and yet makes disingenuous appeals. The second type of disingenuous bipartisanship, however, operates by rigging the system, creating a disingenuous definition of partisanship itself. Here, a party refuses to support an effort—often sabotaging that effort through delays, filibusters, and frivolous claims—while accusing the other party of partisanship. Essentially, as long as a party can control all its members, by withholding support it can paint any policy supported by the other party as partisan and thus bad. Indeed, as long as bipartisanship is an assumed ultimate good, then a policy without bipartisan support can be assumed bad. As long as a party is cohesive, then, that party can rig the system: withholding support and stymieing efforts at compromise and negotiation—all while accusing the other party of partisanship.

This is an important rhetorical tool because—as political scholar Frances E. Lee explains—parties collectively govern.[70] Although congressional members are individually elected, they do not "win or lose elections solely on the basis of their own personal qualities."[71] They derive significant power from obtaining a party's backing, and voters often vote to deny or grant a party a majority regardless of the individuals involved.[72] For example, reflecting on his own 2006 election loss, former Senator Lincoln Chafee (R-RI) stated, "I give the voters credit: They made the connection between electing even popular Republicans at the cost of leaving the Senate in the hands of a leadership they had learned to mistrust."[73] Here, Chafee characterizes his loss not in terms of his own popularity with constituents—he had a sixty-three percent approval rating when he lost the 2006 election—but with the people of Rhode Island deciding they no longer wanted a Republican majority in the Senate.[74] Legislative parties are institutions, and their members "have shared interests in winning elections and in wielding power."[75] This binds the congressional members to their party: their elections and ability to govern hinge on their party's reputation at least as much as their own.

In a two-party system, then, polishing your own party's reputation is only half the equation. In "electoral terms," it is "often just as valuable to undercut the collective reputation of the opposing party" by embarrassing its members and deriding its initiatives.[76] One clear route to this type of embarrassment and derision—to containment—is to stymie productive compromises, withhold support, and then disingenuously accuse the other party of partisanship.

In many ways, this version of disingenuous bipartisan appeals characterizes how Senator Cornyn (R-TX) described the Affordable Care Act in his speech prior to Obama's 2016 State of the Union address. Describing Obama as having forgotten "that there are people of goodwill on both sides of the aisle," Cornyn stated that Obama "jammed" the Affordable Care Act through "on a purely partisan vote."[77] Cornyn continues by looking ahead to Obama's final year, stating, "The President can decide to double down on his go-it-alone strategy, which has proved to be a disaster."[78] Cornyn is correct in that the Affordable Care Act (H.R. 3590) passed both the House and Senate without a single Republican voting to support the policy.[79]

What is omitted—forgotten, unspoken—in Cornyn's account is that the Affordable Care Act was developed out of Republican senators Chuck Grassley's (R-IA), John Chafee's (R-RI), and Orrin Hatch's (R-UT) 1993–1994 alternative to President Clinton's attempt to reform health care. Starting with the Republican plan as the original template, Senator Max Baucus (D-MT) received "Obama's blessing" to convene a group of three Democrats and three Republicans, including Senator Grassley, to develop what became known as the Affordable Care Act.[80] Then Senator Mitch McConnell (R-KY), who was the Senate minority leader, warned Republicans that "their futures in the Senate would be much dimmer if they moved toward a deal with the

Democrats that would produce legislation to be signed by Barack Obama."[81] Heeding McConnell's warning, Grassley and his colleagues shifted into "shrill anti-reform rhetoric" about "death panels that would kill grandma."[82] McConnell was clear that the Affordable Care Act had to appear as a partisan bill pushed through by Democrats. Reflecting on his strategy, he stated, "It was absolutely critical that everybody [Republicans] be together because if the proponents of the bill were able to say it was bipartisan, it tended to convey to the public that this is OK."[83] Again, when bipartisanship is the mark of good governance, the lack of bipartisanship marks a policy—and the party advocating for it—as bad.

This leads to disingenuous bipartisan rhetoric: to amass and retain their own power, either party can simply refuse to play ball regardless of the issue and then accuse the other party of being partisan. Indeed, this tactic was especially prominent in Republicans' discourse surrounding the closed-door depositions during Trump's 2019 House impeachment proceedings.

Throughout Trump's first impeachment, Republican leaders urged congressional Republicans "to support the president," promoting party unity but also ensuring a "partisan" vote in the House.[84] In what became a high-profile move, Representative Matt Gaetz (R-FL) spearheaded a staged protest that framed Democrats as partisan.[85] He led a troop of Republican representatives into a closed-door deposition, accusing Democrats of partisanship and secretiveness as they deposed witnesses.

The committee deposing these witnesses, however, had the customary majority-minority mix of Democrats and Republicans—meaning Republicans were behind those closed doors.[86] Additionally, closed-door depositions are fairly standard to prevent witnesses from coordinating their testimony; they were used in both Clinton's and Nixon's impeachment proceedings.[87] Despite the traditional use of these closed-door depositions and the presence of Republicans in them, approximately twenty-five Republican representatives forcefully occupied the deposition room—known as the SCIF—as part of a staged protest and subsequent press conference.[88]

Representative Steve King (R-IA) participated in this protest and then made a lengthy speech in the House.[89] He stated,

> They said the other day, what happens if they bring ethics charges against those of us who went down to the SCIF and said we were going to bring sunlight into this basement room where Adam Schiff is holding his secret impeachment hearings in, and some of the Members said, well, gee, it is going to cost us millions of dollars to defend ourselves if they bring ethics charges against us. And I said, it is not going to cost me a dime. Lock me up if that is the case, because we have a Constitution to protect and preserve. We have a country to protect and preserve. *We have a legacy that is handed to us from our Founding Fathers* that requires us to step up and defend our Constitution and the rule of law and the principles of truth, justice, and the American way, no matter how heavy the partisan politics get. And they are heavy. They are so heavy that the history of impeachment is kicked aside by Adam Schiff and Nancy Pelosi.[90]

Here, Representative King begins by suggesting that ethics charges might be brought against him for bringing "sunlight" into the impeachment proceedings. This not only frames him and his Republican colleagues as honest and virtuous but frames Democrats—this speech's Third Persona—as so corrupt they not only hold secret meetings but would attempt to punish Republicans for being virtuous. King then shrugs off the idea of an ethics charge with a manly retort that he is ready to be locked up rather than falter in his calling to "protect and preserve" the Constitution. King uses explicit inheritance logic, stating that "we have a legacy that is handed to us from our Founding Fathers" and that he and other Republicans are defending that legacy against Democrats and their "partisan politics."[91] Moreover, as Representative King builds this speech's us-other binary, he not only contrasts Republicans and Democrats, sunlight and basement rooms, ethical and unethical, manly and weak (or feminine), the founders' heirs and the un-American, but he uses a classic phrase, "rule of law," that has a long history of coded racism, subtly adding white and Black into the us-other binary. Indeed, as rhetorical critic

Ryan Neville-Shepard notes, the rhetoric of "law and order" and "getting tough on crime" has long been part of the Southern Strategy's playbook, offering "coded racism" as a way to court white voters.[92] Slipping the phrase "rule of law" into this speech activates this abstract white-supremacist appeal—activating a racist stereotype that paints Black people as criminals and white Democrats as too weak to control Black people's criminality.

Representative King's speech is masterful in its use of disingenuous bipartisan rhetoric. King and other Republicans had clearly rigged the system, staging a protest simply to paint Democrats as partisan. This speech follows up by situating Representative King and other Republicans as the true inheritors of the founders' "legacy" and framing Democrats as illegitimate heirs because of their "partisan politics." This rhetoric packages together a collective memory of the founders (which relies on selective amnesia, on the unspoken history of starkly partisan bickering during the founding era), the negation and constraint of the Third Persona, and inheritance-based reasoning. Within this rhetoric, "we" are the founders' descendants and must defend our inherited property—the United States of America—from "others" who would despoil it through partisanship. This is, again, a rhetoric of sovereignty: it delineates what good governance is, who can govern, how they should govern, and who "the people" are. And yet, however much debate and bipartisanship are heralded within this rhetoric of sovereignty, bipartisan appeals in congressional discourse are largely disingenuous and often reinforce partisanship through "trained incapacity" if not malintent.[93]

Conclusion

With the general exception of George Washington, the founders were deeply embroiled in factionalism and party politics, and they redesigned the Electoral College in a move that helped them consolidate power through parties.[94] To a large extent, the founders' parties (the Federalists, the Democratic-Republicans, etc.) were motivated by ideology, with some favoring a federalized government with the power to enact significant policies and with others favoring a limited federal government that would locate power primarily with individual white men and the states. To this day, the two-party system in the United States tends to recreate this ideological split between a large or limited federal government.

As Frances E. Lee demonstrates, however, parties are more than ideology, and partisan politics are productive even when there is no ideological divide.[95] Parties are institutions, and they provide collective governance. There is a utility in partisanship that has everything to do with electoral interests and often quite little to do with the policies under consideration. To some extent, this is what Senator Chuck Schumer (D-NY) was pointing out as he harangued Republicans to support proposals for increased electoral cybersecurity: the policy under consideration was not ideologically divisive. In the political landscape of 2019, however, it was absolutely a partisan issue, making Schumer's claims of nonpartisanship rather disingenuous.

Analyzing the appeals surrounding bipartisanship, this chapter specifically attends to how this discourse invokes the "Founding Fathers," linking debate and bipartisanship to their collective memory and making debate and bipartisanship an unquestionable good in US governance. This constructs an ideal in which the notion of dispassionately working together for a common good through the rigorous testing of ideas is enshrined as the founders' design for US government. Regardless of how delightful such an ideal might be, it is made possible only through selective amnesia. Only by forgetting, omitting, and negating the realities of the founding era and the ways in which the US government is now designed for parties and thus designed for partisanship can US politicians and publics remember the founders as nonpartisans who excelled at debate and compromise. Indeed, the analysis in this chapter demonstrates how congressional appeals to debate and bipartisanship draw on this collective memory, even as they invoke the "Founding Fathers" within starkly partisan tactics that seek to contain the other party. Ironically then, congressional politicians often use the ideal of debate and bipartisanship to rig the game and deepen partisan divides.

Yet by wielding the ideal of debate and bipartisanship, congressional politicians burnish their own party's reputation and tarnish the opposing party's reputation. This effect is directly dependent on the way debate and bipartisanship are linked through inheritance logic to the "Founding Fathers" and thus the covenant of American exceptionalism. Consider, for example, how Senator Roger F. Wicker (R-MS) asked his colleagues to imagine the "Founding Fathers" walking amid the Senate chambers while he described Trump's first impeachment as a partisan attack. "Let us ask ourselves today, do Hamilton and Madison and Franklin walk these venerable halls at midnight? Do these Founding Fathers traverse the stone corridors of this great building, this symbol of stability and rule of law? If they do, they caution us, as they always have, to be careful, to avoid rash decisions, to resist the urges of partisanship, and to let the Constitution work. I hope my colleagues will heed their counsel."[96]

Like so much of the inheritance-based appeals that permeate Congress, Wicker emphasizes the *reality* of US governance: its "halls," "stone corridors," and the "building" itself. He links these material realities to abstract concepts that also reverberate with a sense of concreteness. The building is a "symbol of stability" and the "rule of law"; again, a phrase that echoes with racist us-other abstractions. Seemingly Congress inherits a reality that is at once physical and abstract. This inheritance logic is then employed in an appeal to "resist the urges of partisanship," and Wicker actually suggests that this appeal comes directly from the founders, not from him, as he states, "I hope my colleagues will heed *their* counsel." The discourse of bipartisanship derives its power from the way politicians link bipartisanship to the "Founding Fathers." That link itself, however, is disingenuous, as the history of the Electoral College demonstrates.

Ultimately, when congressional politicians denounce partisanship and champion bipartisanship, the payoff is largely for their own party. Bipartisan appeals that draw on the founders' collective memory—replete with its omissions—reinforce and empower the two-party system as they enact us-other binaries. This two-party system, however, is responsible for erasing US voters. Indeed, the two-party system condoned by the Twelfth Amendment and enshrined in states' policies surrounding the Electoral College erases enough votes that several recent presidential candidates have lost the majority of US votes and still become president. Likewise, this two-party, winner-take-all system affects gubernatorial elections and legislative elections at both state and national levels, enabling a system of governance that can regularly ignore nearly half the local population. Appeals to bipartisanship, then, not only contain the other party, but enact a system that contains who *counts* during elections as "the people." Thinking about the ways in which the appeals to the "Founding Fathers" delineate the US family, affecting who can take up the mantle of governance and how that governance is enacted, this analysis of bipartisan congressional discourse suggests that such appeals are not just disingenuous but recreate the very divisions—and inequities—they claim to oppose.

CHAPTER FIVE

Losing Faith

———

WHEN CONGRESSIONAL POLITICIANS INVOKE the "Founding Fathers," they use the past to guide the future. They invoke a collective memory—riddled with selective amnesia—that assumes the United States' founding was exceptionally good and thus serves as a guide for an exceptionally good future. Yet there is more at play here than the veneration of an idealized past.

While revering the founders as *fathers*, the metaphor of fatherhood is activated through clustered terms and techniques, such that this discourse (1) constructs us-other binaries between the real America and everyone else; (2) frames this real America as exceptional; (3) imagines a possessive relationship, in which the "Founding Fathers" belong to "us," and "we" to them; (4) uses material appeals to frame this exceptional America as *real*; and (5) assumes that this real America is inherited by real Americans—the "us." At every turn, the "realness" of the United States is defined by its lineage to the "Founding Fathers." The metaphor of fatherhood, then, normalizes a logic of inheritance, suturing a sense of biological lineage into US democracy.

As fathers, the founders are enshrined over the United States: the collective memory of their values, their bodies, their words, and their assumptions for good governance is not just respected but woven into the metaphorical and legal meaning of the United States. This casts the imagination of "real" Americans in their image. Their image is not just white and male but explicitly—politically—white supremacist and patriarchal. Indeed, they did not just enslave others; they created a government—a social contract—that was built on the disenfranchisement of Black people and depended on chattel slavery to preserve the new republic's economic success. They did not just colonize land; they created a government—a social contract—that rendered Indigenous people as second-class, non-voting people and profited from their relocation and murder. They did not just overlook women; they created a nation-state—a social contract—that depended on women's procreation while denying women the rights of self-governance. When contemporary congressional politicians invoke the "Founding Fathers," employing the metaphor of fatherhood with its attendant clustered terms and techniques, they reestablish a version of the United States that privileges its founding social contract—that privileges whiteness, hegemonic masculinity, and Christian nationalism, ensuring that the United States *belongs* to some more than others.

Throughout this book, I have traced the metaphor of fatherhood *across* congressional discourse. Rather than isolating individual congresspeople to study their speeches or isolating individual speeches on a given topic or within a specific genre, I have foregrounded the work of "Founding Fathers" as a trope that runs throughout Congress. Like an earworm humming through the alcoves and chambers of Congress, "Founding Fathers" permeates congressional discourse. It pops up everywhere. It is the same song, sung by even the most bitter ideological rivals. It is a go-to resource for senators and representatives, conservatives and progressives alike. It is a metaphor that packs a white-supremacist, patriarchal punch. It is a metaphor that creates or imagines "others" and then constrains them.

Indeed, tracing this metaphor through the congressional discourse of "rights and liberties" demonstrates how possessive and material appeals construct a Second and Third Persona within the metaphor of "Founding Fathers." Imagining the founders as *our* "Founding Fathers" and portraying the United States and rights as if they were tangible, real, inheritable things, this discourse constructs a clear sense of "us," where "we" inherit land, rights, and US governance. What goes unspoken is the Third Persona: the "not-us" who do not—cannot, should not—inherit the "Founding Fathers'" property. And yet the silences and assumptions in this discourse create a clear pattern that traces the silhouette, if you will, of the negated Third Persona. Analyzing how the Third Persona operates in congressional invocations of the "Founding Fathers" brings Philip Wander's point into sharp relief: not only are the Second and Third Personae typically divided along sexist and racist distinctions, but they move from discourse into the "world of affairs."[1] That is, Congress makes laws. Congress allocates taxpayer budgets. Congress confirms judges. Congress impeaches federal officers and convicts or acquits those officers. Congress governs in the name of "the people," and when it defines "the people" as the "Founding Fathers'" descendants, it writes the inequities of racism and sexism into the "world of affairs."[2]

The ideology of Christian nationalism circulates throughout congressional invocations of the "Founding Fathers," tilting this Second Persona toward those with Christian and "family" values, where "family" is assumed to be a white, middle-class, married, heteronormative couple and their biological children. Christian nationalism is not a religion but rather an assumption that Christian symbols and values should "inform public policy."[3] Analyzing how the "Founding Fathers" are invoked in the congressional discourse of American exceptionalism, I demonstrate how this venerating discourse draws upon covenantal and jeremiadic discourse. This congressional discourse venerates the founders as the *fathers* of an exceptional nation, fusing the national identity to a logic that moves from origin to telos. Within this framework, the founders function as the gods of a (semi-) secular covenant or as dignitaries within an explicitly Christian covenant. Here, it becomes clear how Christian nationalism's symbols, values, and policies are layered within congressional invocations of the "Founding Fathers," shaping the distinctions between "the people" and the Third Persona. This venerating discourse also brings the inheritance-based logic of the "Founding Fathers" metaphor into sharp relief. That is, if the United States is destined to move from origin to telos, then "our" telos depends on "our" ability to inherit—to maintain, preserve, and defend the "Founding Fathers'" property.

The idea of defending property "we" inherit from the "Founding Fathers" ratchets up invocations of the founders into the rhetoric of containment as seen in congressional discourse that calls for "checks and balances." Indeed, here the delineations of the Second and Third Personae are fully expressed through an us-other binary where the "other" is not only negated but demonized. The goal, then, is to vanquish the "other." Within this framework, "we, the people" cannot be safe unless "we" contain the "other." Here, a variety of binaries characterize the "us-other" distinction: "we" are white, rich, strong, masculine, Christian (or Christian adjacent), and civilized; the "other" is not-white, poor, weak, feminine, secular or pagan, and uncivilized. Here, invocations of the "Founding Fathers" function to channel power—the right to govern—toward "us" and away from "others." That is, "we" inherit the founders' power by upholding their supposed vision for governance. And here, "our" right to inherit, to rule, is typically demonstrated by the ability to contain—and perhaps annihilate—racialized and feminized "others."

Given the two-party system and the ways in which parties collectively govern, however, congressional discourse also invokes the "Founding Fathers" to contain the other party, as seen most clearly (and ironically) in the calls for debate and bipartisanship. The thread of American exceptionalism—woven throughout congressional invocations of the "Founding Fathers"—again comes to the forefront as congresspeople draw upon a collective memory steeped in selective amnesia in order to contain the other party by disingenuously appealing to bipartisanship. The founders' memories are invoked to enshrine debate and bipartisanship as an ideal form of US governance. With this ideal in place, the parties can lambast each other for being partisan and can coerce their own members into withholding support from a policy and then lambast the other party for being partisan, regardless of that party's attempts at bipartisanship.

Whether strategically deployed or a "trained incapacity," these disingenuous appeals to bipartisanship—especially within election cycles—not only contain or attempt to contain the other party but also negate large populations within the United States.[4] That is, the combination of parties' collective governance with states' winner-take-all policies (think of primaries as well as elections for all levels of governance) and the Electoral College's condoning of party politics enshrined in the Twelfth Amendment coalesces into a government wherein large portions of US voters are negated in the outcome of every election. On a personal note, I was quite simply gobsmacked when realizing how this congressional discourse contains "the people," especially since these negations are so effective and virtually unnoticed within mainstream news coverage. That is, news stories often cover issues of enfranchisement, with stories about polling places, felons' rights, immigration, and so on. What goes seemingly unnoticed and certainly unsaid is the reality in which US governance also operates through the containment of its voters. Through selective amnesia (the forgetting of the founding era's partisanship, the historic disenfranchisement of people of color and women, the ongoing de facto disenfranchisement of poor people and people of color, and the policy changes that facilitate partisan politics), congressional discourse invokes the founders' collective memory, fixating bipartisanship as the idealized form of governance. These appeals contain the other party by painting that other party as partisan. Containing the other party, however, only heightens partisanship, and partisanship—again—negates large portions of US voters, especially as candidates win slim majorities.

The current governance-by-party system was designed, and it can be redesigned. For instance, states could follow Nebraska's and Maine's examples and reapportion their votes within the Electoral College by congressional district.[5] This would reduce the winner-take-all aspect of the Electoral College, and it could ultimately help decouple the tight links between presidential candidates' party affiliations and party politics in congressional elections. Additionally, congresspeople could be elected by ranked-choice voting, which has a proven track record of decreasing partisanship.[6] Likewise, primaries could change. Currently, only sixteen states have "open" primaries; a handful of states have complicated but fairly nonpartisan processes, but the rest are "closed" or semi-closed primaries.[7] Closed primaries require that "voters must be registered to vote with a party" in order to "vote in that party's primary."[8] This creates political echo chambers. Notoriously, primary voters tend to be small groups of "hardcore" partisans who often advance more partisan candidates into the general elections.[9] States could, instead, open their primaries. These reforms would fundamentally reshape Congress and—alongside expanding voting rights—would end the routine partisan negation of nearly half "the people" and sometimes more than half "the people" in US politics.

Additionally, I strongly encourage more public address scholars to focus their attention on Congress and the *Congressional Record*. While presidents and social-movement leaders tend to command national—and thus frequent—scholarly attention, Congress makes this nation's laws. As a collective, its discourse is fragmented, layered, and multivoiced. Congresspeople are interacting through their speeches. Yet this discourse follows strict rules of decorum, and congressional politicians routinely serve for decades, setting the rhetorical norms for US governance. By studying congressional discourse, public address scholars can better understand the rhetoric of US sovereignty. As such, by tracing the metaphor of fatherhood across the *Congressional Record*, this book models three methodological contributions for public address scholarship.

First, by foregrounding the function of tropes—such as the "Founding Fathers"—within a discourse community, this book highlights the agency of tropes themselves. Here, I worked to demonstrate how the trope of "Founding Fathers" structures and organizes thought. That is, for many congresspeople, I imagine "Founding Fathers" is simply a readily available turn of phrase, and the surrounding rhetorical clusters and techniques are likewise worn paths for congressional argumentation. Indeed, after a thorough analysis, I doubt many congresspeople are consciously aware of the inheritance logic at work in their discourse and the ways in which it constitutes "the people" in terms of white supremacy, patriarchy, and Christian nationalism. Such ignorance is an indictment of "trained incapacity," not an excuse.[10] Such willful ignorance demonstrates a much larger problem—one born not of a few bad actors but a deeply embedded and effective pattern of exclusion, negation, and constraint that is at work in US governance. Here, this book demonstrates that by attending to deeply embedded tropes—what some might even call ideographs—scholars can apprehend the agency of tropes themselves within a discourse community. Second, by tracing the metaphor of fatherhood across the *Congressional Record*, this book models a methodology that works *with* not against the fragmented, layered, and multivoiced nature of contemporary US public address. Finally, third, this book models a critical approach to public address scholarship—recognizing and articulating a burgeoning trend within such scholarship. Problematizing the myth of American exceptionalism and attending to the white supremacy, patriarchy, and Christian nationalism lurking within seemingly benign monoliths of US discourse—phrases such as the "Founding Fathers"—this book identifies a rhetoric of sovereignty within US public address.

The Rhetoric of Sovereignty

Congress is a legislative body. It routinely debates immigration policies, abortion rights, LGBTQ+ rights, school-voucher programs, refugee programs, military policies, Title IX policies, safety-net policies, health-care programs, and a million other policies—like the efforts to create safe nesting places for the American Bald Eagle that are annually celebrated on Bald Eagle Day. These policies are ground zero as Republicans and Democrats argue about the United States' future, and while there are consequential differences and disagreements between the parties, this research demonstrates that both parties' rhetoric reinforces the assumptions of whiteness, patriarchy, and the intertwinement of Christian nationalism and "family" values. Indeed, in hundreds of speeches during the recent election cycles, both Republican and Democratic leaders such as Mitch McConnell (R-KY) and Chuck Schumer (D-NY), as well as rank-and-file party members, employed the metaphor of "Founding Fathers" in similar ways and toward similar ends. Within the *Congressional Record*, members of the House and Senate invoke the trope of "Founding Fathers" across four domains—when advocating for rights and liberties, when celebrating American exceptionalism, when calling for "checks and balances," and when appealing for bipartisan support in often disingenuous ways.

What I want to emphasize here is that these four domains pertain to what it means to be American and what type of government the United States should have. The discussion of Americans' rights and liberties is explicitly about what it means to be American—about what type of lives are or should be possible in the United States and for whom. The discourse celebrating the United States, whether commemorating Constitution Day or National Bible Week, defines what it means to be American. Like most epideictic speeches, this discourse praises that which it deems praiseworthy. In so doing, this celebratory discourse defines what it means to be American as it celebrates American exceptionalism. Likewise, the discussion of "checks and balances" establishes what type of government the United States should have. And the appeals for debate and bipartisan collaboration similarly enshrine a specific type of governance as the ideal form of governance. The metaphor of "Founding Fathers" operates across these four domains, turning each of them toward whiteness, patriarchy, and Christian nationalism while delineating the American family and the nature of US democracy.

By tracing the trope or metaphor of "Founding Fathers" across congressional discourse, then, I have identified and analyzed a rhetoric of sovereignty. Sovereignty is the concept of how a nation-state wields authoritative power over "a territorial entity."[11] Sovereignty is typically concerned with borders, which symbolize a government's claim to "authority."[12] The metaphor of fatherhood offers white patriarchal Americans with "family" values a winsome, deeply resonant, and easily accessible "border." It divides between descendant and foreigner, insider and outsider, American and un-American, real and imposter, civilized and uncivilized, us and other. By negating the Third Persona when advocating for rights and liberties, honoring "our" future in celebrations of American exceptionalism, constraining the "other" in defensive calls for "checks and balances," and deploying selective amnesia in bipartisan appeals that negate the other party—and US voters—this congressional discourse constructs *borders* around who can be "the people" and who can govern "the people." This is the rhetoric of sovereignty within a democratic republic: by invoking the "Founding Fathers," congressional politicians bolster their authority, their right to rule, by circumscribing who matters—who can be "the people" and thus in whose name and for whose benefit congresspeople rule.

It is no accident that the metaphor of "Founding Fathers" reinforces patriarchy, white supremacy, and the ideology of Christian nationalism—legally benefiting white heteronormative men with "family" values and the women who support them. After all, this is the United States' originating social contract.[13] The rhetoric of sovereignty at work within the metaphor of "Founding Fathers" reinscribes the same borders of personhood—of what it means to be fully human—seen in the racist glaring omissions and the sexist on-the-page specifications penned in the Declaration of Independence's preamble, "We hold these truths to be self-evident, that all *men* are created equal, that they are endowed by their Creator with certain unalienable Rights, that among these are Life, Liberty and the pursuit of Happiness."[14] Essentially, when drawing on the "Founding Fathers" in order to enact a rhetoric of sovereignty, congressional politicians reaffirm the United States' founding exclusions.

These borders, these exclusions matter especially because Congress is a legislative body. Its discourse not only establishes the norms and contours of US culture, but it creates the laws, policies, and actual borders that constitute the United States. Again, Congress confirms federal judges, commemorates national and religious holidays, uses the power of the purse to obstruct executive orders, impeaches and acquits federal officials, and, of course, creates the laws of the land. That is to say, as pedantic, prolific, and sometimes petulant as Congress shows itself to be in its *Congressional Record*, it is also a body with teeth. Congress's words become US reality.

Beneficiaries: White Men, Family Values, and Violence

There are innumerable ways in which I—and others more or less like me—have benefited from the current structure of US governance and the rhetoric of sovereignty enacted in congressional invocations of the "Founding Fathers." As an evangelical, white, middle-class woman in a heteronormative nuclear family, I benefit either directly or circuitously from most if not all this congressional "Founding Fathers" discourse.

Thinking back to my childhood and adolescence, I remember—in a hazy and taken-for-granted sort of way—commemorating the likes of George Washington, Thomas Jefferson, James Madison, Alexander Hamilton, John Adams, and Benjamin Franklin. Thinking back to these years, I half recall ditties, books, poems, museum visits, and the like celebrating these men as *our* "Founding Fathers." As a mother, I see it again in my children's books, music recitals, and school curricula. As a scholar, I now recognize this as the work of collective memory, selective amnesia, and political tropes. My hope today is that many, including those who were raised as I was and perhaps identify as I do—as white, middle class, and Christian—might recognize the pernicious effects of the "Founding Fathers" metaphor and the mythical nature of American exceptionalism.

To that end, as I conclude this book, I want to demonstrate how pernicious this discourse is and how dire its consequences can be. As such, I want to draw attention to those who inhabit the fullest expressions of this inheritance discourse: to white men, often with Christian-nationalist ideologies, who perpetrate gun violence primarily against people of color in the United States. Indeed, the repercussions of this fatherhood metaphor with its inheritance logic become most apparent as this discourse is taken up and violently embodied in men's rights groups, white-supremacist groups, and Christian-nationalist politics—especially as these groups overlap to promote the conspiracy theory of the "great replacement."

Replacement theory is family-centric—operating through both sexism and racism. This conspiracy generally argues that white women are birthing too few children and that white people in Western nations are being "replaced" by Black people, Latinx people, Jews, Arabs, or people of Asian descent. For example, the tiki-torch wielding white-supremacist terrorists in Charlottesville, Virginia, chanted, "You will not replace us," in 2017. Patrick Crusius killed twenty-two people of primarily Latinx descent in a Walmart in El Paso, Texas, and published a manifesto about the "great replacement" in 2019. Likewise, the gunman who killed ten people in a Black neighborhood supermarket in Buffalo, New York, published a replacement-theory manifesto in 2022. White supremacy and patriarchy are embroiled with each other: they depend on controlling white women's procreation and violently subjugating people of color.

Replacement theory widely circulates in masculinist, white-supremacist groups within the United States, building on the "fourteen words" white-supremacist mantra. This mantra states: "We must secure the existence of our people and a future for white children," and is often followed by the phrase "because the beauty of the White Aryan woman must not perish from the earth."[15] This mantra was coined by David Lane, a white supremacist who developed his ideology within Protestant contexts such as the Ku Klux Klan, Christian Identity, and other Christian groups and churches affiliated with the Aryan Nation.[16] Contemporary mass shootings reinforce this mantra and its combination of racism, Christian nationalism, and sexism. Indeed, Dylann Roof—a professing Christian—referenced the "fourteen words" throughout his writings before killing nine African Americans at the Emanuel African Methodist Episcopal Church in Charleston, South Carolina, in 2015.[17]

While the "fourteen words" make it clear that white women's procreation is of the utmost importance—combining white supremacy and the patriarchal control of women's bodies—replacement theory emphasizes the urgency latent within the "fourteen words." That is, while the "fourteen words" state the need to "secure the existence" of the white "race" and to prevent the "beauty of the White Aryan woman" from perishing "from the earth," as a conspiracy, replacement theory foregrounds urgency: supposedly, a plot is afoot to replace the white "race."

Here, men's rights groups, Christian-nationalist ideology, and white-supremacy groups in the United States are united in blaming feminism for declining birth rates among white women. This can result in unusual jealousies: for instance, even as white-supremacist groups in the United States spout Islamophobia, they can also uphold Muslim men for having "got their women where they need to be," positioning fundamentalist Muslim patriarchy as an icon to emulate.[18] This is—ultimately—inheritance logic. It circles back around to fatherhood: white men must dominate white women in order to father white children, demonstrating that "white" civilization is better than others and therefore has the right to inherit the United States and oppress all others.

News pundits—such as Tucker Carlson—promote these ideas, opining that the "collapse of families" is the "biggest issue facing this country" and arguing that women outearning men is a major cause of this collapse.[19] Indeed, the hysteria around "families" is largely about white-supremacist fatherhood—it is about inheritance and power.

And here, it becomes clear that as embroiled as white supremacy and patriarchy are with each other, they are also entangled with institutionalized and politicized Christianity. Many evangelical or "born again" versions of Christianity in the United States largely define themselves through an adherence to Complementarian doctrine—claiming the Bible mandates that men are created for leadership and women for submission.[20] Stressing the importance of procreation and child-rearing, these churches and denominations enact the central feature of religious fundamentalism: defining women by the ability to produce new life and valorizing the production of new life to the extent it limits women's participation in "social, economic, political, and religious" arenas, ultimately suggesting women are innately unsuited for "participating in these spheres."[21]

Consider, for example, how the Gospel Coalition's Kevin DeYoung argued that the way to win the "culture wars" was for Christians to "have more children and disciple them like crazy."[22] Bemoaning the Supreme Court's ruling that the protected category "sex" includes "sexual orientation and gender identity" in 2020, DeYoung encouraged Christians to fight back, urging them to "strongly consider having more children than you think you can handle."[23] Indeed, DeYoung directly engaged in "replacement" language, stating, "In the not-too-distant future, the only couples *replacing* themselves in America will be religious couples," and concluding that "the future belongs to the fecund."[24] What DeYoung does not say is that such procreation largely prevents women from engaging in anything outside the home. But he does valorize such child-rearing, reminding readers that "a child's soul will last forever," and he dabbles in Christian nationalism, stating that by "focusing on the family" Christians can bring "the kingdom to bear on the world, one baby at a time."[25] This puts enormous—eternal—weight on (white) women to procreate and engage in intensive mothering, shaping children into the next generation of (white) Christian Americans. The fundamentalist insistence on biological children not only constrains (white) women's lives; it ensures the "fourteen words," securing "the existence of our people and a future for white children."

While Representative Steve King (R-IA) tweeted in 2017, "We can't restore our civilization with somebody else's babies," few senators or representatives openly endorse replacement theory.[26] Indeed, many Democrats call for its repudiation. For instance, Senator Chuck Schumer (D-NY) wrote an open letter to Rupert Murdoch and Fox News's top executives, calling them to "immediately cease the reckless amplification of the so-called 'Great Replacement' theory on your network's broadcasts" after the white-supremacist attack in Buffalo, New York.[27] As this book has amply demonstrated, however, congressional politicians lay the groundwork for this patriarchal white-supremacist violence as they wield the metaphor of fatherhood and its inheritance-based logic. Indeed, Schumer himself routinely invokes the founders as fathers, relying on the assumptions of inheritance.

To be clear, then, I encourage a shift away from the phrase "Founding Fathers," but I do not think this shift alone will set things right.

Substituting "founders" or "framers" instead of "Founding Fathers" would—for a while—likely operate just as cover, window dressing that leaves the underlying logic of inheritance unchanged. I would argue that political discourse already uses the terms "founders" or "framers" in this way: it is not unusual for congressional politicians to use some combination of the terms "Founding Fathers," "founders," "forefathers," and "framers" in the same speech. Indeed, while writing this book I struggled for an appropriate term by which to refer to this supposed cohort of men—who were *not* a cohort during their own time. I am not particularly fond of the term "founders" as used throughout this book, but there was no obvious alternative within the current range of discursive options. At this point, however, I hope it is apparent that words matter, and thus I hope that by shifting away from the metaphor of fatherhood, the people who live in the United States and congressional politicians might begin to chip away at the logic of inheritance that structures US politics—might even articulate better, more realistic, more equitable discursive frameworks through which to remember the politics of the founding era.

Strategic Cynicism

Indeed, some of this work has already begun: there are dissenting voices within Congress. Some congressional discourse—especially among members of the Congressional Black Caucus—provides guidance for how politicians might transition away from the metaphor of fatherhood. First, when advocating for the right to vote and freedom of the press, congressional Democrats avoided many of the rhetorical techniques wrapped up in the metaphor of fatherhood. Talking about what the founders wanted rather than what they made, this discourse framed the "Founding Fathers" more in terms of leadership. This strategy still celebrates the US founding as exceptional and extols the founders, but it operates through a logic of expansion in which the founders lead the United States toward the expansion of rights and liberties, whereas the logic of inheritance would limit those rights to the "Founding Fathers'" true descendants.

Second, Democrats such as Cory Booker (D-NJ) and Thomas R.

Carper (D-DE) modeled a rhetoric that leaned on American exceptionalism while positing the founding as unfinished—interweaving just a hint of cynicism. This discourse celebrates US greatness while insisting that there is work to do in order to continue in the vein of greatness. This discourse disavows inheritance-based reasoning, arguing that instead of working to *preserve* something pristine, Americans must intervene in current politics to chart a path toward a more perfect union.

These first two strategies generally attempt to divorce inheritance-based logic from the covenant of American exceptionalism. That is, these discourses leave the covenant of exceptionalism intact, assuming that the US founding had a kernel of greatness and framing the "Founding Fathers" as generally good, if imperfect, leaders. These strategies more or less weaken the metaphor of fatherhood while still honoring the founders and generally warding off backlash by voicing a clear faith in American exceptionalism.

The third strategy rejects both the founders' fatherhood and American exceptionalism. This is racial realism expressed in the rhetoric of cynicism. Again, I foreground the concept of cynicism because it calls attention to the sense of a loss of faith. This particular aspect to "cynicism" is useful because it highlights the myth of American exceptionalism and the routine veneration of the "Founding Fathers" as a faith—by which I mean, Americans *believe* in American exceptionalism and the "Founding Fathers," not that this constitutes a religion.

Expressing a loss of faith in the "Founding Fathers" reveals how fundamental such a faith is to US collective memory. In so doing, this discourse of realistic cynicism can offer a counternarrative. For instance, Representative Barbara Lee (D-CA) offered such a counternarrative, re-centering the United States' freedom-based identity in Black resistance as she read Nikole Hannah-Jones's essay for "The 1619 Project" into the *Congressional Record*. In this discourse, congressional politicians note that the founders' designed a system of governance rooted in oppression, while cloaking that governance in the language of equality, opportunity, and merit. This third strategy bears the most risk. As such, currently, congressional politicians rarely use this strategy and tend to do so in cautious ways.

This caution is justified. Although Obama was the first president to use the phrase "American exceptionalism" in a major speech, stating, "I believe in American exceptionalism with every fiber of my being," and he emphasized American exceptionalism more than his predecessors, he was routinely attacked by Republicans for not loving America.[28] For instance, Rudy Giuliani stated that he did not hear from Obama "what a great country we are, what an exceptional country we are," and Dick Cheney stated that prior presidents believed "the US did have a role to play in the world as the exceptional nation," but that "Barack Obama clearly doesn't believe that."[29] Historically, Republican presidents have been considered far more "patriotic" than Democratic presidents, perhaps laying the groundwork for Republicans' accusations that Obama was deficient in his love for and belief in American exceptionalism despite his heightened rhetoric.[30]

Yet the type of American exceptionalism Obama voiced was the type that spoke of "a more perfect union."[31] That is, Obama tended to use the second strategy outlined above, revering the founders as leaders who were good but imperfect and calling for ongoing activism. If he faced such intense backlash while still overtly committing himself to the narrative of American exceptionalism, congressional politicians could face even more extreme backlash for expressing realistic cynicism, disassociating themselves from the (false) faith of the "Founding Fathers."

And yet, such cynicism is warranted. The founders are not Americans' fathers, and they were no gods. They were largely rich and well educated, with the privileges of whiteness and maleness in white-supremacist, patriarchal colonies. Some were Christians, some were deists, and others more skeptical, but they routinely touted Christian values, upholding a religious institution that was instrumental in the colonies' creation and codification of race, racism, and patriarchy.[32]

Analyzing the metaphor of fatherhood in congressional discourse, my conclusion is that this metaphor and its attendant appeals are irredeemable. The metaphor rigs the game, rendering the "Founding

Fathers'" most obvious descendants—white men with Christian-nationalist ideologies—as the first among equals. This reinforces both the hierarchy and the pretense of equality that has shaped the United States since its founding. More frighteningly, it normalizes a logic that oppresses women and torments people of color, wreaking violence—both mundane legislative violence and more obvious acts of genocidal terror—across this country.

NOTES

Introduction

1. Mitch McConnell (KY), "Impeachment," *Congressional Record* 166, no. 10 (January 16, 2020): S255–S256, https://www.congress.gov/116/crec/2020/01/16/CREC-2020-01-16-pt1-PgS255-6.pdf.

2. Chuck Schumer (NY), "Impeachment," *Congressional Record* 166, no. 12 (January 21, 2020): S288–S289, https://www.congress.gov/116/crec/2020/01/21/CREC-2020-01-21-pt1-PgS288-2.pdf.

3. David Sehat, *The Jefferson Rule: How the Founding Fathers Became Infallible and Our Politics Inflexible* (New York: Simon & Schuster, 2015), 116; for a discussion of Harding's RNC speech, see Richard B. Bernstein, *The Founding Fathers Reconsidered* (New York: Oxford University Press, 2009), 3–5.

4. Sehat, *The Jefferson Rule*, 116; Bernstein, *The Founding Fathers Reconsidered*, 3–5.

5. Anne E. Burnette and Rebekah L. Fox, "My Three Dads: The Rhetorical Construction of Fatherhood in the 2012 Republican Presidential Primary," *Journal of Contemporary Rhetoric* 2, no. 3–4 (2012): 90.

6. Harlow Giles Unger, *"Mr. President" George Washington and the Making of the Nation's Highest Office* (Boston: Da Capo Press, 2013), 60; Jay A. Parry and Andrew M. Allison, *The Real George Washington: The True Story of America's Most Indispensable Man* (Washington, DC: National Center for Constitutional Studies, 1991), xi.

7. Henry Knox to George Washington, March 19, 1787, in *Papers of George Washington: Confederation Series 1784–1788*, ed. W. W. Abbott (Charlottesville, VA: University Press of Virginia, 1997), 5:995–998.

8. Sehat, *The Jefferson Rule*.

9. Sehat, *The Jefferson Rule*.

10. Abraham Lincoln, "Address Delivered at the Dedication of the Cemetery at Gettysburg," November 19, 1863, in *The Collected Works of Abraham Lincoln*, ed. Roy P. Basler (New Brunswick, NJ: Rutgers University Press, 1953–1955), 7:23, emphasis added.

11. "The Constitution: How Was It Made?" National Archives, accessed October 9, 2023, https://www.archives.gov/founding-docs/constitution/how-was-it-made; "Meet the Framers of the Constitution," National Archives, accessed October 9, 2023, https://www.archives.gov/founding-docs/founding-fathers.

12. "Session Dates of Congress," United States House of Representatives, accessed October 10, 2023, https://history.house.gov/Institution/Session-Dates/110-Current/.

13. I. A. Richards, *The Philosophy of Rhetoric* (London: Oxford University Press, 1936), 93; Leah Ceccarelli, *On the Frontier of Science: An American Rhetoric of Exploration and Exploitation* (East Lansing, MI: Michigan State University Press, 2013), 19.

14. Ceccarelli, *On the Frontier of Science*, 19.

15. George Lakoff and Mark Johnson, *Metaphors We Live By* (Chicago: University of Chicago Press, 1980).

16. See J. David Cisneros, "Contaminated Communities: The Metaphor of 'Immigrant as Pollutant' in Media Representations of Immigration," *Rhetoric & Public Affairs* 11, no. 4 (2008): 569–601.

17. Emily Martin, "The Egg and the Sperm: How Science has Constructed a Romance Based on Stereotypical Male-Female Roles," *Signs* 16, no. 3 (1991): 501.

18. These days, there are no definitive start dates for election cycles; since I focused on the 2016 and 2020 election cycles, I marked the start of these cycles by the months in which Donald Trump and Joseph Biden officially began their campaigns, respectively.

19. Frances. E. Lee, *Beyond Ideology: Politics, Principles and Partisanship in the US Senate* (Chicago: University of Chicago Press, 2009), 8.

20. George Lakoff, *The Political Mind: Why You Can't Understand 21st Century Politics with an 18th Century Brain* (New York: Viking, 2008).

21. Mari Boor Tonn and Valerie A. Endress, "Looking Under the Hood and Tinkering with Voter Cynicism: Ross Perot and 'Perspective by Incongruity,'" *Rhetoric & Public Affairs* 4, no. 2 (2001): 288, 283.

22. Derrick Bell, "Racial Realism," *Connecticut Law Review* 24, no. 2 (1992): 363–379; Andre E. Johnson and Anthony J. Stone, Jr., "'The Most Dangerous Negro in America': Rhetoric, Race and the Prophetic Pessimism of Martin Luther King Jr.," *Journal of Communication and Religion* 41, no. 1 (2018): 8–22; Frank B. Wilderson III, *Afropessimism* (New York: Liveright Publishing, 2020).

23. Bell, "Racial Realism," 363.

24. Bell, "Racial Realism," 373–374.

25. Stephen J. Hartnett and Bryan R. Reckard, "Sovereign Tropes: A Rhetorical Critique of Contested Claims in the South China Sea," *Rhetoric & Public Affairs* 20, no. 2 (2017): 295; see also Anne Demo, "Sovereignty Discourse and Contemporary Immigration Politics," *Quarterly Journal of Speech* 91, no. 3 (2005): 295.

26. Demo, "Sovereignty Discourse," 295.

27. See Michael J. Lee and Jarrod Atchison, *We Are Not One People: Secession and Separatism in American Politics Since 1776* (New York: Oxford University Press, 2022).

28. Paul Elliot Johnson, *I the People: The Rhetoric of Conservative Populism in the United States* (Tuscaloosa, AL: University of Alabama Press, 2022), 2; Nadia Urbinati, *Me the People: How Populism Transforms Democracy* (Cambridge, MA: Harvard University Press, 2019).

29. Johnson, *I the People*, 3–4.
30. Lee and Atchison, *We Are Not One People*.
31. Johnson, *I the People*, 15–16.
32. Johnson, *I the People*, 15–16.
33. Johnson, *I the People*, 15–16.
34. Johnson, *I the People*, 15–16.
35. Johnson, *I the People*, 15–16.
36. Johnson, *I the People*, 15–16.
37. Barbie Zelizer, "Reading the Past against the Grain: The Shape of Memory Studies," *Critical Studies in Mass Communication* 12, no. 2 (1995): 214.
38. Trevor Parry-Giles, "Fame, Celebrity and the Legacy of John Adams," *Western Journal of Communication* 72, no. 1 (2008): 86.
39. John K. Amory, "George Washington's Infertility: Why Was the Father of Our Country Never a Father?" *Fertility and Sterility* 81, no. 3 (2004): 495–499.
40. *The Washington Family*, 1789–1796, National Gallery of Art, accessed October 10, 2023, https://www.nga.gov/collection/art-object-page.561.html.
41. Amory, "George Washington's Infertility," 498.
42. Lorri Glover, *The Founders as Fathers: The Private Lives and Politics of the American Revolutionaries* (New Haven, CT: Yale University Press), 9.
43. Glover, *The Founders as Fathers*, 9.
44. Glover, *The Founders as Fathers*, 9.
45. Glover, *The Founders as Fathers*, 9.
46. Glover, *The Founders as Fathers*, 9.
47. Glover, *The Founders as Fathers*, 9.
48. Glover, *The Founders as Fathers*, 22.
49. Glover, *The Founders as Fathers*, 2.
50. Glover, *The Founders as Fathers*, 2.
51. Glover, *The Founders as Fathers*, 2.
52. Glover, *The Founders as Fathers*, 3.
53. Glover, *The Founders as Fathers*, 3.
54. Carole Blair, "Communication as Collective Memory," in *Communication as . . . Perspectives on Theory*, ed. Gregory J. Shepherd, Jeffrey St. John, and Ted Striphas (Thousand Oaks: Sage, 2006), 53.
55. Sehat, *The Jefferson Rule*; Derigan Silver, "The Framers' First Amendment: Originalist Citations in US Supreme Court Freedom of Expression Opinions," *Journalism & Mass Communication Quarterly* 88, no. 1 (2011): 101.
56. Sehat, *The Jefferson Rule*, 1.
57. Sehat, *The Jefferson Rule*, 2.
58. Sehat, *The Jefferson Rule*, 114.
59. Sehat, *The Jefferson Rule*, 19; James Madison to Thomas Jefferson, September 2, 1793, in *The Papers of James Madison*, ed. William Thomas Hutchinson and William M. E. Rachal (Chicago: University of Chicago Press, 1962–1991), 15:93.
60. Mark Anthony Hoffman, "The Materiality of Ideology: Cultural Consump-

tion and Political Thought After the American Revolution," *American Journal of Sociology* 125, no. 1 (2019): 2.

61. Robert P. Saldin, "William McKinley and the Rhetorical Presidency," *Presidential Studies Quarterly* 14, no. 1 (2010): 121; Jeffrey K. Tulis, *The Rhetorical Presidency* (Princeton, NJ: Princeton University Press, 1987).

62. Saldin, "William McKinley and the Rhetorical Presidency"; Tulis, *The Rhetorical Presidency*.

63. Daniel Dreisbach, "Micah 6:8 in the Literature of the American Founding Era: A Note on Religion and Rhetoric," *Rhetoric & Public Affairs* 12, no. 1 (2009): 91; Donald S. Lutz, *A Preface to American Political Theory* (Lawrence, KS: University Press of Kansas, 1992), 136.

64. Dreisbach, "Micah 6:8," 91.

65. Dreisbach, "Micah 6:8," 91; Daniel L. Dreisbach, *Reading the Bible with the Founding Fathers* (New York: Oxford University Press, 2017), 1.

66. See Dreisbach, *Reading the Bible*, 7.

67. Dreisbach, *Reading the Bible*, 27–28.

68. Dreisbach, *Reading the Bible*, 28.

69. See Sehat, *The Jefferson Rule*, 73.

70. Helen Sterk, "How Rhetoric Becomes Real: Religious Sources of Gender Identity," *Journal of Communication and Religion* 12, no. 2 (1989): 30.

71. Sterk, "How Rhetoric Becomes Real," 30.

72. Sterk, "How Rhetoric Becomes Real," 25.

73. Sterk, "How Rhetoric Becomes Real," 25.

74. Mary Beth Norton, "'Either Married or to Bee Married': Women's Legal Inequality in Early America," in *Inequality in Early America*, ed. Carla Gardina Pestana and Sharon V. Salinger (Hanover, NH: University Press of New England, 1999), 25–45.

75. Cheryl I. Harris, "Whiteness as Property," *Harvard Law Review* 106, no. 8 (1993): 1720–1721.

76. Harris, "Whiteness as Property," 1715.

77. Harris, "Whiteness as Property," 1715.

78. Harris, "Whiteness as Property," 1716.

79. Harris, "Whiteness as Property," 1714.

80. Harris, "Whiteness as Property," 1725.

81. James Madison, *The Writings of James Madison*, ed. Gaillard Hunt (New York: G. P. Putnam's Sons, 1906), 101; Harris, "Whiteness as Property," 1726.

82. Harris, "Whiteness as Property," 1731–1737; Jessica C. Harris, Ryan P. Barone, and Hunter Finch, "The Property Functions of Whiteness within Fraternity and Sorority Culture and Its Impact on Campus," *New Directions of Student Services* 2019, no. 165 (2019): 18.

83. Peggy McIntosh, "White Privilege: Unpacking the Invisible Knapsack," in *Introduction to Women's, Gender and Sexuality Studies: Interdisciplinary and*

Intersectional Approaches, ed. L. Ayu Saraswati, Barbara L. Shaw, and Heather Rellihan (New York: Oxford University Press, 2018), 72–75.

84. McIntosh, "White Privilege."
85. Harris, Barone, and Finch, "The Property Functions of Whiteness," 18.
86. See Harris, "Whiteness as Property," 1719.
87. Carole Pateman and Charles W. Mills, *Contract and Domination* (Cambridge, UK: Polity Press, 2007), 5.
88. John Locke, *Two Treatises of Government*, 3rd ed., ed. William Seal Carpenter (London: Dent, 1924, 1698), 130; see Harris, "Whiteness as Property," 1735.
89. Harris, Barone, and Finch, "The Property Functions of Whiteness," 18; Harris "Whiteness as Property."
90. Carole Pateman, *The Sexual Contract* (Stanford, CA: Stanford University Press, 1988); Charles W. Mills, *The Racial Contract* (Ithaca, NY: Cornell University Press, 1997); Charles W. Mills, *Black Rights/White Wrongs: The Critique of Racial Liberalism* (New York: Oxford University Press, 2017); Pateman and Mills, *Contract and Domination*; Hortense J. Spillers, "Mama's Baby, Papa's Maybe: An American Grammar Book," *Diacritics* 17, no. 2 (1987): 64–81; Saidiya V. Hartman, *Scenes of Subjection: Terror, Slavery and Self-Making in Nineteenth-Century America* (New York: Oxford University Press, 1997); Harris, "Whiteness as Property," 1715.
91. Pateman, *The Sexual Contract*; Mills, *The Racial Contract*; Mills, *Black Rights/White Wrongs*; Pateman and Mills, *Contract and Domination*.
92. See Pateman, *The Sexual Contract*, 7.
93. Pateman, *The Sexual Contract*; Mills, *The Racial Contract*; Mills, *Black Rights/White Wrongs*; Pateman and Mills, *Contract and Domination*.
94. Pateman and Mills, *Contract and Domination*, 2.
95. Pateman, *The Sexual Contract*; Mills, *The Racial Contract*; Mills, *Black Rights/White Wrongs*; Pateman and Mills, *Contract and Domination*.
96. Spillers, "Mama's Baby, Papa's Maybe," 68.
97. Spillers, "Mama's Baby, Papa's Maybe."
98. Spillers, "Mama's Baby, Papa's Maybe."
99. Spillers, "Mama's Baby, Papa's Maybe," 75.
100. Spillers, "Mama's Baby, Papa's Maybe," 74, emphasis in the original.
101. Spillers, "Mama's Baby, Papa's Maybe," 74.
102. Hartman, *Scenes of Subjection*, 6.
103. Hartman, *Scenes of Subjection*, 5.
104. Hartman, *Scenes of Subjection*, 6.
105. Anna Cornelia Fahey, "French and Feminine: Hegemonic Masculinity and the Emasculation of John Kerry in the 2004 Presidential Race," *Critical Studies in Media Communication* 24, no. 2 (2007): 134.
106. See Nick Trujillo, "Hegemonic Masculinity on the Mound: Media Representations of Nolan Ryan and American Sports Culture," *Critical Studies in Mass Communication* 8, no. 3 (1991): 290–308.

107. Fahey, "French and Feminine," 133.

108. Jim Crow laws largely kept these privileges reserved for white men. For a discussion of "muscular" Christianity during this era, see Roxanne Mountford, *The Gendered Pulpit: Preaching in American Protestant Spaces* (Carbondale, IL: Southern Illinois University Press, 2003); Gail Bederman, *Manliness and Civilization: A Cultural History of Gender and Race in the United States, 1880–1917* (Chicago: University of Chicago Press, 1995).

109. Bederman, *Manliness and Civilization*; see also Kristin Kobes Du Mez, *Jesus and John Wayne: How White Evangelicals Corrupted a Faith and Fractured a Nation* (New York: Liveright, 2020), 16.

110. Du Mez, *Jesus and John Wayne*, 17.

111. Du Mez, *Jesus and John Wayne*, 30–32.

112. Du Mez, *Jesus and John Wayne*, 30–31.

113. Du Mez, *Jesus and John Wayne*, 30–31.

114. Sage Mikkelsen and Sarah Kornfield, "Girls Gone Fundamentalist: Feminine Appeals of White Christian Nationalism," *Women's Studies in Communication* 44, no. 4 (2021): 565.

115. Jerry Falwell, quoted in Matt Stearns, "Jerry Falwell Brought Religious Conservatives into US Politics," *Mercury News*, May 16, 2007, https://www.mercurynews.com/2007/05/16/jerry-falwell-brought-religious-conservatives-into-u-s-politics/.

116. Mikkelsen and Kornfield, "Girls Gone Fundamentalist," 566.

117. Rebecca Goetz, *The Baptism of Early Virginia: How Christianity Created Race* (Baltimore: Johns Hopkins University Press, 2012).

118. Mark Ward Sr., "Sermons as Social Interaction: Pulpit Speech, Power and Gender," *Women & Language* 42, no. 2 (2019): 285–316; Seth Dowland, "'Family Values' and the Formation of a Christian Right Agenda," *Church History* 78, no. 3 (2009): 606–631; and Du Mez, *Jesus and John Wayne*.

119. Denny Burk, "The Roles of Men and Women," *The Gospel Coalition*, 2022, https://www.thegospelcoalition.org/essay/the-roles-of-men-and-women/.

120. Mikkelsen and Kornfield, "Girls Gone Fundamentalist."

121. For a discussion of "purity" in connection to white supremacy, see Myra Washington, "Interracial Intimacy: Hegemonic Construction of Asian American and Black Relationships on TV Medical Dramas," *Howard Journal of Communications* 23, no. 3 (2012): 253–271.

122. For a discussion of white Christian political activism regarding sex education, see Casey Ryan Kelly, "Chastity for Democracy: Surplus Repression and the Rhetoric of Sex Education," *Quarterly Journal of Speech* 102, no. 4 (2016): 353–375. For a discussion of declining white birth rates and *Roe v. Wade*, see Odette Yousef, "Supremacy Movements Unite Over Abortion Restriction, Though for Different Reasons," NPR.com, May 12, 2022, https://www.npr.org/2022/05/12/1098585429/supremacy-movements-unite-over-abortion-restriction-though-for-different-reasons; Gretchen Livingston and D'Vera Cohn, "Childness Up Among All Women; Down Among Women with Advanced Degrees," Pew Research Center, June 25, 2010,

https://www.pewresearch.org/social-trends/2010/06/25/childlessness-up-among-all-women-down-among-women-with-advanced-degrees/; Jens Manuel Krogstad, Amina Dunn, and Jeffrey S. Passel, "Most Americans Say the Declining Share of White People in the US Is Neither Good nor Bad for Society," Pew Research Center, August 23, 2021, https://www.pewresearch.org/fact-tank/2021/08/23/most-americans-say-the-declining-share-of-white-people-in-the-u-s-is-neither-good-nor-bad-for-society/.

123. Andrew L. Whitehead and Samuel L. Perry, *Taking America Back for God: Christian Nationalism in the United States* (New York: Oxford University Press, 2020), x; Kristina M. Lee, "'In God We Trust?': Christian Nationalists' Establishment and Use of Theistnormative Legislation," *Rhetoric Society Quarterly* 52, no. 5 (2022): 419.

124. John Fea, *Believe Me: The Evangelical Road to Donald Trump* (Grand Rapids, MI: William B. Eerdmans Publishing Company, 2018), 6–7.

125. Kristina M. Lee, "'In God We Trust?'"

126. Megan Foley, "Sound Bites: Rethinking the Circulation of Speech from Fragment to Fetish," *Rhetoric & Public Affairs* 15, no. 4 (2012): 613.

127. Foley, "Sound Bites," 613.

128. Foley, "Sound Bites," 614.

129. Jonathan Alter, "How the Media Blew It," *Newsweek*, November 21, 1988, 24; Foley, "Sound Bites," 616.

130. Ersula Ore, *Lynching: Violence, Rhetoric, and American Identity* (Jackson, MS: University Press of Mississippi, 2019); Johnson, *I the People*; Lee and Atchison, *We Are Not One People*.

131. Judy Schneider, "House and Senate Rules of Procedure: A Comparison," Congressional Research Service, April 16, 2008, 6, https://crsreports.congress.gov/product/pdf/RL/RL30945.

132. Schneider, "House and Senate Rules," 5.

133. Schneider, "House and Senate Rules," 5.

134. Barry Loudermilk (GA), "Our Documents of Freedom," *Congressional Record* 161, no. 98 (June 18, 2015): H4536–H4537, https://www.congress.gov/114/crec/2015/06/18/CREC-2015-06-18-pt1-PgH4536-2.pdf.

135. Loudermilk (GA), "Our Documents of Freedom."

136. Loudermilk (GA), "Our Documents of Freedom."

137. Loudermilk (GA), "Our Documents of Freedom."

138. Loudermilk (GA), "Our Documents of Freedom."

139. Loudermilk (GA), "Our Documents of Freedom."

140. Catherine Shoichet and Michael Pearson, "Garland, Texas, Shooting Suspect Linked Himself to ISIS in Tweets," CNN.com, May 4, 2015, https://www.cnn.com/2015/05/04/us/garland-mohammed-drawing-contest-shooting/index.html.

141. Shoichet and Pearson, "Garland, Texas, Shooting Suspect," https://www.cnn.com/2015/05/04/us/garland-mohammed-drawing-contest-shooting/index.html.

142. Loudermilk (GA), "Our Documents of Freedom."

143. Loudermilk (GA), "Our Documents of Freedom," emphasis added.

144. Loudermilk (GA), "Our Documents of Freedom," emphasis added.
145. Loudermilk (GA), "Our Documents of Freedom," emphasis added.
146. "Moses, Relief Portrait," Architect of the Capitol, accessed October 10, 2023, https://www.aoc.gov/explore-capitol-campus/art/moses-relief-portrait; "Relief Portrait Plaques of Lawgivers," Architect of the Capitol, accessed October 10, 2023, https://www.aoc.gov/explore-capitol-campus/art/relief-portrait-plaques-lawgivers.
147. Loudermilk (GA), "Our Documents of Freedom," emphasis added.
148. Loudermilk (GA), "Our Documents of Freedom."
149. Loudermilk (GA), "Our Documents of Freedom."
150. Loudermilk (GA), "Our Documents of Freedom."
151. Loudermilk (GA), "Our Documents of Freedom."
152. Loudermilk (GA), "Our Documents of Freedom."
153. Loudermilk (GA), "Our Documents of Freedom."
154. Loudermilk (GA), "Our Documents of Freedom."
155. Loudermilk (GA), "Our Documents of Freedom."
156. Loudermilk (GA), "Our Documents of Freedom."
157. Loudermilk (GA), "Our Documents of Freedom."
158. Loudermilk (GA), "Our Documents of Freedom."
159. Loudermilk (GA), "Our Documents of Freedom."
160. Loudermilk (GA), "Our Documents of Freedom."
161. See Jessie Kratz, "Pieces of History: The National Archives' Larger-Than-Life Statues," National Archives, May 22, 2018, https://prologue.blogs.archives.gov/2018/05/22/the-national-archives-larger-than-life-statues/.
162. "Furniture," History, Art & Archives: United States House of Representatives, accessed October 10, 2023, https://history.house.gov/Exhibitions-and-Publications/House-Chamber/Rostrum/; "Eternal vigilance is the price of liberty (Spurious Quotation)," Monticello, accessed October 10, 2023, https://www.monticello.org/site/research-and-collections/eternal-vigilance-price-liberty-spurious-quotation.
163. Loudermilk (GA), "Our Documents of Freedom," emphasis added.
164. Loudermilk (GA), "Our Documents of Freedom."
165. Loudermilk (GA), "Our Documents of Freedom."
166. Loudermilk (GA), "Our Documents of Freedom."
167. Loudermilk (GA), "Our Documents of Freedom."
168. Loudermilk (GA), "Our Documents of Freedom."
169. Loudermilk (GA), "Our Documents of Freedom."
170. Loudermilk (GA), "Our Documents of Freedom."
171. Harris, "Whiteness as Property," 1731–1734.
172. Mills, *Black Rights / White Wrongs*, xxi.
173. See Nicholas Confessore, "Schumer Calls on Murdoch and Fox News Executives to Stop Amplifying Replacement Theory," *NYTimes.com*, May 17, 2022, https://www.nytimes.com/2022/05/17/nyregion/schumer-fox-news-replacement-theory-murdoch.html?smid=url-share; Nellie Bowles, "'Replacement Theory,' a Racist, Sexist Doctrine, Spreads in Far-Right Circles," *NYTimes.com*, March 18, 2019, https://

www.nytimes.com/2019/03/18/technology/replacement-theory.html?smid=url-share; Lauretta Charlton, "What Is the Great Replacement?" *NYTimes.com*, August 6, 2019, https://www.nytimes.com/2019/08/06/us/politics/grand-replacement-explainer.html?smid=url-share.

Chapter 1. Rights and Liberty

1. Although the position of superintendent of Indian Affairs has evolved into the Bureau of Indian Affairs, it originated as a role within the War Department, and Thomas L. McKenney was its first appointee, at the behest of Secretary of War John C. Calhoun. See James Madison, *The Letters of James Madison, 1816–1828* (New York: Townsend MacCoun, 1884), 3:515–516; see also Richard Drinnon, *Facing West: The Metaphysics of Indian-Hating and Empire-Building* (New York: Meridian/New American Library, 1980), 99.

2. Madison, *The Letters of James Madison*, 516.

3. See Drinnon, *Facing West*.

4. Madison, *The Letters of James Madison*, 516.

5. Charles W. Mills, "Body Politic, Bodies Impolitic," *Social Research* 78, no. 2 (2011): 594.

6. Mills, "Body Politic, Bodies Impolitic," 594–595; see also George Fredrickson, *White Supremacy: A Comparative Study in American and South African History* (New York: Oxford University Press, 1981), xii.

7. Edwin Black, "The Second Persona," *Quarterly Journal of Speech* 56, no. 2 (1970): 109–119; Philip Wander, "The Third Persona: An Ideological Turn in Rhetorical Theory," *Central States Speech Journal* 35, no. 4 (1984): 197–216.

8. Don J. Waisanen and Amy B. Becker, "The Problem with Being Joe Biden: Political Comedy and Circulating Personae," *Critical Studies in Media Communication* 32, no. 4 (2015): 258.

9. Black, "The Second Persona," 111.

10. Wander, "The Third Persona," 209.

11. Black, "The Second Persona," 112.

12. Black, "The Second Persona," 112, 119.

13. Black, "The Second Persona," 119.

14. Wander, "The Third Persona," 209.

15. Wander, "The Third Persona," 209.

16. Wander, "The Third Persona," 209.

17. Wander, "The Third Persona," 209.

18. Wander, "The Third Persona," 210.

19. Wander, "The Third Persona," 216.

20. "Bill of Rights (1791)," Bill of Rights Institute, accessed October 13, 2023, https://billofrightsinstitute.org/primary-sources/bill-of-rights.

21. "Bill of Rights (1791)."

22. "Bill of Rights (1791)," emphasis added.

23. "Bill of Rights (1791)," emphasis added.

24. "Bill of Rights (1791)," emphasis added.
25. Marci A. Hamilton and Michael McConnell, "The Establishment Clause: Common Interpretation," National Constitution Center, accessed October 13, 2023, https://constitutioncenter.org/the-constitution/amendments/amendment-i/interpretations/264.
26. Geoffrey R. Stone and Eugene Volokh, "Freedom of Speech and the Press: Common Interpretation," National Constitution Center, accessed October 13, 2023, https://constitutioncenter.org/the-constitution/amendments/amendment-i/interpretations/266.
27. Hamilton and McConnell, "The Establishment Clause: Common Interpretation."
28. Orrin Hatch (UT), "Religious Freedom," *Congressional Record* 161, no. 147 (October 7, 2015): S7212, https://www.congress.gov/114/crec/2015/10/07/CREC-2015-10-07-pt1-PgS7195.pdf.
29. Hatch (UT), "Religious Freedom."
30. Hatch (UT), "Religious Freedom."
31. Hatch (UT), "Religious Freedom."
32. Hatch (UT), "Religious Freedom."
33. Hatch (UT), "Religious Freedom."
34. Hatch (UT), "Religious Freedom."
35. Orrin Hatch (UT), "Religious Liberty," *Congressional Record* 161, no. 173 (December 1, 2015): S8206, https://www.congress.gov/114/crec/2015/12/01/CREC-2015-12-01-pt1-PgS8206.pdf, emphasis added.
36. Hatch (UT), "Religious Liberty," emphasis added.
37. Hatch (UT), "Religious Liberty."
38. Hatch (UT), "Religious Liberty," emphasis added.
39. Emphasis added.
40. Sheila Jackson Lee (TX), "General Leave," *Congressional Record* 165, no. 97 (June 11, 2019): H4407, https://www.congress.gov/116/crec/2019/06/11/CREC-2019-06-11-pt1-PgH4402-2.pdf.
41. Hatch (UT), "Religious Liberty."
42. Hatch (UT), "Religious Liberty."
43. Hatch (UT), "Religious Liberty."
44. John M. Murrin, "Religion and Politics in America from the First Settlements to the Civil War," in *Religion and American Politics: From the Colonial Period to the 1980s*, ed. Mark A. Noll (New York: Oxford University Press, 1990), 35.
45. Hatch (UT), "Religious Liberty."
46. Alexander Mooney (WV), "Religious Liberties," *Congressional Record* 161, no. 163 (November 3, 2015): H7396, https://www.congress.gov/114/crec/2015/11/03/CREC-2015-11-03-pt1-PgH7395-2.pdf.
47. Mooney (WV), "Religious Liberties," emphasis added.
48. Mooney (WV), "Religious Liberties."
49. Mooney (WV), "Religious Liberties," emphasis added.

50. Adam Liptak, "Supreme Court Sides with Coach over Prayers at the 50-Yard Line," *NYTimes.com*, June 27, 2022, https://www.nytimes.com/2022/06/27/us/politics/supreme-court-coach-prayers.html?smid=url-share.

51. Hatch (UT), "Religious Freedom."

52. Jeffrey Rosen and David Rubenstein, "The Declaration, the Constitution, and the Bill of Rights," National Constitution Center, accessed October 13, 2023, https://constitutioncenter.org/the-constitution/white-papers/the-declaration-the-constitution-and-the-bill-of-rights.

53. Rosen and Rubenstein, "The Declaration."

54. "Declaration of Independence: A Transcription," National Archives, accessed October 12, 2023, https://www.archives.gov/founding-docs/declaration-transcript.

55. Daniel L. Dreisbach, *Reading the Bible with the Founding Fathers* (New York: Oxford University Press, 2017), 125–126; see also Worthington Chauncey Ford, ed., *Journals of the Continental Congress, 1774–1789* (Washington, DC: Government Printing Office, 1906), August 20, 1776, 5:690.

56. Rosen and Rubenstein, "The Declaration"; Carole Pateman, *The Sexual Contract* (Stanford, CA: Stanford University Press, 1988); Charles W. Mills, *The Racial Contract* (Ithica, NY: Cornell University Press, 1997); Charles W. Mills, *Black Rights/White Wrongs: The Critique of Racial Liberalism* (New York: Oxford University Press, 2017); Carole Pateman and Charles W. Mills, *Contract and Domination* (Cambridge, UK: Polity Press, 2007); Hortense J. Spillers, "Mama's Baby, Papa's Maybe: An American Grammar Book," *Diacritics* 17, no. 2 (1987): 64–81; Saidiya V. Hartman, *Scenes of Subjection: Terror, Slavery and Self-Making in Nineteenth-Century America* (New York: Oxford University Press, 1997).

57. Rosen and Rubenstein, "The Declaration."

58. Peter Manseau, "The Myth of the 'Good Guy With a Gun' Has Religious Roots," *NYTimes.com*, June 23, 2022, https://www.nytimes.com/2022/06/23/opinion/uvalde-evangelicals-guns.html?smid=url-share.

59. Rosen and Rubenstein, "The Declaration."

60. Rosen and Rubenstein, "The Declaration."

61. Rosen and Rubenstein, "The Declaration."

62. Brad Wenstrup (OH), "Pro-Life Movement," *Congressional Record* 162, no. 4 (January 7, 2016): H154, https://www.congress.gov/114/crec/2016/01/07/CREC-2016-01-07-pt1-PgH154-3.pdf, emphasis added.

63. John Ratcliffe (TX), "Pro-Life," *Congressional Record* 162, no. 7 (January 12, 2016): H289, https://www.congress.gov/114/crec/2016/01/12/CREC-2016-01-12-pt1-PgH289.pdf, emphasis added.

64. Ratcliffe (TX), "Pro-Life," emphasis added.

65. Steve King (IA), "National Security, The Rule of Law, and Planned Parenthood Videos," *Congressional Record* 161, no. 120 (July 28, 2015): H5583–H5587, https://www.congress.gov/114/crec/2015/07/28/161/120/CREC-2015-07-28-pt1-PgH5583.pdf, emphasis added.

66. Ted Yoho (FL), "The 47th Annual March for Life," *Congressional Record* 166,

no. 9 (January 15, 2020): H281–H287, https://www.congress.gov/116/crec/2020/01/15/CREC-2020-01-15-pt1-PgH281.pdf, emphasis added.

67. Barry Loudermilk (GA), "On the Rights of Persons," *Congressional Record* 162, no. 4 (January 7, 2016): H154, https://www.congress.gov/114/crec/2016/01/07/CREC-2016-01-07-pt1-PgH154-5.pdf.

68. Loudermilk (GA), "On the Rights of Persons," emphasis added.

69. Loudermilk (GA), "On the Rights of Persons," emphasis added.

70. Malcolm Levene, David I. Tudehope, and M. John Thearle, *Essentials of Neonatal Medicine*, 3rd ed. (Somerset, NJ: Blackwell, 2000), 8.

71. Loudermilk (GA), "On the Rights of Persons," emphasis added.

72. Loudermilk (GA), "On the Rights of Persons."

73. Trent Franks (AZ), "Born-Alive Abortion Survivors Protection Act" *Congressional Record* 161, no. 135 (September 18, 2015): H6143, https://www.congress.gov/114/crec/2015/09/18/CREC-2015-09-18-pt1-PgH6143-4.pdf.

74. Franks (AZ), "Born-Alive Abortion Survivors Protection Act"; Trent Franks (AZ), "Condemning the Actions of Planned Parenthood," *Congressional Record* 161, no. 114 (July 21, 2015): H5325, https://www.congress.gov/114/crec/2015/07/21/CREC-2015-07-21-pt1-PgH5325.pdf.

75. Franks (AZ), "Condemning the Actions of Planned Parenthood."

76. Franks (AZ), "Born-Alive Abortion Survivors Protection Act."

77. Adrienne Davis, "Don't Let Nobody Bother Yo' Principle," in *Sister Circle: Black Women and Work*, eds. Sharon Harley and the Black Women and Work Collective (New Brunswick, NJ: Rutgers University Press, 2002), 103–127.

78. See Loretta J. Ross et al., eds., *Radical Reproductive Justice: Foundations, Theory, Practice, Critique* (New York: First Feminist Press, 2017).

79. Nathan S. Chapman and Kenji Yoshino, "The Fourteenth Amendment Due Process Clause," National Constitution Center, accessed October 13, 2023, https://constitutioncenter.org/interactive-constitution/interpretation/amendment-xiv/clauses/701.

80. Chapman and Yoshino, "The Fourteenth Amendment Due Process Clause."

81. Franks (AZ), "Condemning the Actions of Planned Parenthood."

82. Amanda J. Stevenson et al., "The Impact of Contraceptive Access on High School Graduation," *Science Advances* 7, no. 19 (2021): https://doi.org/10.1126/sciadv.abf6732; Liana Christin Landivar, "First-Birth Timing and the Motherhood Wage Gap in 140 Occupations," *Socius: Sociological Research for a Dynamic World* 6 (2020): https://doi.org/10.1177/2378023120939424.

83. Quoctrung Bui and Claire Cain Miller, "The Age That Women Have Babies: How a Gap Divides America," *NYTimes.com*, August 4, 2018, https://www.nytimes.com/interactive/2018/08/04/upshot/up-birth-age-gap.html; Naomi Cahn and June Carbone, *Red Families v. Blue Families: Legal Polarization and the Creation of Culture* (New York: Oxford University Press, 2010).

84. Alex DiBranco, "The Long History of the Anti-Abortion Movement's Links

to White Supremacists," *Nation*, February 3, 2020, https://www.thenation.com/article/politics/anti-abortion-white-supremacy/.

85. Nicquel Terry Ellis, "'Pushed to the Margins': Why Some Activists and Lawmakers Say Abortion Bans Are a Form of White Supremacy," CNN.com, May 18, 2022, https://www.cnn.com/2022/05/18/us/abortion-ban-women-of-color/index.html; see also Katherine Kortsmit et al., "Abortion Surveillance—United States, 2019," Surveillance Summaries, Centers for Disease Control and Prevention, November 26, 2021, https://www.cdc.gov/mmwr/volumes/70/ss/ss7009a1.htm.

86. William H. Frey, "New 2020 Census Results Show Increased Diversity Countering Decade-Long Declines in America's White and Youth Populations," Brookings Institute, August 13, 2021, https://www.brookings.edu/research/new-2020-census-results-show-increased-diversity-countering-decade-long-declines-in-americas-white-and-youth-populations/.

87. Loudermilk (GA), "On the Rights of Persons."

88. DiBranco, "The Long History."

89. Sage Mikkelsen and Sarah Kornfield, "Girls Gone Fundamentalist: Feminine Appeals of White Christian Nationalism," *Women's Studies in Communication* 44, no. 4 (2021): 365; Robert Jones, *White Too Long: The Legacy of White Supremacy in American Christianity* (New York: Simon & Schuster, 2020), 103.

90. DiBranco, "The Long History"; see also Randall Balmer, "The Religious Right and the Abortion Myth," *Politico*, May 10, 2022, https://www.politico.com/news/magazine/2022/05/10/abortion-history-right-white-evangelical-1970s-00031480.

91. Steve King, quoted in Nellie Bowles, "'Replacement Theory,' a Racist, Sexist Doctrine, Spreads in Far-Right Circles," *NYTimes.com*, March 18, 2019, https://www.nytimes.com/2019/03/18/technology/replacement-theory.html?smid=url-share, emphasis added; Steve King, quoted in Ari M. Brostoff, "How White Nationalists Aligned Themselves with the Antiabortion Movement," *Washington Post*, August 27, 2019, https://www.washingtonpost.com/outlook/2019/08/27/how-white-nationalists-aligned-themselves-with-antiabortion-movement/, emphasis added.

92. Mary Miller, quoted in Caroline Linton, "Trump-Backed Rep. Mary Miller Says at Rally That Overturning *Roe v. Wade* Is a 'Victory for White Life'; Campaign Says She Misspoke," CBS News, June 28, 2022, https://www.cbsnews.com/news/mary-miller-victory-for-white-life-roe-v-wade-overturned-donald-trump/.

93. Michael T. Morley and Franita Tolson, "Elections Clause," National Constitution Center, accessed October 13, 2023, https://constitutioncenter.org/interactive-constitution/interpretation/article-i/clauses/750.

94. Morley and Tolson, "Elections Clause."

95. Morley and Tolson, "Elections Clause."

96. Bradley A. Smith and Daniel P. Tokaji, "Article I, Section 2: Common Interpretation," National Constitution Center, accessed October 13, 2023, https://constitutioncenter.org/interactive-constitution/interpretation/article-i/clauses/762;

see also Alexander Keyssar, *The Right to Vote: The Contested History of Democracy in the United States* (New York: Basic Books, 2000/2009), 15, 23–24.

97. Richard H. Pildes and Bradley A. Smith, "The Fifteenth Amendment: Common Interpretation," National Constitution Center, accessed October 13, 2023, https://constitutioncenter.org/the-constitution/amendments/amendment-xv/interpretations/141.

98. "Voting Rights Act of 1965," NAACP, accessed October 13, 2023, https://naacp.org/find-resources/history-explained/legislative-milestones/voting-rights-act-1965.

99. Terri A. Sewell (AL), "60th Anniversary of Montgomery Bus Boycott," *Congressional Record* 161, no. 177 (December 8, 2015): H9031, https://www.congress.gov/114/crec/2015/12/08/CREC-2015-12-08-pt1-PgH9031.pdf.

100. Sewell (AL), "60th Anniversary of Montgomery Bus Boycott."

101. Sewell (AL), "60th Anniversary of Montgomery Bus Boycott."

102. John Seven, "The Exclusionary History of Voter Registration Dates to 1800," History.com, October 22, 2018, https://www.history.com/news/voter-registration-elections-president-midterms.

103. Seven, "The Exclusionary History of Voter Registration."

104. Emphasis added.

105. Sewell (AL), "60th Anniversary of Montgomery Bus Boycott."

106. Sewell (AL), "60th Anniversary of Montgomery Bus Boycott."

107. Sewell (AL), "60th Anniversary of Montgomery Bus Boycott."

108. Sewell (AL), "60th Anniversary of Montgomery Bus Boycott."

109. Sheila Jackson Lee (TX), "Committee Consideration," *Congressional Record* 165, no. 168 (October 23, 2019): H8398–H8403, https://www.congress.gov/116/crec/2019/10/23/CREC-2019-10-23-pt1-PgH8398-4.pdf.

110. Jackson Lee (TX), "Committee Consideration."

111. Jackson Lee (TX), "Committee Consideration."

112. Jackson Lee (TX), "Committee Consideration."

113. Akhil Reed Amar and John C. Harrison, "The Citizenship Clause: Common Interpretation," National Constitution Center, accessed October 13, 2023, https://constitutioncenter.org/interactive-constitution/interpretation/amendment-xiv/clauses/700; "Voting Rights for Native Americans," Library of Congress, accessed October 13, 2023, https://www.loc.gov/classroom-materials/elections/right-to-vote/voting-rights-for-native-americans/.

114. Sewell (AL), "60th Anniversary of Montgomery Bus Boycott."

115. See Thomas Healy, "The Justice Who Changed His Mind: Oliver Wendell Holmes, Jr., and the Story behind *Abrams v. United States*," *Journal of Supreme Court History* 39, no. 1 (2014): 38.

116. Healy, "The Justice Who Changed His Mind," 38.

117. Geoffrey R. Stone and Eugene Volokh, "Freedom of Speech and the Press: Common Interpretation," National Constitution Center, accessed October 13, 2023, https://constitutioncenter.org/blog/a-common-interpretation-freedom-of-speech-and-the-press.

118. Stone and Volokh, "Freedom of Speech and the Press: Common Interpretation."
119. Stone and Volokh, "Freedom of Speech and the Press: Common Interpretation."
120. Stone and Volokh, "Freedom of Speech and the Press: Common Interpretation."
121. Stone and Volokh, "Freedom of Speech and the Press: Common Interpretation."
122. Robert Menendez (NJ), "Submitted Resolutions," *Congressional Record* 165, no. 71 (May 1, 2019): S2573–S2575, https://www.congress.gov/116/crec/2019/05/01/CREC-2019-05-01-pt1-PgS2573.pdf.
123. Menendez (NJ), "Submitted Resolutions."
124. Menendez (NJ), "Submitted Resolutions."
125. Menendez (NJ), "Submitted Resolutions."
126. Menendez (NJ), "Submitted Resolutions."
127. Menendez (NJ), "Submitted Resolutions."
128. Menendez (NJ), "Submitted Resolutions."
129. Menendez (NJ), "Submitted Resolutions."
130. Menendez (NJ), "Submitted Resolutions."
131. Menendez (NJ), "Submitted Resolutions."
132. Menendez (NJ), "Submitted Resolutions."
133. Ron Wyden (OR), "Death of Jamal Khashoggi," *Congressional Record* 165, no. 106 (June 24, 2019): S4470–S4472, https://www.congress.gov/116/crec/2019/06/24/CREC-2019-06-24-pt1-PgS4470.pdf.
134. Wyden (OR), "Death of Jamal Khashoggi."
135. Wyden (OR), "Death of Jamal Khashoggi."
136. Wyden (OR), "Death of Jamal Khashoggi."
137. Wyden (OR), "Death of Jamal Khashoggi."
138. Wyden (OR), "Death of Jamal Khashoggi."
139. Wyden (OR), "Death of Jamal Khashoggi."
140. Wyden (OR), "Death of Jamal Khashoggi."
141. Wyden (OR), "Death of Jamal Khashoggi."
142. Wyden (OR), "Death of Jamal Khashoggi."
143. Steve Russell (OK), "Protecting Our Second Amendment Rights," *Congressional Record* 162, no. 4 (January 7, 2016): H171–H173, https://www.congress.gov/114/crec/2016/01/07/CREC-2016-01-07-pt1-PgH171.pdf; Louie Gohmert (TX), "Issues of the Day," *Congressional Record* 165, no. 109 (June 27, 2019): H5252–H5254, https://www.congress.gov/116/crec/2019/06/27/CREC-2019-06-27-pt1-PgH5252-7.pdf; Dana Rohrabacher (CA), "Innovation Act," *Congressional Record* 161, no. 102 (June 24, 2015): H4639–H4643, https://www.congress.gov/114/crec/2015/06/24/CREC-2015-06-24-pt1-PgH4639.pdf.
144. Madison, *The Letters of James Madison*, 515–516.

Chapter 2. Veneration and Cynicism

1. Sheldon Stern, "Did the Founding Fathers Believe in American Exceptionalism?" History News Network, August 14, 2015, https://historynewsnetwork.org/article/160334.

2. See Joseph J. Ellis, *Passionate Sage: The Character and Legacy of John Adams* (New York: Norton, 1993), 106–107.

3. Peter S. Onuf, "American Exceptionalism and National Identity," *American Political Thought* 1, no. 1 (2012): 94; Jacob E. Cook, ed., *The Federalist* (Middletown, CT: Wesleyan University Press, 1961).

4. Merrill D. Peterson, ed., *Thomas Jefferson Writings* (New York: Library of America, 1984), 494.

5. Onuf, "American Exceptionalism," 79.

6. Onuf, "American Exceptionalism," 79.

7. Onuf, "American Exceptionalism," 79.

8. Onuf, "American Exceptionalism," 81.

9. Onuf, "American Exceptionalism," 81.

10. Onuf, "American Exceptionalism," 81.

11. Onuf, "American Exceptionalism," 79.

12. Onuf, "American Exceptionalism," 80.

13. Onuf, "American Exceptionalism," 80; Daniel J. Boorstin, *The Genius of American Politics* (Chicago: University of Chicago Press, 1953).

14. Kim R. Holmes, "Why American Exceptionalism Is Different from Other Countries' 'Nationalisms,'" Heritage Foundation, September 29, 2020, https://www.heritage.org/american-founders/commentary/why-american-exceptionalism-different-other-countries-nationalisms.

15. Holmes, "Why American Exceptionalism Is Different."

16. Holmes, "Why American Exceptionalism Is Different."

17. Holmes, "Why American Exceptionalism Is Different."

18. Holmes, "Why American Exceptionalism Is Different."

19. Holmes, "Why American Exceptionalism Is Different."

20. Holmes, "Why American Exceptionalism Is Different."

21. Onuf, "American Exceptionalism," 95.

22. Onuf, "American Exceptionalism," 95.

23. Andrew L. Whitehead and Samuel L. Perry, *Taking America Back for God: Christian Nationalism in the United States* (New York: Oxford University Press, 2020), x; Kristina M. Lee, "'In God We Trust?': Christian Nationalists' Establishment and Use of Theistnormative Legislation," *Rhetoric Society Quarterly* 52, no. 5 (2022): 419.

24. Whitehead and Perry, *Taking America Back for God*, x; Lee, "'In God We Trust?,'" 419.

25. Christopher Davis, "Flow of Business: A Typical Day on the Senate Floor," Congressional Research Service, September 16, 2015, 2, https://crsreports.congress.gov/product/pdf/RS/98-865; Richard J. McKinney, "An Overview of the Congressional Record and Its Predecessor Publications: A Research Guide," Law Librarians' Society of Washington, DC, May 2020, https://www.llsdc.org/congressional-record-overview.

26. Lee, "'In God We Trust?,'" 419; Whitehead and Perry, *Taking America Back for God*, x.

27. Lee, "'In God We Trust?,'" 419.

28. John Fea, *Believe Me: The Evangelical Road to Donald Trump* (Grand Rapids, MI: William B. Eerdmans Publishing Company, 2018), 6–7.

29. Fea, *Believe Me*, 6–7.

30. Fea, *Believe Me*, 60.

31. Fea, *Believe Me*, 61.

32. Fea, *Believe Me*, 61.

33. Fea, *Believe Me*, 10.

34. Mari Boor Tonn and Valerie A. Endress, "Looking Under the Hood and Tinkering with Voter Cynicism: Ross Perot and 'Perspective by Incongruity,'" *Rhetoric & Public Affairs* 4, no. 2 (2001): 288, 283; Derrick Bell, "Racial Realism," *Connecticut Law Review* 24, no. 2 (1992): 363–379.

35. Chuck Schumer (NY), "Recognition of the Minority Leader," *Congressional Record* 165, no. 109 (June 27, 2019): S4589–S4590, https://www.congress.gov/116/crec/2019/06/27/CREC-2019-06-27-pt1-PgS4589-3.pdf; Chuck Schumer (NY), "Election Security," *Congressional Record* 165, no. 126 (July 25, 2019): S5078, https://www.congress.gov/116/crec/2019/07/25/CREC-2019-07-25-pt1-PgS5078.pdf.

36. Chuck Schumer (NY), "The Trump Administration," *Congressional Record* 165, no. 162 (October 15, 2019): S5777–S5778, https://www.congress.gov/116/crec/2019/10/15/CREC-2019-10-15-pt1-PgS5777-4.pdf.

37. Steve King (IA), "Full-Scale Impeachment History," *Congressional Record* 165, no. 172 (October 30, 2019): H8668–H8675, https://www.congress.gov/116/crec/2019/10/30/CREC-2019-10-30-pt1-PgH8668.pdf.

38. Steve Daines (MT), "Recognition of the Minority Leader," *Congressional Record* 166, no. 23 (February 4, 2020): S835–S836, https://www.congress.gov/116/crec/2020/02/04/CREC-2020-02-04-pt1-PgS815.pdf.

39. Mike Rounds (SD), "Recognition of the Minority Leader," *Congressional Record* 166, no. 23 (February 4, 2020): S836–S837, https://www.congress.gov/116/crec/2020/02/04/CREC-2020-02-04-pt1-PgS815.pdf.

40. James E. Risch (ID), "Impeachment," *Congressional Record* 166, no. 24 (February 5, 2020): S891, https://www.congress.gov/116/crec/2020/02/05/CREC-2020-02-05-pt1-PgS873.pdf.

41. Ron Johnson (WI), "Impeachment," *Congressional Record* 166, no. 24 (February 5, 2020): S919–S922, https://www.congress.gov/116/crec/2020/02/05/CREC-2020-02-05-pt1-PgS873.pdf.

42. Thomas R. Carper (DE), "Recognition of the Minority Leader," *Congressional Record* 166, no. 23 (February 4, 2020): S830–S831, https://www.congress.gov/116/crec/2020/02/04/CREC-2020-02-04-pt1-PgS815.pdf.

43. James Lankford (OK), "Impeachment," *Congressional Record* 166, no. 37 (February 25, 2020): S1144–S1152, https://www.congress.gov/116/crec/2020/02/25/CREC-2020-02-25-pt1-PgS1144.pdf.

44. "Is the NIV Gender Neutral?," New International Version, accessed October 17, 2023, https://www.thenivbible.com/niv-gender-neutral/.

45. Emphasis added.

46. "Preface to the English Standard Version," English Standard Version, 2001–2022, https://www.esv.org/preface/.

47. Emphasis added.

48. Helen Sterk, "How Rhetoric Becomes Real: Religious Sources of Gender Identity," *Journal of Communication and Religion* 12, no. 2 (1989): 25, 30.

49. Lloyd Stilley, "Sermon: The Wisdom of God—Romans 16, 1 Corinthians 1," Lifeway.com, January 1, 2014, https://www.lifeway.com/en/articles/sermon-wisdom-god-romans-16-1-corinthians-1.

50. Stilley, "Sermon: The Wisdom of God"; Ken Leaman, "Fathers Imparting Wisdom," Young Adults of Worth, July 8, 2017, https://yaow.org/2017/07/fathers-imparting-wisdom/.

51. Gary Peters (MI), "Michigan Productivity and Innovation," *Congressional Record* 161, no. 97 (June 17, 2015): S4215–S4217, https://www.congress.gov/114/crec/2015/06/17/CREC-2015-06-17-pt1-PgS4215-3.pdf.

52. Peters (MI), "Michigan."

53. Peters (MI), "Michigan."

54. Peters (MI), "Michigan."

55. Peters (MI), "Michigan."

56. Peters (MI), "Michigan."

57. Ronald Reagan, "Bicentennial Year of the American Bald Eagle and National Bald Eagle Day," Statute 96, p. 2693, Proclamation 4893, January 28, 1982, https://www.gpo.gov/fdsys/pkg/STATUTE-96/pdf/STATUTE-96-Pg2693.pdf.

58. Lamar Alexander (TN), "Submitted Resolutions," *Congressional Record* 162, no. 92 (June 17, 2015): S4252–S4253, https://www.congress.gov/114/crec/2015/06/17/CREC-2015-06-17-pt1-PgS4252.pdf; Lamar Alexander (TN), "Senate Resolution 257," *Congressional Record* 165, no. 104 (June 20, 2019): S4178–S4179, https://www.congress.gov/116/crec/2019/06/20/CREC-2019-06-20-pt1-PgS4178.pdf.

59. Alexander (TN), "Submitted Resolutions"; Alexander (TN), "Senate Resolution 257."

60. David P. Roe (TN), "Celebrating American Eagle Day," *Congressional Record* 165, no. 104 (June 20, 2019): H4928–H4929, https://www.congress.gov/116/crec/2019/06/20/CREC-2019-06-20-pt1-PgH4928-6.pdf; David P. Roe (TN), "Commemorating American Eagle Day," *Congressional Record* 161, no. 98 (June 18, 2015): H4497, https://www.congress.gov/114/crec/2015/06/18/CREC-2015-06-18-pt1-PgH4497.pdf.

61. Joni Ernst (IA), "Constitution Day," *Congressional Record* 165, no. 150 (September 18, 2019): H5556–H5557, https://www.congress.gov/116/crec/2019/09/18/CREC-2019-09-18-pt1-PgS5553-2.pdf.

62. Ernst (IA), "Constitution Day."

63. Steve Daines (MT), "Constitution Day," *Congressional Record* 165, no. 150 (September 18, 2019): S5557, https://www.congress.gov/116/crec/2019/09/18/CREC-2019-09-18-pt1-PgS5553-2.pdf.

64. James Lankford (OK), "Constitution Day," *Congressional Record* 165, no. 150 (September 18, 2019): S5557–S5558, https://www.congress.gov/116/crec/2019/09/18/CREC-2019-09-18-pt1-PgS5553-2.pdf.

65. David Andrew Dean, "Covenant, Conditionality, and Consequence: New Terminology and a Case Study in the Abrahamic Covenant," *Journal of the Evangelical Theological Society* 57, no. 2 (2014): 290.

66. John Winthrop, "A Modell of Christian Charity (1630)," University of Texas, accessed October 17, 2023, https://minio.la.utexas.edu/webeditor-files/coretexts/pdf/16302omodel20of20christian20charity.pdf; Jason A. Edwards, "Contemporary Conservative Constructions of American Exceptionalism," *Journal of Contemporary Rhetoric* 1, no. 2 (2011): 42.

67. Stephen Howard Browne, "Close Textual Analysis: Approaches and Applications," in *Rhetorical Criticism: Perspectives in Action*, ed. Jim A. Kuypers (Lanham, MD: Rowman & Littlefield, 2009), 63–76.

68. For a discussion of the white secularization of jeremiads in political discourse, see Meg Kunde, "Making the Free Market Moral: Ronald Reagan's Covenantal Economy," *Rhetoric & Public Affairs* 22, no. 2 (2019): 217–252. For a discussion of Black American jeremiads, see Kirt H. Wilson, "Political Paradoxes and the Black Jeremiad: Frederick Douglass's Immanent Theory of Rhetorical Protest," *Howard Journal of Communications* 29, no. 3 (2018): 251; David Howard-Pitney, "The Jeremiads of Frederick Douglass, Booker T. Washington, and W. E. B. Du Bois and Changing Patterns of Black Messianic Rhetoric, 1841–1920," *Journal of American Ethnic History* 6, no. 1 (1986): 47–61; Wilson J. Moses, *Black Messiahs and Uncle Toms: Social and Literary Manipulations of a Religious Myth* (University Park, PA: Pennsylvania State University Press, 1982), 31.

69. Kunde, "Making the Free Market Moral," 217–252.

70. Kunde, "Making the Free Market Moral," 224; Kurt Ritter, "American Political Rhetoric and the Jeremiad Tradition: Presidential Nomination Acceptance Addresses, 1960–1976," *Central States Speech Journal* 31, no. 3 (1980): 161.

71. Kunde, "Making the Free Market Moral," 238.

72. Edwards, "Contemporary Conservative Constructions," 44.

73. Whitehead and Perry, *Taking America Back for God*, x; Lee, "'In God We Trust?,'" 419.

74. Sheldon Whitehouse (RI), "Climate Change," *Congressional Record* 161, no. 102 (June 24, 2015): S4570–S4571, https://www.congress.gov/114/crec/2015/06/24/CREC-2015-06-24-pt1-PgS4559-2.pdf.

75. Whitehouse (RI), "Climate Change."

76. Whitehouse (RI), "Climate Change."

77. Robert Dold (IL), "Persecution of Christians," *Congressional Record* 161, no. 110 (July 15, 2015): H5186, https://www.congress.gov/114/crec/2015/07/15/CREC-2015-07-15-pt1-PgH5186-4.pdf.

78. Dold (IL), "Persecution of Christians."

79. Valerie Richardson, "Kamala Harris, Mazie Hirono Target Brian Buescher Knights of Columbus Membership," *Washington Times*, December 30, 2018, https://www.washingtontimes.com/news/2018/dec/30/kamala-harris-mazie-hirono-target-brian-buescher-k/.

80. Deb Fischer (NE), "Nomination of Brian C. Buescher," *Congressional Record* 165, no. 125 (July 24, 2019): S5041–S5042, https://www.congress.gov/116/crec/2019/07/24/CREC-2019-07-24-pt1-PgS5038.pdf.

81. Fischer (NE), "Nomination of Brian C. Buescher."

82. Fischer (NE), "Nomination of Brian C. Buescher."

83. Fischer (NE), "Nomination of Brian C. Buescher."

84. Fea, *Believe Me*, 61.

85. Virginia Foxx (NC), "Commemorating Constitution Day," *Congressional Record* 165, no. 149 (September 17, 2019): H7717–H7718, https://www.congress.gov/116/crec/2019/09/17/CREC-2019-09-17-pt1-PgH7717-4.pdf.

86. Foxx (NC), "Commemorating Constitution Day," emphasis added.

87. Foxx (NC), "Commemorating Constitution Day."

88. Foxx (NC), "Commemorating Constitution Day."

89. Foxx (NC), "Commemorating Constitution Day."

90. Doug Lamborn (CO), "National Bible Week," *Congressional Record* 165, no. 186 (November 20, 2019): H9104–H9110, https://www.congress.gov/116/crec/2019/11/20/CREC-2019-11-20-pt1-PgH9104-4.pdf.

91. Davis, "Flow of Business: A Typical Day on the Senate Floor"; McKinney, "An Overview of the Congressional Record and Its Predecessor Publications."

92. Brian Babin (TX), "National Bible Week," *Congressional Record* 165, no. 186 (November 20, 2019): H9105, https://www.congress.gov/116/crec/2019/11/20/CREC-2019-11-20-pt1-PgH9104-4.pdf.

93. Lamborn (CO), "National Bible Week."

94. "National Bible Week," *Congressional Record* 165, no. 186 (November 20, 2019): H9104–H9110, https://www.congress.gov/116/crec/2019/11/20/CREC-2019-11-20-pt1-PgH9104-4.pdf.

95. Lamborn (CO), "National Bible Week."

96. Glenn Grothman (WI), "National Bible Week," *Congressional Record* 165, no. 186 (November 20, 2019): H9108–H9109, https://www.congress.gov/116/crec/2019/11/20/CREC-2019-11-20-pt1-PgH9104-4.pdf.

97. Lamborn (CO), "National Bible Week."

98. Lamborn (CO), "National Bible Week."

99. Lamborn (CO), "National Bible Week."

100. Fea, *Believe Me*, 8, 10.

101. Boor Tonn and Endress, "Looking under the Hood and Tinkering with Voter Cynicism," 288, 283.

102. Robin Kelly (IL), "Congressional Black Caucus: Race Relations in America," *Congressional Record* 161, no. 168 (November 16, 2015): H8228, https://www.congress.gov/114/crec/2015/11/16/CREC-2015-11-16-pt1-PgH8228-2.pdf.

103. Kelly (IL), "Congressional Black Caucus."

104. Kelly (IL), "Congressional Black Caucus."

105. Brenda L. Lawrence (MI), "Removing Deadline for Ratification of Equal Rights Amendment," *Congressional Record* 166, no. 30 (February 13, 2020): H1137, https://www.congress.gov/116/crec/2020/02/13/CREC-2020-02-13-pt1-PgH1129-3.pdf.

106. Lawrence (MI), "Removing Deadline."

107. Lawrence (MI), "Removing Deadline," emphasis added.

108. Hakeem S. Jeffries (NY), "Congressional Black Caucus," *Congressional Record* 161, no. 108 (July 13, 2015): H5112–H5113, https://www.congress.gov/114/crec/2015/07/13/CREC-2015-07-13-pt1-PgH5109.pdf.

109. Jeffries (NY), "Congressional Black Caucus."

110. Jeffries (NY), "Congressional Black Caucus."

111. "About Barbara," Barbara Lee, May 2, 2022, https://lee.house.gov/about/biography?1.

112. Nikole Hannah-Jones, quoted in Barbara Lee (CA), "400th Anniversary of First Enslaved Africans Brought to America," *Congressional Record* 165, no. 146 (September 12, 2019): E1143–E1147, https://www.congress.gov/116/crec/2019/09/12/CREC-2019-09-12-pt1-PgE1143-2.pdf.

113. Hannah-Jones, quoted in Lee (CA), "400th Anniversary."

114. Hannah-Jones, quoted in Lee (CA), "400th Anniversary."

115. Hannah-Jones, quoted in Lee (CA), "400th Anniversary."

116. Hannah-Jones, quoted in Lee (CA), "400th Anniversary."

117. Hannah-Jones, quoted in Lee (CA), "400th Anniversary."

118. Hannah-Jones, quoted in Lee (CA), "400th Anniversary."

119. Hannah-Jones, quoted in Lee (CA), "400th Anniversary."

120. Hannah-Jones, quoted in Lee (CA), "400th Anniversary."

121. Hannah-Jones, quoted in Lee (CA), "400th Anniversary."

122. Hannah-Jones, quoted in Lee (CA), "400th Anniversary."

123. Rick Scott (FL), "Maiden Speech," *Congressional Record* 165, no. 163 (October 16, 2019): S5815–S5816, https://www.congress.gov/116/crec/2019/10/16/CREC-2019-10-16-pt1-PgS5815-2.pdf.

124. Scott (FL), "Maiden Speech."

125. Scott (FL), "Maiden Speech."

126. Scott (FL), "Maiden Speech."

127. Dumas Malone, *Jefferson and the Ordeal of Liberty* (Boston: Little, Brown, 1962), 3:481.

128. Kristin Kobes Du Mez, *Jesus and John Wayne: How White Evangelicals Corrupted a Faith and Fractured a Nation* (New York: Liveright, 2020); "Gender Composition: Religious Landscape Study," Pew Research Center, accessed October 17, 2023, https://www.pewresearch.org/religion/religious-landscape-study/gender-composition/; Besheer Mohamed et al., "Faith Among Black Americans," Pew Research Center, February 16, 2021, https://www.pewresearch.org/religion/2021/02/16/faith-among-black-americans/; Anthea D. Butler, *White Evangelical Racism:*

The Politics of Morality in America (Chapel Hill, NC: University of North Carolina Press, 2021).

129. Sage Mikkelsen and Sarah Kornfield, "Girls Gone Fundamentalist: Feminine Appeals of White Christian Nationalism," *Women's Studies in Communication* 44, no. 4 (2021): 567.

130. Mikkelsen and Kornfield, "Girls Gone Fundamentalist," 566; see Rebecca Goetz, *The Baptism of Early Virginia: How Christianity Created Race* (Baltimore: Johns Hopkins University Press, 2012).

131. Deborah Gray White, *Ar'n't I a Woman? Female Slaves in the Plantation South* (New York: Norton, 1985); James H. Cone, *The Cross and the Lynching Tree* (Maryknoll, NY: Orbis Books, 2017); Robert Jones, *White Too Long: The Legacy of White Supremacy in American Christianity* (New York: Simon & Schuster, 2020).

132. Mikkelsen and Kornfield, "Girls Gone Fundamentalist," 567.

133. Fea, *Believe Me*, 6–7; Lee, "'In God We Trust?'," 419.

Chapter 3. Checks and Balances

1. See "Handout A: Montesquieu—Excerpts from the Spirit of Laws (1748)," Bill of Rights Institute, accessed October 17, 2023, https://billofrightsinstitute.org/activities/handout-a-montesquieu-excerpts-from-the-spirit-of-laws-1748.

2. "The Separation of Powers—Battles of the Branches," National Constitution Center, accessed October 17, 2023, https://constitutioncenter.org/education/classroom-resources-by-topic/separation-of-powers.

3. See Andrew Lintott, "Aristotle and the Mixed Constitution," in *Alternatives to Athens: Varieties of Political Organization and Community in Ancient Greece*, ed. Roger Brock and Stephen Hodkinson (Oxford: Oxford University Press, 2002).

4. Polibius, *The Rise of the Roman Empire*, trans. Ian Scott-Kilvert (London: Penguin Classics, 1979).

5. Bruce E. Johansen, "Dating the Iroquois Confederacy," *Akswesasne Notes New Series*, 1, no. 3–4 (1995): 62–63, https://ratical.org/many_worlds/6Nations/DatingIC.html; "Iroquois Confederacy," *Encyclopedia Britannica*, October 4, 2018, https://www.britannica.com/topic/Iroquois-Confederacy.

6. Terri Hansen, "How the Iroquois Great Law of Peace Shaped US Democracy," Native America, PBS, December 13, 2018, https://www.pbs.org/native-america/blogs/native-voices/how-the-iroquois-great-law-of-peace-shaped-us-democracy/.

7. Becky Little, "The Native American Government That Inspired the US Constitution," History.com, November 9, 2020, https://www.history.com/news/iroquois-confederacy-influence-us-constitution.

8. Little, "The Native American Government."

9. Benjamin Franklin, "From Benjamin Franklin to James Parker, 20 March 1751," National Archives, accessed October 17, 2023, https://founders.archives.gov/documents/Franklin/01-04-02-0037.

10. See "Articles of Confederation (1777)," National Archives, March 8, 2022, https://www.archives.gov/milestone-documents/articles-of-confederation.

11. James Madison, "Federalist Papers No. 51 (1788)," Bill of Rights Institute, accessed October 17, 2023, https://billofrightsinstitute.org/primary-sources/federalist-no-51.

12. Steven G. Calabresi and Michael J. Gerhardt, "Article I, Section 3: Common Interpretation," National Constitution Center, accessed October 17, 2023, https://constitutioncenter.org/interactive-constitution/interpretation/article-i/clauses/765.

13. Calabresi and Gerhardt, "Article I, Section 3: Common Interpretation."

14. Calabresi and Gerhardt, "Article I, Section 3: Common Interpretation."

15. Calabresi and Gerhardt, "Article I, Section 3: Common Interpretation."

16. Calabresi and Gerhardt, "Article I, Section 3: Common Interpretation."

17. Calabresi and Gerhardt, "Article I, Section 3: Common Interpretation."

18. Chuck Grassley (IA), "The United States Senate," *Congressional Record* 165, no. 154 (September 24, 2019): S5635, https://www.congress.gov/116/crec/2019/09/24/CREC-2019-09-24-pt1-PgS5635-4.pdf.

19. Kristan Poirot, "Domesticating the Liberated Woman: Containment Rhetorics of Second Wave Radical/Lesbian Feminism," *Women's Studies in Communication* 32, no. 3 (2009): 266; see also Karrin Vasby Anderson, "'Rhymes with Rich': Bitch as a Tool of Containment in Contemporary American Politics," *Rhetoric & Public Affairs* 2, no. 4 (1999): 599–623.

20. Poirot, "Domesticating the Liberated Woman," 266; Anderson, "'Rhymes with Rich.'"

21. "The Impeachment of Bill Clinton," Bill of Rights Institute, accessed October 17, 2023, https://billofrightsinstitute.org/e-lessons/the-impeachment-of-bill-clinton.

22. Anderson, "'Rhymes with Rich,'" 601; Poirot, "Domesticating the Liberated Woman"; Lisa A. Flores, "Introduction: Of Gendered/Racial Boundaries and Borders," *Women's Studies in Communication* 40, no. 4 (2017): 317–320.

23. Anderson, "'Rhymes with Rich,'" 600.

24. Anderson, "'Rhymes with Rich,'" 601.

25. Anderson, "'Rhymes with Rich,'" 601.

26. Anderson, "'Rhymes with Rich,'" 601; David Campbell, *Writing Security: United States Foreign Policy and the Politics of Identity* (Minneapolis: University of Minnesota Press, 1992), 116, 121, 127; Alan Nadel, *Containment Culture: American Narratives, Postmodernism, and the Atomic Age* (Durham, NC: Duke University Press, 1995), 6; Elaine Tyler May, *Homeward Bound: American Families in the Cold War Era* (New York: Basic Books, 1988), 10.

27. Anderson, "'Rhymes with Rich,'" 601; Campbell, *Writing Security*, 116, 121, 127; May, *Homeward Bound*, 10

28. Anderson, "'Rhymes with Rich,'" 601.

29. Flores, "Introduction: Of Gendered/Racial Boundaries and Borders," 317.

30. Karlyn Kohrs Campbell, *Man Cannot Speak for Her* (New York: Greenwood Press, 1989), 1:12; Anderson, "'Rhymes with Rich,'" 601.

31. Susan J. Douglas, *Where the Girls Are: Growing Up Female with the Mass Media* (New York: Random House, 1994), 189; see also Anderson, "'Rhymes with Rich,'" 601.

32. Anderson, "'Rhymes with Rich'"; Karrin Vasby Anderson, "'Rhymes with Blunt': Pornification and US Political Culture," *Rhetoric and Public Affairs* 14, no. 2 (2011): 327–368; Joan Faber McAlister, "_____ Trash in the White House: Michelle Obama, Post-Racism, and the Pre-Class Politics of Domestic Style," *Communication & Critical/Cultural Studies* 6, no. 3 (2009): 311–315; Ralina L. Joseph, "'Hope Is Finally Making a Comeback': First Lady Reframed," *Communication, Culture & Critique* 4, no. 1 (2011): 56–77; Maureen Ebben and Teresita Garza, "When They Go Low, We Go High: First Lady Michelle Obama's Feminist Rhetoric of Inclusion," *Women & Language* 40, no. 1 (2017–2018): 83–100.

33. Poirot, "Domesticating the Liberated Woman," 265.

34. See Poirot, "Domesticating the Liberated Woman," 263.

35. Poirot, "Domesticating the Liberated Woman," 263.

36. Lisa A. Flores and Logan Rae Gomez, "Disciplinary Containment: Whiteness and the Academic Scarcity Narrative," *Communication and Critical/Cultural Studies* 17, no. 2 (2020): 237.

37. Flores and Gomez, "Disciplinary Containment," 237, 240.

38. Lisa A. Flores and Mary Ann Villarreal, "Unmasking 'Ignorance,'" *Quarterly Journal of Speech* 106, no. 3 (2020): 312.

39. See Carole Pateman and Charles W. Mills, *Contract and Domination* (Cambridge, UK: Polity Press, 2007), 5; see also Judith Butler, *Gender Trouble: Feminism and the Subversion of Identity* (New York: Routledge, 1990).

40. Marlin A. Stutzman (IN), "Gun Control and Americans' Second Amendment Rights," *Congressional Record* 162, no. 3 (January 6, 2016): H94–H99, https://www.congress.gov/114/crec/2016/01/06/CREC-2016-01-06-pt1-PgH94-3.pdf.

41. "The United States Constitution," National Constitution Center, accessed October 17, 2023, https://constitutioncenter.org/the-constitution/full-text.

42. Nelson Lund and Adam Winkler, "The Second Amendment: Common Interpretation," National Constitution Center, accessed October 17, 2023, https://constitutioncenter.org/the-constitution/amendments/amendment-ii/interpretations/99.

43. Lund and Winkler, "The Second Amendment."

44. Lund and Winkler, "The Second Amendment."

45. See Calabresi and Gerhardt, "Article I, Section 3: Common Interpretation."

46. Lund and Winkler, "The Second Amendment."

47. Lund and Winkler, "The Second Amendment."

48. Lund and Winkler, "The Second Amendment."

49. German Lopez, "President Obama's Boldest Action on Guns Yet, Explained," Vox.com, January 7, 2016, https://www.vox.com/2016/1/4/10708324/obama-gun-control-executive-order; see also "Fact Sheet: New Executive Actions to Reduce Gun Violence and Make Our Communities Safer," The White House, January 4, 2016, https://obamawhitehouse.archives.gov/the-press-office/2016/01/04/fact-sheet-new-executive-actions-reduce-gun-violence-and-make-our.

50. "The United States Constitution."

51. "FAQ's About Executive Orders," Office of the Federal Register, National Archives, accessed October 17, 2023, https://www.archives.gov/federal-register/executive-orders/about.html#orders; Vivian S. Chu and Todd Garvey, "Executive Orders: Issuance, Modification, and Revocation," Congressional Research Service, April 16, 2014, p. 1, https://fas.org/sgp/crs/misc/RS20846.pdf.

52. Chu and Garvey, "Executive Orders: Issuance, Modification, and Revocation."

53. Lopez, "President Obama's Boldest Action on Guns"; "Fact Sheet: New Executive Actions to Reduce Gun Violence."

54. Barry Loudermilk (GA), "Gun Control and Americans' Second Amendment Rights," *Congressional Record* 162, no. 3 (January 6, 2016): H97, https://www.congress.gov/114/crec/2016/01/06/CREC-2016-01-06-pt1-PgH94-3.pdf.

55. Steve Russell (OK), "Protecting Our Second Amendment Rights," *Congressional Record* 162, no. 4 (January 7, 2016): H171–H173, https://www.congress.gov/114/crec/2016/01/07/CREC-2016-01-07-pt1-PgH171.pdf.

56. John Abney Culberson (TX), "Our Second Amendment Rights," *Congressional Record* 162, no. 8 (January 13, 2016): H358, https://www.congress.gov/114/crec/2016/01/13/CREC-2016-01-13-pt1-PgH358-4.pdf; Loudermilk (GA), "Gun Control."

57. Paul Singer, "The US House May Be the Only Place with Rules Against Calling the President Racist," GBH.com, October 15, 2019, https://www.wgbh.org/news/politics/2019-07-17/the-us-house-may-be-the-only-place-with-rules-against-calling-the-president-racist.

58. Lynn A. Westmoreland (GA), "Obama's Executive Action on Guns," *Congressional Record* 162, no. 4 (January 7, 2016): H112–H113, https://www.congress.gov/114/crec/2016/01/07/CREC-2016-01-07-pt1-PgH112-2.pdf.

59. Westmoreland (GA), "Obama's Executive Action on Guns."

60. Maryann Erigha and Camille Z. Charles, "Other, Uppity Obama: A Content Analysis of Race Appeals in the 2008 US Presidential Election," *Du Bois Review* 9, no. 2 (2012): 441.

61. Erigha and Charles, "Other, Uppity Obama," 441.

62. Erigha and Charles, "Other, Uppity Obama," 441, emphasis in original.

63. Earl Carter (GA), "Gun Control Executive Orders," *Congressional Record* 162, no. 5 (January 8, 2016): H180, https://www.congress.gov/114/crec/2016/01/08/CREC-2016-01-08-pt1-PgH180-5.pdf.

64. Billy Corriher, "Court Finally Says 'Boy' Comments Are Racist," *Harvard Law & Policy Review*, December 21, 2011, https://journals.law.harvard.edu/lpr/2011/12/21/court-finally-says-boy-comments-are-racist/#more-1114.

65. Russell (OK), "Protecting Our Second Amendment Rights."

66. See Tommy J. Curry, *The Man-Not: Race, Class, Genre, and the Dilemmas of Black Manhood* (Philadelphia: Temple University Press, 2017).

67. Russell (OK), "Protecting Our Second Amendment Rights."

68. Loudermilk (GA), "Gun Control."

69. Russell (OK), "Protecting Our Second Amendment Rights."
70. Loudermilk (GA), "Gun Control"; Russell (OK), "Protecting Our Second Amendment Rights."
71. Russell (OK), "Protecting Our Second Amendment Rights."
72. Loudermilk (GA), "Gun Control."
73. Loudermilk (GA), "Gun Control."
74. Loudermilk (GA), "Gun Control."
75. Loudermilk (GA), "Gun Control."
76. Russell (OK), "Protecting Our Second Amendment Rights."
77. Gail Bederman, *Manliness and Civilization: A Cultural History of Gender and Race in the United States, 1880–1917* (Chicago: University of Chicago Press, 1995).
78. Russell (OK), "Protecting Our Second Amendment Rights."
79. Karlyn Kohrs Campbell, "The Discursive Performance of Femininity: Hating Hillary," *Rhetoric & Public Affairs* 1, no. 1 (1998): 5; Bonnie Dow and Mari Boor Tonn, "'Feminine Style' and Political Judgment in the Rhetoric of Ann Richards," *Quarterly Journal of Speech* 79, no. 3 (1993): 289.
80. Russell (OK), "Protecting Our Second Amendment Rights."
81. Russell (OK), "Protecting Our Second Amendment Rights."
82. Carter (GA), "Gun Control Executive Orders."
83. Loudermilk (GA), "Gun Control."
84. Carter (GA), "Gun Control Executive Orders."
85. Westmoreland (GA), "Obama's Executive Action on Guns."
86. Loudermilk (GA), "Gun Control."
87. Russell (OK), "Protecting Our Second Amendment Rights."
88. Carter (GA), "Gun Control Executive Orders."
89. Russell (OK), "Protecting Our Second Amendment Rights."
90. Westmoreland (GA) "Obama's Executive Action on Guns."
91. Loudermilk (GA), "Gun Control."
92. Culberson (TX), "Our Second Amendment Rights."
93. Culberson (TX), "Our Second Amendment Rights."
94. "The United States Constitution."
95. "The United States Constitution."
96. Michael D. Ramsey and Stephen I. Vladeck, "Commander in Chief Clause: Common Interpretation," National Constitution Center, October 17, 2023, https://constitutioncenter.org/interactive-constitution/interpretation/article-ii/clauses/345.
97. Ramsey and Vladeck, "Commander in Chief Clause: Common Interpretation."
98. Michael D. Ramsey and Stephen I. Vladeck, "Declare War Clause: Common Interpretation," National Constitution Center, October 17, 2023, https://constitutioncenter.org/interactive-constitution/interpretation/article-i/clauses/753.
99. Ramsey and Vladeck, "Declare War Clause: Common Interpretation."
100. Ramsey and Vladeck, "Declare War Clause: Common Interpretation."
101. Ramsey and Vladeck, "Declare War Clause: Common Interpretation."
102. Stephen I. Vladeck, "Congress's Statutory Abdication of Its Declare War

Power," National Constitution Center, October 17, 2023, https://constitutioncenter
.org/interactive-constitution/interpretation/article-i/clauses/753#congresss-statutory
-abdication-of-its-declare-war-power-vladeck.

103. Vladeck, "Congress's Statutory Abdication."

104. Vladeck, "Congress's Statutory Abdication."

105. "The Rule XIX Call to Order for Disorderly Language in Senate Debate," Congressional Research Service, June 27, 2018, https://www.everycrsreport.com/reports/R45241.html/

106. Rand Paul (KY), "Motion to Discharge—S.J. Res. 20 and S.J. Res. 26," *Congressional Record* 165, no. 99 (June 13, 2019): S3457–S3459, https://www.congress.gov/116/crec/2019/06/13/CREC-2019-06-13-pt1-PgS3457.pdf.

107. Paul (KY), "Motion to Discharge."

108. Chuck Schumer (NY), "Executive Session, January 6, 2020: Iran," *Congressional Record* 166, no. 2 (January 6, 2020): S13–S15, https://www.congress.gov/116/crec/2020/01/06/CREC-2020-01-06-pt1-PgS13-5.pdf.

109. Schumer (NY), "Executive Session, January 6, 2020: Iran."

110. Schumer (NY), "Executive Session, January 6, 2020: Iran."

111. Richard J. Durbin (IL), "Executive Session: Iran," *Congressional Record* 166, no. 4 (January 8, 2020): S65–S66, https://www.congress.gov/116/crec/2020/01/08/CREC-2020-01-08-pt1-PgS64-4.pdf.

112. Paul (KY), "Motion to Discharge"; Chuck Schumer (NY), "Executive Session, January 9, 2020: Iran," *Congressional Record* 166, no. 5 (January 9, 2020): S100–S101, https://www.congress.gov/116/crec/2020/01/09/CREC-2020-01-09-pt1-PgS100-3.pdf; Durbin (IL), "Executive Session: Iran"; Mike Lee (UT), "S.J. Res. 7," *Congressional Record* 165, no. 72 (May 2, 2019): S2588–S2589, https://www.congress.gov/116/crec/2019/05/02/CREC-2019-05-02-pt1-PgS2585-2.pdf; and Bernie Sanders (VT), "S.J. Res. 7," *Congressional Record* 165, no. 72 (May 2, 2019): S2589–S2590, https://www.congress.gov/116/crec/2019/05/02/CREC-2019-05-02-pt1-PgS2585-2.pdf.

113. Schumer (NY), "Executive Session, January 6, 2020: Iran."

114. Durbin (IL), "Executive Session: Iran"; and Sanders (VT), "S.J. Res. 7."

115. Campbell, "The Discursive Performance of Femininity: Hating Hillary"; Dow and Boor Tonn, "'Feminine Style' and Political Judgment."

116. Lee (UT), "S.J. Res. 7."

117. Paul (KY), "Motion to Discharge."

118. Durbin (IL), "Executive Session: Iran."

119. Durbin (IL), "Executive Session: Iran."

120. Lee (UT), "S.J. Res. 7"; Sanders (VT), "S.J. Res. 7."

121. Paul (KY), "Motion to Discharge."

122. Paul (KY), "Motion to Discharge," and Schumer (NY), "Executive Session, January 9, 2020: Iran."

123. Sanders (VT), "S.J. Res. 7."

124. Sanders (VT), "S.J. Res. 7."

125. Tasha N. Dubriwny, "First Ladies and Feminism: Laura Bush as Advocate

for Women's and Children's Rights," *Women's Studies in Communication* 28, no. 1 (2005): 84–114.

126. Lee (UT), "S.J. Res. 7."
127. Lee (UT), "S.J. Res. 7."
128. Lee (UT), "S.J. Res. 7."
129. Durbin (IL), "Executive Session: Iran."
130. Schumer (NY), "Executive Session, January 9, 2020: Iran," emphasis added.
131. Lee (UT), "S.J. Res. 7," emphasis added.
132. Lee (UT), "S.J. Res. 7"; Paul (KY), "Motion to Discharge."
133. Paul (KY), "Motion to Discharge."
134. "The United States Constitution."
135. "The United States Constitution."
136. "The United States Constitution."
137. "The United States Constitution."
138. Neil J. Kinkopf and Keith E. Whittington, "Article II, Section 4: Common Interpretation," National Constitution Center, October 17, 2023, https://constitutioncenter.org/interactive-constitution/interpretation/article-ii/clauses/349.
139. Kinkopf and Whittington, "Article II, Section 4: Common Interpretation."
140. Kinkopf and Whittington, "Article II, Section 4: Common Interpretation."
141. Kinkopf and Whittington, "Article II, Section 4: Common Interpretation."
142. Kinkopf and Whittington, "Article II, Section 4: Common Interpretation."
143. See Kinkopf and Whittington, "Article II, Section 4: Common Interpretation."
144. Robin Kelly (IL), "Impeaching Donald John Trump, President of the United States, for High Crimes and Misdemeanors," *Congressional Record* 165, no. 205 (December 18, 2019): H12153, https://www.congress.gov/116/crec/2019/12/18/CREC-2019-12-18-pt1-PgH12130.pdf, emphasis added.
145. Kelly (IL), "Impeaching Donald John Trump," emphasis added.
146. Chuck Schumer (NY), "The Trump Administration," *Congressional Record* 165, no. 162 (October 15, 2019): S5777–S5778, https://www.congress.gov/116/crec/2019/10/15/CREC-2019-10-15-pt1-PgS5777-4.pdf.
147. Carolyn B. Maloney (NY), "Impeaching Donald John Trump, President of the United States, for High Crimes and Misdemeanors," *Congressional Record* 165, no. 205 (December 18, 2019): H12173, https://www.congress.gov/116/crec/2019/12/18/CREC-2019-12-18-pt1-PgH12130.pdf.
148. Gregory W. Meeks (NY), "Impeaching Donald John Trump, President of the United States, for High Crimes and Misdemeanors," *Congressional Record* 165, no. 205 (December 18, 2019): H12174, https://www.congress.gov/116/crec/2019/12/18/CREC-2019-12-18-pt1-PgH12130.pdf.
149. Gwen Moore (WI), "Impeaching Donald John Trump, President of the United States, for High Crimes and Misdemeanors," *Congressional Record* 165, no. 205 (December 18, 2019): H12154, https://www.congress.gov/116/crec/2019/12/18/CREC-2019-12-18-pt1-PgH12130.pdf.

150. Suzanne Bonamici (OR), "In Support of H. Res. 660, Impeachment Inquiry Resolution," *Congressional Record* 165, no. 181 (November 13, 2019): E1431, https://www.congress.gov/116/crec/2019/11/13/CREC-2019-11-13-pt1-PgE1431-5.pdf.

151. James R. Langevin (RI), "Impeaching Donald John Trump, President of the United States, for High Crimes and Misdemeanors," *Congressional Record* 165, no. 205 (December 18, 2019): H12149, https://www.congress.gov/116/crec/2019/12/18/CREC-2019-12-18-pt1-PgH12130.pdf.

152. Chuck Schumer (NY), "Executive Session: Impeachment," *Congressional Record* 166, no. 5 (January 9, 2020): S101, https://www.congress.gov/116/crec/2020/01/09/CREC-2020-01-09-pt1-PgS100-3.pdf.

153. Juan Vargas (CA), "Impeaching Donald John Trump, President of the United States, for High Crimes and Misdemeanors," *Congressional Record* 165, no. 208 (December 26, 2019): E1643, https://www.congress.gov/116/crec/2019/12/26/CREC-2019-12-26-pt1-PgE1643-2.pdf.

154. Vargas (CA), "Impeaching Donald John Trump."

155. Cory Booker (NJ), "Recognition of the Minority Leader," *Congressional Record* 166, no. 23 (February 4, 2020): S842–S845, https://www.congress.gov/116/crec/2020/02/04/CREC-2020-02-04-pt1-PgS815.pdf.

156. Booker (NJ), "Recognition of the Minority Leader."

157. Thomas R. Carper (DE), "Recognition of the Minority Leader," *Congressional Record* 166, no. 23 (February 4, 2020): S830–S831, https://www.congress.gov/116/crec/2020/02/04/CREC-2020-02-04-pt1-PgS815.pdf.

158. Carper (DE), "Recognition of the Minority Leader."

159. Carper (DE), "Recognition of the Minority Leader."

160. Carper (DE), "Recognition of the Minority Leader."

161. Michael Guest (MS), "Support Nation's Farmers and Ranchers," *Congressional Record* 165, no. 181 (November 13, 2019): H8814–H8815, https://www.congress.gov/116/crec/2019/11/13/CREC-2019-11-13-pt1-PgH8814-6.pdf.

162. Guest (MS), "Support Nation's Farmers and Ranchers."

163. Denver Riggleman (VA), "Impeaching Donald John Trump, President of the United States, for High Crimes and Misdemeanors," *Congressional Record* 165, no. 205 (December 18, 2019): H12151–H12152, https://www.congress.gov/116/crec/2019/12/18/CREC-2019-12-18-pt1-PgH12130.pdf.

164. Gregory Murphy (NC), "Impeaching Donald John Trump, President of the United States, for High Crimes and Misdemeanors," *Congressional Record* 165, no. 205 (December 18, 2019): H12152, https://www.congress.gov/116/crec/2019/12/18/CREC-2019-12-18-pt1-PgH12130.pdf.

165. Murphy (NC), "Impeaching Donald John Trump."

166. Lance Gooden (TX), "Impeaching Donald John Trump, President of the United States, for High Crimes and Misdemeanors," *Congressional Record* 165, no. 205 (December 18, 2019): H12154, https://www.congress.gov/116/crec/2019/12/18/CREC-2019-12-18-pt1-PgH12130.pdf, emphasis added.

167. Gooden (TX), "Impeaching Donald John Trump."

168. Tim Walberg (MI), "Impeaching Donald John Trump, President of the United States, for High Crimes and Misdemeanors," *Congressional Record* 165, no. 205 (December 18, 2019): H12170, https://www.congress.gov/116/crec/2019/12/18/CREC-2019-12-18-pt1-PgH12130.pdf.

169. Gooden (TX), "Impeaching Donald John Trump."

170. Vern Buchanan (FL), "Impeaching Donald John Trump, President of the United States, for High Crimes and Misdemeanors," *Congressional Record* 165, no. 205 (December 18, 2019): H12157, https://www.congress.gov/116/crec/2019/12/18/CREC-2019-12-18-pt1-PgH12130.pdf.

171. Chris Stewart (UT), "Impeaching Donald John Trump, President of the United States, for High Crimes and Misdemeanors," *Congressional Record* 165, no. 205 (December 18, 2019): H12142, https://www.congress.gov/116/crec/2019/12/18/CREC-2019-12-18-pt1-PgH12130.pdf.

172. Mitch McConnell (KY), "Impeachment," *Congressional Record* 166, no. 10 (January 16, 2020): S255–S256, https://www.congress.gov/116/crec/2020/01/16/CREC-2020-01-16-pt1-PgS255-6.pdf.

173. McConnell (KY), "Impeachment."

174. Mike Lee (UT), "Impeachment," *Congressional Record* 166, no. 24 (February 5, 2020): S888–S890, https://www.congress.gov/116/crec/2020/02/05/CREC-2020-02-05-pt1-PgS873.pdf.

175. Steve Daines (MT), "Recognition of the Minority Leader," *Congressional Record* 166, no. 23 (February 4, 2020): S835–S836, https://www.congress.gov/116/crec/2020/02/04/CREC-2020-02-04-pt1-PgS815.pdf.

176. See Jim Hagedorn (MN), "Impeaching Donald John Trump, President of the United States, for High Crimes and Misdemeanors," *Congressional Record* 165, no. 205 (December 18, 2019): H12201–H12203, https://www.congress.gov/116/crec/2019/12/18/CREC-2019-12-18-pt1-PgH12130.pdf; Joe Wilson (SC), "Letter from President Trump," *Congressional Record* 165, no. 205 (December 18, 2019): E1605–E1607, https://www.congress.gov/116/crec/2019/12/18/CREC-2019-12-18-pt1-PgE1605-4.pdf; Gregory Steube (FL), "Letter from President Trump," *Congressional Record* 166, no. 4 (January 8, 2020): E11–E13, https://www.congress.gov/116/crec/2020/01/08/CREC-2020-01-08-pt1-PgE11-3.pdf.

177. Emphasis added, see Hagedorn (MN), "Impeaching Donald John Trump"; Wilson (SC), "Letter from President Trump"; Steube (FL), "Letter from President Trump."

178. Greg Walden (OR), "Impeaching Donald John Trump, President of the United States, for High Crimes and Misdemeanors," *Congressional Record* 165, no. 205 (December 18, 2019): H12187, https://www.congress.gov/116/crec/2019/12/18/CREC-2019-12-18-pt1-PgH12130.pdf, emphasis added.

179. James E. Risch (ID), "Impeachment," *Congressional Record* 166, no. 24 (February 5, 2020): S891, https://www.congress.gov/116/crec/2020/02/05/CREC-2020-02-05-pt1-PgS873.pdf, emphasis added.

180. Risch (ID), "Impeachment," emphasis added.

181. Robert B. Aderholt (AL), "Impeaching Donald John Trump, President of the

United States, for High Crimes and Misdemeanors," *Congressional Record* 165, no. 205 (December 18, 2019): H12180, https://www.congress.gov/116/crec/2019/12/18/CREC-2019-12-18-pt1-PgH12130.pdf, emphasis added.

Chapter 4. Debate and Bipartisanship

1. D. Jason Berggren, "Presidential Election of 1789," George Washington's Mount Vernon, accessed October 17, 2023, https://www.mountvernon.org/library/digital history/digital-encyclopedia/article/presidential-election-of-1789/.

2. Berggren, "Presidential Election of 1789."

3. Sanford V. Levinson, "A Common Interpretation: The Twelfth Amendment and the Electoral College," National Constitutional Center, December 14, 2016, https://constitutioncenter.org/blog/a-common-interpretation-the-12th-amendment-and-the-electoral-college.

4. George Washington, "Farewell Address, September 19, 1796," Library of Congress, accessed October 17, 2023, https://www.loc.gov/exhibits/creating-the-united-states/formation-of-political-parties.html.

5. Levinson, "A Common Interpretation: The Twelfth Amendment."

6. Levinson, "A Common Interpretation: The Twelfth Amendment."

7. Levinson, "A Common Interpretation: The Twelfth Amendment."

8. Devin McCarthy, "How the Electoral College Became Winner-Take-All," Fair Vote, August 21, 2012, https://www.fairvote.org/how-the-electoral-college-became-winner-take-all.

9. Notably, however, only 29 states have laws requiring electors to vote for the state's majority winner. See "Summary: State Laws Regarding Presidential Electors," National Association of Secretaries of State, November 2016, https://www.google.com/url?sa=t&rct=j&q=&esrc=s&source=web&cd=&ved=2ahUKEwjyjuva7832AhVoHzQIHSCqB3AQFnoECEQQAQ&url=https%3A%2F%2Fwww.nass.org%2Fsites%2Fdefault%2Ffiles%2Fsurveys%2F2017-08%2Fresearch-state-laws-pres-electors-nov16.pdf&usg=AOvVaw1FBMW6_dAKFuxfYxrWR4F4.

10. "Black Population by State 2022," World Population Review, accessed October 17, 2023, https://worldpopulationreview.com/state-rankings/black-population-by-state.

11. Barbara Sinclair, *Party Wars: Polarization and the Politics of National Policy Making* (Norman, OK: University of Oklahoma Press, 2006), 18; Philip Bump, "When Did Black Americans Start Voting So Heavily Democratic?" *Washington Post*, July 7, 2015, https://www.washingtonpost.com/news/the-fix/wp/2015/07/07/when-did-black-americans-start-voting-so-heavily-democratic/.

12. See Paul Finkelman, "The Founders and Slavery: Little Ventured, Little Gained," *Yale Journal of Law & the Humanities* 13, no. 2 (2001): 413–499.

13. "What Is the 3/5 Compromise?" ConstitutionUS.com, accessed October 17, 2023, https://constitutionus.com/constitution/what-is-the-3-5-compromise/#Disproportionate_Representation_of_Southern_States.

14. "What Is the 3/5 Compromise?" ConstitutionUS.com.

15. Brian D. Humes et al., "Representation of the Antebellum South in the House of Representatives: Measuring the Impact of the Three-Fifths Clause," in *Party, Process and Political Change in Congress: New Perspectives on the History of Congress*, ed. David W. Brady and Matthew D. McCubbins (Stanford, CA: Stanford University Press, 2002), 464; Abby Watkins, "How the Three-Fifths Compromise Skewed Counts of the US Population," Population Education, December 2, 2020, https://populationeducation.org/how-the-three-fifths-compromise-skewed-counts-of-the-u-s-population/.

16. Kristen Hoerl, "Selective Amnesia and Racial Transcendence in News Coverage of President Obama's Inauguration," *Quarterly Journal of Speech* 98, no. 2 (2012): 178–202.

17. Barbie Zelizer, "Reading the Past Against the Grain: The Shape of Memory Studies," *Critical Studies in Mass Communication* 12, no. 2 (1995): 214; Trevor Parry-Giles, "Fame, Celebrity and the Legacy of John Adams," *Western Journal of Communication* 72, no. 1 (2008): 86; Carole Blair, "Communication as Collective Memory," in *Communication as . . . Perspectives on Theory*, ed. Gregory J. Shepherd, Jeffrey St. John, and Ted Striphas (Thousand Oaks, CA: Sage, 2006), 53.

18. Bradford Vivian, "Review Essay: On the Language of Forgetting," *Quarterly Journal of Speech* 95, no. 1 (2009): 89–104.

19. Andre E. Johnson and Anthony J. Stone Jr., "'The Most Dangerous Negro in America': Rhetoric, Race and the Prophetic Pessimism of Martin Luther King Jr.," *Journal of Communication and Religion* 41, no. 1 (2018): 8–22; Hoerl, "Selective Amnesia," 181.

20. Barbara Biesecker, "Remembering World War II: The Rhetoric and Politics of National Commemoration at the Turn of the 21st Century," *Quarterly Journal of Speech* 88, no. 4 (2002): 406.

21. Philip C. Wander, "The Third Persona: An Ideological Turn in Rhetorical Theory," *Central States Speech Journal* 35, no. 4 (1984): 210.

22. Ryan Neville-Shepard, "Rand Paul at Howard University and the Rhetoric of the New Southern Strategy," *Western Journal of Communication* 82, no. 1 (2018): 20–39.

23. Neville-Shepard, "Rand Paul at Howard University," 25.

24. Kenneth Burke, *Permanence and Change*, 3rd ed. (Berkeley, CA: University of California Press, 1954/1984), 7.

25. Burke, *Permanence and Change*, 10.

26. Hoerl, "Selective Amnesia"; Neville-Shepard, "Rand Paul at Howard University."

27. Kristan Poirot, "Domesticating the Liberated Woman: Containment Rhetorics of Second Wave Radical/Lesbian Feminism," *Women's Studies in Communication* 32, no. 3 (2009): 263–292; Karrin Vasby Anderson, "'Rhymes with Rich': Bitch as a Tool of Containment in Contemporary American Politics," *Rhetoric & Public Affairs* 2, no. 4 (1999): 599–623; Lisa A. Flores, "Introduction: Of Gendered/Racial Boundaries and Borders," *Women's Studies in Communication* 40, no. 4 (2017):

317–320; Lisa A. Flores and Logan Rae Gomez, "Disciplinary Containment: Whiteness and the Academic Scarcity Narrative," *Communication and Critical/Cultural Studies* 17, no. 2 (2020): 236–244; Lisa A. Flores and Mary Ann Villarreal, "Unmasking 'Ignorance,'" *Quarterly Journal of Speech* 106, no. 3 (2020): 310–315.

28. John Cornyn (TX), "The President's State of the Union Address," *Congressional Record* 162, no. 7 (January 12, 2016): S50–S52, https://www.congress.gov/114/crec/2016/01/12/CREC-2016-01-12-pt1-PgS50.pdf.

29. Cornyn (TX), "The President's State of the Union Address."

30. Michael Conaway (TX), "Lifting Ban on Oil Exports," *Congressional Record* 161, no. 148 (October 8, 2015): H6925–H6926, https://www.congress.gov/114/crec/2015/10/08/CREC-2015-10-08-pt1-PgH6925.pdf.

31. Conaway (TX), "Lifting Ban on Oil Exports."

32. Ron Wyden (OR), "Trade Act of 2015," *Congressional Record* 161, no. 161 (October 30, 2015): S7666–S7667, https://www.congress.gov/114/crec/2015/10/30/CREC-2015-10-30-pt1-PgS7665-6.pdf.

33. David Sehat, *The Jefferson Rule: How the Founding Fathers Became Infallible and Our Politics Inflexible* (New York: Simon & Schuster, 2015).

34. Alcee Lamar Hastings (FL), "General Leave," *Congressional Record* 161, no. 96 (June 16, 2016): H4390–H4392, https://www.congress.gov/114/crec/2015/06/16/CREC-2015-06-16-pt1-PgH4389-6.pdf.

35. Louise McIntosh Slaughter (NY), "General Leave," *Congressional Record* 161, no. 169 (November 17, 2015): H8255, https://www.congress.gov/114/crec/2015/11/17/CREC-2015-11-17-pt1-PgH8254-3.pdf.

36. Slaughter (NY), "General Leave."

37. Chuck Schumer (NY), "Election Security," *Congressional Record* 165, no. 96 (June 10, 2019): S3278, https://www.congress.gov/116/crec/2019/06/10/CREC-2019-06-10-pt1-PgS3276-3.pdf.

38. Chuck Schumer (NY), "The National Defense Authorization Act and Election Security," *Congressional Record* 165, no. 102 (June 18, 2019): S3639, https://www.congress.gov/116/crec/2019/06/18/CREC-2019-06-18-pt1-PgS3639.pdf.

39. Chuck Schumer (NY), "Election Security," *Congressional Record* 165, no. 115 (July 10, 2019): S4745–S4746, https://www.congress.gov/116/crec/2019/07/10/CREC-2019-07-10-pt1-PgS4745-3.pdf.

40. Chuck Schumer (NY), "Election Security," *Congressional* Record 165, no. 126 (July 25, 2019): S5074–S5075, https://www.congress.gov/116/crec/2019/07/25/CREC-2019-07-25-pt1-PgS5074-3.pdf.

41. Chuck Schumer (NY), "Defense Appropriations," *Congressional Record* 165, no. 191 (December 2, 2019): S6738, https://www.congress.gov/116/crec/2019/12/02/CREC-2019-12-02-pt1-PgS6781-7.pdf.

42. Schumer (NY), "Defense Appropriations."

43. Richard Durbin (IL), "Iran," *Congressional Record* 165, no. 108 (June 26, 2019): S4549–S4550, https://www.congress.gov/116/crec/2019/06/26/CREC-2019-06-26-pt1-PgS4531.pdf.

44. Cornyn (TX), "The President's State of the Union Address."
45. Cornyn (TX), "The President's State of the Union Address."
46. Cornyn (TX), "The President's State of the Union Address."
47. Cornyn (TX), "The President's State of the Union Address."
48. Cornyn (TX), "The President's State of the Union Address."
49. Cornyn (TX), "The President's State of the Union Address."
50. Cornyn (TX), "The President's State of the Union Address."
51. Ted Yoho (FL), "Impeachment Timeline," *Congressional Record* 166, no. 8 (January 14, 2020): H233, https://www.congress.gov/116/crec/2020/01/14/CREC-2020-01-14-pt1-PgH231.pdf.
52. Kevin Cramer (ND), "Impeachment," *Congressional Record* 166, no. 39 (February 27, 2020): S1210–S1212, https://www.congress.gov/116/crec/2020/02/27/CREC-2020-02-27-pt1-PgS1184.pdf.
53. Jon Tester (MT), "Nomination of Lawrence VanDyke," *Congressional Record* 165, no. 197 (December 10, 2019): S6914–S6915, https://www.congress.gov/116/crec/2019/12/10/CREC-2019-12-10-pt1-PgS6910-2.pdf; Christopher Murphy (CT), "Nomination of Lawrence VanDyke," *Congressional Record* 165, no. 197 (December 10, 2019): S6936–S6937, https://www.congress.gov/116/crec/2019/12/10/CREC-2019-12-10-pt1-PgS6930.pdf.
54. Tester (MT), "Nomination of Lawrence VanDyke."
55. Tester (MT), "Nomination of Lawrence VanDyke."
56. Tester (MT), "Nomination of Lawrence VanDyke."
57. "Roll Call Vote 116th Congress—1st Session: December 11, 2019," United States Senate, accessed October 17, 2023, https://www.senate.gov/legislative/LIS/roll_call_votes/vote1161/vote_116_1_00391.htm.
58. Bill Cassidy (LA), "Trial of Donald J. Trump, President of the United States," *Congressional Record* 166, no. 20 (January 30, 2020): S713, https://www.congress.gov/116/crec/2020/01/30/CREC-2020-01-30-pt1-PgS693-2.pdf.
59. Pat Cipollone, "Trial of Donald J. Trump, President of the United States," *Congressional Record* 166, no. 8 (January 28, 2020): S713, https://www.congress.gov/116/crec/2020/01/28/CREC-2020-01-28-pt1-PgS619-2.pdf; Cassidy (LA), "Trial of Donald J. Trump, President of the United States."
60. "The Constitution and the Federal Budget Process," National Constitution Center, March 1, 2017, https://constitutioncenter.org/blog/the-constitution-and-the-federal-budget-process.
61. Peter Baker, "Trump Declares a National Emergency, and Provokes a Constitutional Clash," *New York Times*, February 15, 2019, https://www.nytimes.com/2019/02/15/us/politics/national-emergency-trump.html.
62. Baker, "Trump Declares a National Emergency."
63. Baker, "Trump Declares a National Emergency."
64. Chuck Schumer (NY), "Declaration of National Emergency," *Congressional Record* 165, no. 154 (September 24, 2019): S5637–S5638, https://www.congress.gov/116/crec/2019/09/24/CREC-2019-09-24-pt1-PgS5636-5.pdf.

65. Schumer (NY), "Declaration of National Emergency."
66. Schumer (NY), "Declaration of National Emergency."
67. Durbin (IL), "Iran."
68. Tester (MT), "Nomination of Lawrence VanDyke."
69. Schumer (NY), "Declaration of National Emergency."
70. Frances E. Lee, *Beyond Ideology: Politics, Principles and Partisanship in the US Senate* (Chicago: University of Chicago Press, 2009).
71. Lee, *Beyond Ideology*, 8.
72. Lee, *Beyond Ideology*, 8.
73. Quoted in Scott MacKay, "Chafee's New Book Is Tough on Pro-War Democrats, Republicans, President Bush," *Providence Journal*, January 27, 2008, https://www.google.com/url?sa=t&rct=j&q=&esrc=s&source=web&cd=&ved=2ahUKEwiOtID_gN_2AhUEHM0KHZUIBz0QFnoECAMQAQ&url=https%3A%2F%2Flibrary.salve.edu%2Fnewsletter%2FLincoln_Chafee_01-27-08_projo.pdf&usg=AOvVaw2QJntcKzuJC1vrlk9ne8Hn; Lee, *Beyond Ideology*, 8.
74. MacKay, "Chafee's New Book Is Tough on Pro-War Democrats."
75. Lee, *Beyond Ideology*, 7.
76. Lee, *Beyond Ideology*, 9
77. Cornyn (TX), "The President's State of the Union Address."
78. Cornyn (TX), "The President's State of the Union Address."
79. "Final Vote Results for Roll Call 165: March 21, 2010," House Clerk, accessed October 17, 2023 , https://clerk.house.gov/evs/2010/roll165.xml; "Roll Call Vote 111th Congress—1st Session: December 24, 2009," United States Senate, accessed October 17, 2023, https://www.senate.gov/legislative/LIS/roll_call_votes/vote1111/vote_111_1_00396.htm.
80. Norm Ornstein, "The Real Story of Obamacare's Birth," *Atlantic*, July 6, 2015, https://www.theatlantic.com/politics/archive/2015/07/the-real-story-of-obamacares-birth/397742/.
81. Ornstein, "The Real Story of Obamacare's Birth."
82. Ornstein, "The Real Story of Obamacare's Birth."
83. Quoted in Ornstein, "The Real Story of Obamacare's Birth."
84. Bart Jansen and Ledyard King, "'Betrayal': Powerful GOP Support for Trump's Impeachment Shows Major Republican Shift After Capitol Riot," *USAToday.com*, January 14, 2021, https://www.usatoday.com/story/news/politics/elections/2021/01/13/house-gop-impeachment-trump/6637559002/.
85. "Congressman Matt Gaetz to Lead Members of Congress in a Press Conference Demanding Transparency in Impeachment Inquiry," GaetzHouse.com, October 22, 2019, https://archive.ph/2at2D.
86. Li Zhou and Ella Nilsen, "House Republicans' Impeachment Stunt Is an Attempt to Distract from the Allegations against Trump," Vox.com, October 23, 2019, https://www.vox.com/policy-and-politics/2019/10/23/20929023/house-republicans-impeachment-stunt-trump.
87. Zhou and Nilsen, "House Republicans' Impeachment Stunt."

88. "Congressman Matt Gaetz to Lead Members of Congress," GaetzHouse.com.

89. Mike Lillis et al., "Republicans Storm Closed-Door Hearing to Protest Impeachment Inquiry," *TheHill.com*, October 23, 2019, https://thehill.com/homenews/house/467092-republicans-storm-into-house-hearing-to-break-up-trump-impeachment-testimony.

90. Steve King (IA), "Full-Scale Impeachment History," *Congressional Record* 165, no. 172 (October 30, 2019): H8668–H8675, https://www.congress.gov/116/crec/2019/10/30/CREC-2019-10-30-pt1-PgH8668.pdf, emphasis added.

91. King (IA), "Full-Scale Impeachment History."

92. Neville-Shepard, "Rand Paul at Howard University," 24, 27.

93. Burke, *Permanence and Change*, 7.

94. Sehat, *The Jefferson Rule*.

95. Lee, *Beyond Ideology*.

96. Roger F. Wicker (MS), "Recognition of the Minority Leader," *Congressional Record* 166, no. 23 (February 4, 2020): S817–S818, https://www.congress.gov/116/crec/2020/02/04/CREC-2020-02-04-pt1-PgS815.pdf.

Chapter 5. Losing Faith

1. Philip Wander, "The Third Persona: An Ideological Turn in Rhetorical Theory," *Central States Speech Journal* 35, no. 4 (1984): 210.

2. Wander, "The Third Persona," 210.

3. Kristina M. Lee, "'In God We Trust?': Christian Nationalists' Establishment and Use of Theistnormative Legislation," *Rhetoric Society Quarterly* 52, no. 5 (2022): 419; Andrew L. Whitehead and Samuel L. Perry, *Taking America Back for God: Christian Nationalism in the United States* (New York: Oxford University Press, 2020), x.

4. Kenneth Burke, *Permanence and Change*, 3rd ed. (Berkeley, CA: University of California Press, 1954/1984), 7. Burke, *Permanence and Change*, 10.

5. "Summary: State Laws Regarding Presidential Electors," National Association of Secretaries of State, November 2016, https://www.google.com/url?sa=t&rct=j&q=&esrc=s&source=web&cd=&ved=2ahUKEwjyjuva7832AhVoHzQIHSCqB3AQFnoECEQQAQ&url=https%3A%2F%2Fwww.nass.org%2Fsites%2Fdefault%2Ffiles%2Fsurveys%2F2017-08%2Fresearch-state-laws-pres-electors-nov16.pdf&usg=AOvVaw1FBMW6_dAKFuxfYxrWR4F4.

6. Anne-Marie Slaughter, "Ranked-Choice Voting," Politico.com, accessed October 17, 2023, https://www.politico.com/interactives/2019/how-to-fix-politics-in-america/polarization/ranked-choice-voting/.

7. "State Primary Election Types," National Conference of State Legislatures, June 22, 2023, https://www.ncsl.org/elections-and-campaigns/state-primary-election-types#Open.

8. Arnold Schwarzenegger, "Ban Partisan Gerrymandering and Enact Open Primaries Nationwide," Politico.com, accessed October 17, 2023, https://www.politico.com/interactives/2019/how-to-fix-politics-in-america/polarization/ban-partisan-gerrymandering-enact-open-primaries-nationwide/.

9. Schwarzenegger, "Ban Partisan Gerrymandering and Enact Open Primaries Nationwide."

10. Burke, *Permanence and Change*, 10.

11. Anne Demo, "Sovereignty Discourse and Contemporary Immigration Politics," *Quarterly Journal of Speech* 91, no. 3 (2005): 295.

12. Stephen J. Hartnett and Bryan R. Reckard, "Sovereign Tropes: A Rhetorical Critique of Contested Claims in the South China Sea," *Rhetoric & Public Affairs* 20, no. 2 (2017): 295; Demo, "Sovereignty Discourse and Contemporary Immigration Politics," 295.

13. Carole Pateman, *The Sexual Contract* (Stanford, CA: Stanford University Press, 1988); Charles W. Mills, *The Racial Contract* (Ithaca, NY: Cornell University Press, 1997); Charles W. Mills, *Black Rights/White Wrongs: The Critique of Racial Liberalism* (New York: Oxford University Press, 2017); Carole Pateman and Charles W. Mills, *Contract and Domination* (Cambridge, UK: Polity Press, 2007); Hortense J. Spillers, "Mama's Baby, Papa's Maybe: An American Grammar Book," *Diacritics* 17, no. 2 (1987): 64–82; Saidiya V. Hartman, *Scenes of Subjection: Terror, Slavery and Self-Making in Nineteenth-Century America* (New York: Oxford University Press, 1997).

14. "Declaration of Independence: A Transcription," National Archives, accessed October 17, 2023, https://www.archives.gov/founding-docs/declaration-transcript, emphasis added.

15. See George Michael, "David Lane and the Fourteen Words," *Totalitarian Movements and Political Religions* 10, no. 1 (2009): 43–61.

16. David Lane converted to Norse paganism before his death in 2007, embracing what he understood as an even "whiter" religion than American Protestant Christianity. See Michael, "David Lane and the Fourteen Words," 43–61.

17. Clara Jeffery and James West, "The Deeply Racist References in Dylann Roof's Apparent Manifesto, Decoded," *MotherJones.com*, June 20, 2015, https://www.motherjones.com/politics/2015/06/references-dylann-roof-manifesto-explained-1488/.

18. Arun Kundnani quoted in Nellie Bowles, "'Replacement Theory,' a Racist, Sexist Doctrine, Spreads in Far-Right Circles," *NYTimes.com*, March 18, 2019, https://www.nytimes.com/2019/03/18/technology/replacement-theory.html?smid=url-share.

19. See Bowles, "'Replacement Theory,' a Racist, Sexist Doctrine."

20. Mark Ward Sr., "Sermons as Social Interaction: Pulpit Speech, Power and Gender," *Women & Language* 42, no. 2 (2019): 285–316.

21. Maxine L. Margolis, *Women in Fundamentalism* (Lanham, MD: Rowman & Littlefield, 2020), 2.

22. Kevin DeYoung, "It's Time for a New Culture War Strategy," Gospel Coalition, June 17, 2020, https://www.thegospelcoalition.org/blogs/kevin-deyoung/its-time-for-a-new-culture-war-strategy/.

23. DeYoung, "It's Time for a New Culture War Strategy."

24. DeYoung, "It's Time for a New Culture War Strategy."

25. DeYoung, "It's Time for a New Culture War Strategy."

26. Steve King (IA), quoted in Bowles, "'Replacement Theory,' a Racist, Sexist Doctrine."

27. Chuck Schumer (NY), quoted in Nicholas Confessore, "Schumer Calls on Murdoch and Fox News Executives to Stop Amplifying Replacement Theory," *NYTimes.com*, May 17, 2022, https://www.nytimes.com/2022/05/17/nyregion/schumer-fox-news-replacement-theory-murdoch.html?smid=url-share.

28. Jason Gilmore, Penelope Sheets, and Charles Rowling, "Make No Exception, Save One: American Exceptionalism, the American Presidency, and the Age of Obama," *Communication Monographs* 83, no. 4 (2016): 505–520.

29. Rudy Giuliani, quoted in Lindsey Bever, "Report: Rudy Giuliani Tells Private Dinner 'I Do Not Believe That the President Loves America," *Washington Post*, February 19, 2015, https://www.washingtonpost.com/news/morning-mix/wp/2015/02/19/report-rudy-giuliani-tells-private-dinner-i-do-not-believe-that-the-president-loves-america/; Dick Cheney, quoted in Bill Hoffman, "Cheney to Newsmax: 'Obama Doesn't Believe in an Exceptional America,'" Newsmax.com, September 2, 2015, https://www.newsmax.com/Headline/Dick-Cheney-Newsmax-TV-Obama-Iran/2015/09/02/id/673213/.

30. Jason Gilmore and Charles M. Rowling, "Partisan Patriotism in the American Presidency: American Exceptionalism, Issue Ownership, and the Age of Trump," *Mass Communication and Society* 22, no. 3 (2019): 396–397.

31. Julie Husband, "Multicultural American Exceptionalism in the Speeches of Frederick Douglass and Barack Obama," *Howard Journal of Communications* 29, no. 3 (2018): 225–242.

32. Rebecca Goetz, *The Baptism of Early Virginia: How Christianity Created Race* (Baltimore: Johns Hopkins University Press, 2012).

INDEX

Adams, John, 73–74, 86, 163, 164
Adams, John Quincy, 50, 164
Aderholt, Robert B., 160–61
Affordable Care Act (ACA), 56, 60–61, 178, 185–86
Afropessimism, 7
Alexander, Lamar, 97
American exceptionalism: and bipartisanship discourse, 190, 195; and celebrations, 95–100, 106–9, 117, 199–200, 201; and Christian nationalism, 89–91, 102–10, 117–19, 194–95; and covenant rhetoric, 42, 45, 47, 100–110, 116–17, 151, 194, 205–6; and cynicism discourse, 7–8, 44, 45, 91–92, 110–17, 119, 205–6, 207; and impeachment discourse, 151, 155–56; and inheritance, 53, 99–100, 112, 119, 151, 192; from Loudermilk, 33, 37–40, 43; and othering, 124–25; overview of usage, 86–92, 199–200; and rights discourse, 53, 56–57, 61, 67, 68, 80, 84–85; as term, 88–89; veneration of, 45, 92–95, 192–93; and whiteness, 89–91, 101, 106, 107, 117–19, 199
Americanness: of Black people, 6, 114–15, 206; and cynicism, 115–17; and purity tests, 17, 119; and veneration, 91, 119
Amory, John, 11–12
anti-abortion. *See* life, right to
Anti-Federalists, 54, 129, 163–64, 188–89
anti-miscegenation laws, 20, 21
argumentation and containment rhetoric, 137–39
Aristotle, 121
Articles of Confederation, 155
Aryan Nation, 202
Atchison, Jarrod, 9, 32
Attucks, Crispus, 114–15

Atwater, Lee, 169
authority: and American exceptionalism, 37; and bipartisanship discourse, 176–77; and Complementarianism, 28; and containment rhetoric, 128, 132–34; of Founding Fathers, 5–6, 17; of the people, 8. *See also* sovereignty
Authorization for Use of Military Force (AUMF), 143, 146

Babin, Brian, 108
backwardness and othering, 127, 146
bald eagle, 97–98, 100, 198
Baucus, Max, 185
belittling, 132–34, 140–41, 143–46, 154, 158
Bell, Derrick, 7
Bible: and masculinity, 153; National Bible Week, 107–9, 117; translations and gendered language, 93–94; use of, by Founding Fathers, 16
Bill of Rights, 53–54, 129
bipartisanship discourse: and American exceptionalism, 190, 195; and containment rhetoric, 170, 174, 175–82, 195–96; and disingenuous rhetoric, 46, 182–88, 190, 195–96, 199; and ideal governance, 170–77, 189; and inheritance, 170–77, 179, 187–88, 190; overview of, 44, 45–46, 163–70, 199–200; and rigging of system, 184–89
birthing of nation: and gender, 5–6, 43; and inheritance, 53, 99, 100
Black, Edwin, 51–52
Black people: and Americanness, 6, 114–15, 206; and citizenship, 22, 76; and emotionality, 134; and "fatherlessness," 23–24; and inheritance, 18–19, 23–24; and right-to-vote discourse, 76;

247

Black people (*cont.*)
and Third Persona, 52, 59, 68, 69, 84; and "uppity" discourse, 133–34, 178. *See also* Congressional Black Caucus; race; slavery

Black resistance, 114–15, 206. *See also* cynicism as counter-discourse

Blackstone, William, 66, 121, 135, 138

blasphemy, 55, 77

Bob Jones University, 27, 70

Bonamici, Suzanne, 153

Booker, Cory, 155, 162, 205

border wall, 181–82, 183

Bryan, William Jennings, 156

Buchanan, Vern, 158

budgetary powers, 181–82

Buescher, Brian, 105

Burr, Aaron, 164

Burr, Richard, 151

Bush, George H. W., 142, 143

Byrd, Robert, 98

capitalism, 9, 101

Carlson, Tucker, 203

Carper, Thomas R., 92–93, 155–56, 162, 205–6

Carter, Earl "Buddy," 131, 134, 138, 139–40

Cassidy, Bill, 151, 180–81

celebrations: of American exceptionalism and Founding Fathers, 95–100, 106–9, 117, 199–200, 201; of bipartisanship, 170–77; and cynicism as counter-discourse, 206

Chafee, John, 185

Chafee, Lincoln, 184

Charlottesville, VA, rally (2017), 47, 202

checks and balances: and bipartisanship discourse, 195–96; and confrontational language, 137–39; in Constitution, 122; and cynicism as counter-discourse, 45, 154–57, 162; and gun rights, 128, 129–41, 161; and impeachment, 128, 149–61; and Iroquois Confederacy, 121–22; overview of usage, 44, 45, 120–28, 199–200; phrase origins, 120–21; relation to separation of powers, 120–21; and war powers, 128, 141–48, 161, 176, 183. *See also* containment rhetoric

Cheney, Dick, 207

Chisholm, Shirley, 112

Christianity: and American exceptionalism, 45, 92–95; and Complementarianism, 28, 203–4; and containment rhetoric, 128, 140–41, 157, 159–62, 195; and control of procreation, 28, 29, 201–4; and covenant rhetoric, 42, 45, 47, 100–110, 116–17, 151, 194, 205–6; of Founding Fathers, 16–17, 45, 200, 207–8; and God as father, 17, 94; and inheritance, 7, 10, 28, 42, 45, 46, 53, 194–95; in Loudermilk's discourse, 10, 37–42; and masculinity, 25–29, 93–94, 118, 153; and patriarchy, 25–29, 62, 90, 94; persecution of, 104–5; privileging of, 193, 200, 207–8; and rights discourse, 53, 56, 59–66, 69, 70–71, 83–85; and Second Persona, 194; and whiteness, 17, 27, 118; and white supremacy, 27, 29, 70, 118, 207–8. *See also* "family" values

Christian nationalism: and American exceptionalism, 89–91, 102–10, 117–19, 194–95, 199; Charlottesville rally (2017), 47, 202; and containment rhetoric, 140–41, 161–62; as ideological framework *vs.* religiosity, 28–29, 90; privileging of, 8, 42, 193, 200; and Second Persona, 71, 194; unconscious use of, 198; and violence, 201–2, 204; and women, 201–4. *See also* replacement theory; white supremacy

Cipollone, Pat, 180–81

citizenship: and Black people, 22, 76; and Native Americans, 76, 125; and whiteness, 20, 50; and women, 22, 125

"city upon a hill" trope, 101, 103, 104–5, 107

civilized *vs.* uncivilized discourse and othering, 124–25, 127, 136–37, 195

Civil Right Act of 1964, 22

civil rights movement, 59, 167

climate change, 102

Clinton, Hillary, 126, 159

Clinton, William Jefferson, 124, 142, 149, 180–81, 185, 186

closed-door depositions, 186–88

closed rule, 173

collective memory: as constructed, 11, 13, 167–70; and cynicism as counter-discourse, 206–7; defined, 11; of Founding Fathers, 10–18, 73, 192–93; of Founding Fathers' nonpartisanship, 46, 167, 172–73, 174, 189, 195; and selective amnesia, 8, 167–70, 192, 195
Collins, Susan, 151
Commander in Chief Clause (Article II), 141–42
Complementarianism, 28, 203–4
Conaway, Michael, 171–72
Confederate symbols, 118
confrontational language, 137–39
Congress: budgetary powers of, 181–82; lawmaking by vs. executive orders, 131; prayer in, 90; and representative vs. direct democracy, 14–15; rule and norms of, 33, 143; as subject, 4; war powers of, 141–43, 148, 176
Congressional Black Caucus: rights discourse, 71–85. See also cynicism as counter-discourse
Congressional Record and methodology, 3, 5
Constitution: Article I, 122, 181; Article II, 130–31; budgetary powers, 181; celebrations of, 98–100, 106–7; checks and balances in, 122; executive orders in, 130–31; impeachment in, 149–50; in Jackson Lee's discourse, 75; and selective amnesia, 168; tensions with Bill of Rights, 54; voting in, 71–72; war powers in, 141–42
Constitution Day, 98–100, 106–7, 117
containment rhetoric: and bipartisanship discourse, 170, 174, 175–82, 185–89, 195–96; and confrontational language, 137–39; and cynicism as counter-discourse, 45, 154–57, 162; and gun rights, 128, 129–41, 161; hierarchies of containment, 128; and impeachment, 128, 149–61; othering in, 33–37, 50–52, 124–28, 131–34, 137, 139–41, 143, 146–47, 152, 157–62, 195; overview of usage, 123–28; theorized by Flores, 124, 127; theorized by Poirot, 124, 126; about voters, 196; and war powers, 128, 141–48, 161, 176, 183. See also checks and balances
Cornyn, John, 171, 177–78, 185
covenant rhetoric: and American exceptionalism, 42, 45, 47, 100–110, 116–17, 151, 194, 205–6; and bipartisanship discourse, 194–95; and containment rhetoric, 141, 151, 155; and cynicism as counter-discourse, 91, 112, 162, 205–6; if-then formula, 100–101
COVID-19 pandemic, ix
Cramer, Kevin, 179
Crusius, Patrick, 47, 202
Culberson, John Abney, 131, 132, 140
cybersecurity, 75, 173–76, 183, 189
cynicism as counter-discourse: about American exceptionalism, 7–8, 44, 45, 91–92, 110–17, 119, 205–6, 207; and containment rhetoric, 45, 154–57, 162; risks of, 115–17, 162; as strategy, 7–8, 46, 48, 205–8

Daines, Steve, 92, 98–99, 100, 159
Danvers Statement, 28
debates and bipartisanship. See bipartisanship discourse
Declaration of Independence: use in discourse, 38, 39, 41, 56, 58–59, 63–66, 67, 68; writing of, 63–64
Declare War Clause (Article I), 141–42
defense discourse: and confrontational language, 137–39; and containment rhetoric, 128, 135–41, 151–61, 195; and gun control, 129–41; and immigration, 83; and impeachment, 151–61; from Loudermilk, 37, 40–42
democracy: and Black resistance, 114–15; classical, 121; and Electoral College as undemocratic, 14–15, 113, 159, 160, 163, 190–91, 196; Founding Fathers as architects of, 14–15; House as undemocratic, 166; and inheritance, 46; in Iroquois Confederacy, 121–22; representative vs. direct, 14–15; Senate as undemocratic, 14, 113, 122–23, 159, 160
Democratic-Republican Party, 164, 188–89
DeYoung, Kevin, 203–4
disposition, right of, 20–21, 28, 42–43, 44

Index 249

District of Columbia v. Heller, 130
doctrine of coverture, 12, 18
Dold, Robert, 104
Durbin, Richard J., 143, 144, 145–46, 148, 176, 183

Election Clause (Constitution), 71–72
elections: of 1800, 164, 166; of 1828, 166; and popular vote, 159; and research focus, 5
Electoral College: and partisanship, 163–67, 188, 190–91, 196; reform suggestions, 196–97; and state electoral systems, 165–66, 196; and three-fifths rule, 166, 168; as undemocratic, 14–15, 113, 159, 160, 163, 166, 190–91, 196
Employment Division v. Smith, 57
Equal Rights Amendment (ERA), 112, 125–26
Ernst, Joni, 98, 99, 100
Establishment Clause (First Amendment), 54–55, 57
ethnicity, elision of, 89
exceptionalism. *See* American exceptionalism
exclude, right to, 20
executive orders: and gun control, 45, 129–41; use of, 130–31
Expatriation Act of 1907, 125

faith. *See* loss of faith and cynicism
Falwell, Jerry, Sr., 27, 70
family: African American, 23–24; and hegemonic masculinity, 26. *See also* inheritance
"family" values: and American exceptionalism, 45, 47, 89, 106, 117–19; from Loudermilk, 10, 43; and masculinity, 25–29; overview of, 6; and patriarchy, 6, 10, 25–29, 198; and rights discourse, 53, 83–85; and whiteness, 47, 53, 83, 89, 119, 194, 198, 199–200; and white supremacy, 6, 10
fatherhood: and "fatherlessness" of Black families, 23–24; God as father, 17, 94; and male fertility, 12; and othering, 132; and Trump, ix; Washington as father of country, 2, 17–18; and wisdom, 94

fear: and containment rhetoric, 125–28; of moral decline, 29, 90–91, 118; of the other, 125, 132
Federalist Papers, 75, 122, 135
Federalists and Federalism: and Bill of Rights, 54; defined, 121; and partisanship, 163–64, 188–89
feminization: of Obama, 131, 133, 134; and war powers, 146. *See also* masculinity
Fifteenth Amendment, 22, 72
Fifth Amendment, 68
First Amendment: and freedom-of-press discourse, 77–78, 82; and freedom-of-religion discourse, 54–55, 57, 58, 60; and right to privacy, 68
First Persona: and bipartisanship discourse, 176, 180; defined, 51
Fischer, Deb, 105
Flores, Lisa, 124, 127
Ford, Gerald, 150
Foucault, Michel, 9
Founding Fathers: as above partisanship, 15–16, 46, 167, 172–73, 174, 189, 195; in collective memory, 10–18, 73, 192–93; distrust of citizenry, 15; enslaved children of, 12, 20–21; partisanship of, 2–3, 13–14, 163–67, 172, 188, 195; possession of, from Loudermilk, 33, 36, 43; religious skepticism by, 117; as slave-owners, ix, 2, 12, 49, 73, 114, 193; social class and wealth of, 2, 12–13; as term, 2, 3, 17–18, 205; veneration of, 44–47, 92–95, 99–100, 104, 106–7, 192–93; volume of invoking, by Congress, 1–2, 3, 43–44, 193, 198–99. *See also* American exceptionalism; bipartisanship discourse; checks and balances; containment rhetoric; rights discourse; veneration
Fourteenth Amendment, 22, 68, 76, 125, 166
"fourteen words" mantra, 202–3, 204
Fourth Amendment, 68
Foxx, Virginia, 106–7
Francis (pope), 102, 103, 117
Franklin, Benjamin, 75, 111, 121–22, 124, 156
Franks, Trent, 67–68
Fraser, James Earle, 40

Free Exercise Clause (First Amendment), 55, 57
Friedan, Betty, 126
frontiersmanship, 26

Gaetz, Matt, 186
gender: and Bible translations, 93–94; and "birthing" of nation, 5–6, 43; and Christian nationalism, 29; and Complementarianism, 28, 203–4; and containment rhetoric, 127–28, 133, 147, 154; and Declaration of Independence, 59; and Founding Fathers as term, 2, 17–18; and inheritance, 18; and personhood, 23–25; and property, 18–19; and purity tests, 17–18; and right to vote, 72, 73; sexist racism, 23–24; as social construct, 127–28; and Third Persona, 52. *See also* masculinity; women
Gitlow v. New York, 78
Giuliani, Rudy, 207
God: covenant with Israelites, 101; as father, 17, 94
Gohmert, Louie, 83
Goldberg, Arthur, 56
Goldwater, Barry, 169
Gooden, Lance, 157, 158
Grassley, Chuck, 123, 124, 185–86
Greek democracy, 121
Griswold v. Connecticut, 68
Grothman, Glenn, 108
Grudem, Wayne, 27–28
Guest, Michael, 157
Gulf of Tonkin Resolution, 142
gun rights, 83, 128, 129–41, 161

Hamilton, Alexander, 157, 164
Hannah-Jones, Nikole, 113–15, 117, 206
Harding, Warren G., 2, 3
Harris, Cheryl I., 19, 20, 42
Hastings, Alcee Lamar, 172–73
Hatch, Orrin, 55–60, 62, 185
Helsinki Accords, 56, 57
Hemings, Robert, 114
heterosexuality: and Complementarianism, 28; and hegemonic masculinity, 26; and othering, 125–27; and Second Persona, 194
high crimes and misdemeanors, 149–50

Hirono, Mazie, 105
Hoerl, Kristen, 167, 170
Holmes, Kim R., 88–89
Holmes, Oliver Wendell, 77
House of Representatives: belittling of, 158; and election decisions, 164; and impeachment role, 123; minimum age for, 123; rule and norms of, 33, 173; as undemocratic, 166

identity: collective, 167; and Second and Third Personae, 51–52
immigration: and border wall, 181–82, 183; and othering, 125, 140; and rights discourse, 83, 135–36, 137; and right to exclude, 20
impeachment: and bipartisanship discourse, 178–79; of Clinton, 124, 149, 180–81, 186; in Constitution, 149–50; and containment rhetoric, 128, 149–61; and House *vs.* Senate powers, 123; of Johnson, 149; and Nixon, 149, 186; and othering, 124, 152, 157–61; and representation, 159–60; of Trump, 1, 45, 92, 149, 150–61, 178–81, 186–88, 190
incapacity, trained, 169, 188, 196, 198
inferential racism, 118
"In God We Trust" motto, 37–41
inheritance: and American exceptionalism, 53, 99–100, 112, 119, 151, 192; and bipartisanship discourse, 170–77, 179, 187–88, 190; and Christianity, 7, 10, 28, 42, 45, 46, 53, 194–95; and containment rhetoric, 128, 131, 151, 161, 162; and covenant rhetoric, 42, 45, 47, 109, 151, 194; effect on democracy, 46; of freedom, 33–43, 44, 53; and impeachment discourse, 151, 154, 160–62; in Loudermilk's discourse, 33–43; and masculinity, 10, 18, 26, 119; overview of, 5–7, 10, 18–25; and property, 18–21, 23–24, 42–43; and race, 18–19, 23–24; and rights discourse, 44, 53, 55–71, 75–76, 83–85; and Third Persona, 193–94; unconscious use of, as logic, 197–98; and veneration, 99–100, 112, 119; and whiteness, 18–21, 42, 43, 45, 50, 119; and white supremacy, 19, 46, 203

Iran and containment rhetoric, 143, 176, 183
Iroquois Confederacy, 121–22
Israelites, 65, 101

Jackson, Andrew, 166
Jackson Lee, Sheila, 59, 75–76
Jay, John, 86
Jefferson, Thomas: on American exceptionalism, 86; and Anti-Federalist leadership, 164; and Declaration of Independence, 63; in discourse, 37, 66, 78–79; and 1800 election, 164, 166; and "eternal vigilance," 40; and father imagery, 2; religious skepticism of, 117; as slave-owner, ix, 114
Jeffries, Hakeem S., 113
jeremiads, 101–2, 103, 106, 116–17, 194
Jesus, 102–3
John Lewis Voting Rights Advancement Act of 2021, 73
Johnson, Andre E., 7, 167
Johnson, Andrew, 149
Johnson, Lyndon B., 142, 177–78
Johnson, Paul Elliot, 8–9, 32
Johnson, Ron, 92
judiciary: and bipartisanship discourse, 179–80; and originalism, 13–14; Trump appointments, 105

Kelly, Robin, 111–12, 152–53
Kennedy v. Bremerton School District, 61–62
Khashoggi, Jamal, 81, 82
King, Martin Luther, Jr., 59, 167
King, Steve, 65, 70, 92, 187–88, 204
Kinkopf, Neil J., 150
kinship, 24

Lakoff, George, 4, 6
Lamborn, Doug, 107–9
Lane, David, 202
Langevin, James R., 153–54
Lankford, James, 93, 98, 99, 100
Lawrence, Brenda L., 112
Leaman, Ken, 94
Lee, Barbara, 113–14, 115, 206
Lee, Frances E., 184, 189
Lee, Kristina M., 90

Lee, Michael J. (scholar), 9, 32
Lee, Mike (senator), 143, 145, 146, 147, 148, 158–59
LGBTQ+ rights, 29, 68, 105, 126, 204
life, right to, 44, 53, 62–71, 83
Lincoln, Abraham, 2–3, 67, 105
Little Sisters of the Poor, 60
Locke, John, 21, 121
Lofgren, Zoe, 180–81
loss of faith and cynicism, 7, 91–92, 110–17, 119, 206–7
Loudermilk, Barry: gun rights discourse, 131, 132, 135–36, 138, 139, 140; inheritance discourse case study, 33–43; right-to-life discourse, 65–67, 69–70

Madison, James: and Anti-Federalist leadership, 164; and Bill of Rights, 53–54; and checks and balances, 122, 123, 135, 138; in discourse, 56, 138; distrust of citizenry, 15; on Native Americans, 49–50, 84; on property, 19–20; and slavery, 49; and war powers, 142
Maloney, Carolyn B., 153
masculinity: and American exceptionalism, 93–94, 118; and bipartisanship discourse, 178, 183, 184, 187, 195; and Christianity, 25–29, 93–94, 118, 153; and civilized *vs.* uncivilized discourse, 135–36; and containment rhetoric, 45, 128, 132–36, 140–41, 144–48, 152–54, 157, 161–62, 195; and defense of property, 135; and "family" values, 25–29; and impeachment, 152, 153, 154, 157; and inheritance, 10, 18, 26, 119; and language, 17–18; and othering, 132, 195; and personhood, 24–25, 39, 200; privileging of, 5–6, 193, 200, 207–8; and rights discourse, 58–59, 77, 80, 81, 82, 128, 132, 134–37, 140–41; traits of hegemonic, 26–29; and violence, 24–25, 201–2, 204; and whiteness, 25–29, 201–2, 204; and white supremacy, 207–8; and wisdom, 93–94
Mason, Crystal, 127
materiality: and bipartisanship discourse, 190; and containment rhetoric,

252 *Index*

135, 148, 160; and cynicism discourse, 112; in Loudermilk's discourse, 33, 37–38, 41, 43, 66, 69–70; and rights discourse, 53, 56–60, 61, 62, 64, 65, 66, 69–70, 83–84; as technique, 33, 192, 194; and veneration, 91, 99, 112
McConnell, Mitch, 1, 158, 174, 175–76, 185–86
McDonald v. City of Chicago, 130
McKenney, Thomas L., 49, 50
McKinley, Sarah, 135
McKinley, William, 15
Meeks, Gregory W., 153
memory. *See* collective memory
Menendez, Robert, 78–80
men's rights groups, 46, 201, 203
metaphors, effect on meaning, 4
methodology, 4–5, 10, 29–32, 193, 197–98
Middle East and war powers, 143, 146–47, 176
Miller, Mary, 70
Mills, Charles W., 22–23, 46
monarchy, 2, 6
Montesquieu, 120–21, 135, 140
Mooney, Alexander, 56, 60–61
Moore, Gwen, 153
morality: and Christian nationalism, 29, 90–91, 118; and Clinton impeachment, 124; and white American jeremiad, 101
Moral Majority, 27, 70, 90–91
Moses, 37
Moynihan, Daniel Patrick, 23–24
Mueller, Robert, 175
Murkowski, Lisa, 151
Murphy, Gregory, 157

National Defense Act of 1916, 130
nationalism: *vs.* American exceptionalism, 88–89. *See also* Christian nationalism
Native Americans: and citizenship, 76, 125; and Founding Fathers, 49–50, 84, 121–22, 124, 193; and inheritance, 18; Iroquois Confederacy, 121–22; othering of, 124–25; and right to vote, 76; and war powers, 142
Naturalization Act of 1790, 20
natural rights, 63–64
Neville-Shepard, Ryan, 168–69, 170, 188

9/11 attacks, 142–43
Nineteenth Amendment, 22, 72
Nixon, Richard, 142, 149, 186

Obama, Barack: on American exceptionalism, 207; belittling of, 133, 140–41; and bipartisanship discourse, 171, 177–78, 185; and containment rhetoric, 45, 129–41, 142, 143, 161; othering of, 131–34, 137, 139, 140–41, 161, 178
Obama, Michelle, 126
Obamacare. *See* Affordable Care Act (ACA)
oil energy bills, 171–72
one-drop laws, 21, 28
Onuf, Peter S., 86, 87, 89
originalism, 13–14
Orms, Arlene, 135
Ortega, Rosa Maria, 127
othering: and American exceptionalism, 124–25; and backwardness, 127, 146; and bipartisanship discourse, 174–77, 183, 187–88; and civilized *vs.* uncivilized discourse, 124–25, 127, 136–37, 195; and containment rhetoric, 33–37, 50–52, 124–28, 131–34, 137, 139–41, 143, 146–47, 152, 157–62, 195; by Loudermilk, 33–37; and masculinity, 132, 195; of Obama, 131–34, 137, 139, 140–41, 161, 178; and possession, 50–52; and race, 6, 124–25, 126, 199–200; and rights discourse, 58, 59, 60–61, 62, 131–34; as technique, 6, 9–10, 192, 195; and Third Persona, 193–94; of Trump, 153; of women, 125–27

pardons, 149
partisanship: of Electoral College, 163–67, 188, 190–91, 196; of Founding Fathers, 2–3, 13–14, 163–67, 172, 188, 195; Founding Fathers as above, 15–16, 46, 167, 172–73, 174, 189, 195; and party tickets, 164–65; utility of, 189. *See also* bipartisanship discourse
Pateman, Carole, 22–23
patent law, 83
patriarchy: and American exceptionalism, 117–19, 199; and Christianity,

Index 253

patriarchy (*cont.*) 25–29, 62, 90, 94; and Christian nationalism, 90; and containment rhetoric, 126–27, 152; and "family" values, 25–29; Founding Fathers as patriarchs, 12–13, 193, 207; and inheritance, 19, 45; and masculinity, 26; and othering, 9–10, 22–23, 43; privileging of, 6, 8, 10, 23, 62, 198–200; and replacement theory, 201–4; and rights discourse, 62, 69, 71, 82, 83–85; and veneration, 45, 47, 94, 117–19; and white supremacy, 202–3, 204; women's role in, 28, 202–3

Paul, Rand, 143, 144, 145, 146, 147, 148

Pelosi, Nancy, 187

people, the: as social construct, 8–9; and sovereignty, 8; as white, 84–85. *See also* othering; personhood

Perry, Samuel L., 29, 90

personhood: and masculinity, 24–25, 39, 200; and race, 22–25, 39, 42; and Second and Third Personae, 51–52, 200

Peters, Gary, 95–96

Pinckney, Charles Cotesworth, 164

Piper, John, 27–28

Planned Parenthood, 67

Poirot, Kristan, 124, 126

possession: Founding Fathers as a, 33, 36, 43; and freedom of religion discourse, 56–57, 83; and ours *vs.* theirs, 50–52; and property, 24–25; and Second and Third Personae, 51–52

prayer, 62, 90

preclearance process, 72–73

presidency: as above partisanship, 15; budgetary powers, 181–82; rhetorical form of, 15–16; war powers, 141–48, 176

press, freedom of, 44, 53, 77–83, 205

primaries, 197

privacy, right to, 68

property: Black slaves as, 19; and containment rhetoric, 135–37; and inheritance, 18–21, 23–24, 42–43; and kinship, 24; and masculinity, 26, 27, 135; and possession, 24–25; right to use and enjoy, 20; as right *vs.* thing, 19–20; whiteness as, 10, 19–20, 27, 28, 52

prophetic pessimism, 7

Protestantism, 16–17

Puritans, 101, 109, 124–25

purity tests, 17, 119

Putin, Vladimir, 175

race: and American exceptionalism discourse, 89; and bipartisanship discourse, 178, 187–88; as determining factor in early republic, 49–50; and Electoral College, 165–66; elision of, 34–37, 89; and emotionality, 134; of enslaved children of Founding Fathers, 20–21; inferential racism, 118; and inheritance, 18–19, 23–24; one-drop laws, 21, 28; and othering, 6, 124–25, 126, 199–200; and othering of Obama, 131–34, 139, 140–41; and personhood, 6, 22–25, 39, 42; replacement theory, 46, 47, 69–71, 201–4; and rights discourse, 68–70, 76–77, 129; and right to vote, 22, 72; and rule-of-law trope, 187–88; and Second and Third Personae, 52, 59, 68, 69, 84, 194; sexist racism, 23–24; and shootings, 34–35, 36, 47; as social construct, 21, 127–28; and three-fifths rule, 166, 168; and "uppity" discourse, 133–34, 178. *See also* Black people; Native Americans; whiteness; white supremacy

racial realism, 7–8, 91–92, 110, 206–8. *See also* cynicism as counter-discourse

ranked-choice voting, 196–97

Ratcliffe, John, 64–65

Reagan, Ronald, 101

refugees, 135–36

religion: and Founding Fathers, 16–17, 45, 117, 200, 207–8; freedom of, 36, 41–42, 44, 53, 55–62, 83; and persecution of Christians, 104–5. *See also* Christianity

replacement theory, 46, 47, 69–71, 201–4

representation: and Electoral College as unrepresentative, 14–15, 113, 159, 160, 163; and impeachment, 159–60; representative *vs.* direct democracy, 14–15; in Senate as undemocratic, 14, 113, 122–23, 159, 160; and three-fifths rule, 166, 168

reputation and status, right to, 21
resistance theology, 63–64
restoration and containment rhetoric, 128, 143–44, 147–48, 161–62
Riggleman, Denver, 157
rights: and Declaration of Independence, 63–64; expansion of, 22, 205; natural, 63–64
rights discourse: and American exceptionalism, 53, 56–57, 61, 67, 68, 80, 84–85; differences in party usages, 53, 83; freedom of press, 44, 53, 77–83, 205; freedom of religion, 36, 41–42, 44, 53, 55–62, 83; gun ownership, 83, 128, 129–41, 161; and inheritance, 44, 53, 55–71, 75–76, 83–85; overview of, 44, 49–53, 199; right to life, 44, 53, 62–71, 83; right to vote, 44, 53, 71–77, 205
Risch, James E., 92, 160, 180–81
Roe, David P., 97
Roe v. Wade, 28, 62, 64, 66, 68, 70
Rohrabacher, Dana, 83
Roman Republic, 121
Romney, Mitt, 150–51, 179
Roof, Dylann, 34–35, 36, 202
Roosevelt, Franklin, 56, 107
Roosevelt, Theodore, 15, 26
Rosen, Jeffrey, 64
Rounds, Mike, 92
Rubenstein, David, 64
rule-of-law trope, 187–88
Russell, Steve, 83, 131, 132, 134–35, 136–39, 140
Russian interference in elections, 75, 175

Sanders, Bernie, 143, 145, 146, 147
sartorial statutes, 12
Sasse, Ben, 151
Saudi Arabia human rights abuses, 146
Schiff, Adam, 187
Schumer, Chuck: bipartisanship discourse, 173–76, 183, 189; on border wall, 182; and containment rhetoric, 143, 144, 145, 146, 148, 153, 154; on replacement theory, 204; and Trump impeachment, 1, 153, 154; and veneration, 92
Scott, Rick, 116–17
Second Amendment, 83, 128, 129–41, 161

Second Persona: defined, 51–52; and freedom-of-press discourse, 80, 81, 82; and freedom-of-religion discourse, 56, 58, 59, 60, 61, 83; and othering, 193–94; and right-to-life discourse, 64, 69, 71, 83; and right-to-vote discourse, 71, 76–77
Sehat, David, 14
selective amnesia: and bipartisanship discourse, 167–70, 174, 177, 181, 188–89, 195; and containment of voters, 196; and negation of Third Persona, 168–69, 170; as technique, 8, 192
self-defense, 134, 135
Senate: impeachment powers, 123; rule and norms of, 33, 143; as undemocratic, 14, 113, 122–23, 159, 160
separation of church and state, 55, 62
separation of powers, 45, 120–21, 176, 183. *See also* checks and balances
Seventeenth Amendment, 123
Sewell, Terri A., 73–75
sexism: and othering, 125–27; and othering of Obama, 131, 133, 134, 139, 140–41; and Second and Third Personae, 52, 194; sexist racism, 23–24
Shelby County v. Holder, 73
Sherman, Roger, 3
shootings, 34–35, 36, 47, 130, 131, 201–2, 204
Slaughter, Louise McIntosh, 173
slavery: abolition of, 22, 59; and Black people as property, 19; and cynicism, 113–15; enslaved children of Founding Fathers, 12, 20–21; Founding Fathers as slave-owners, ix, 2, 12, 49, 73, 114, 193; and inheritance, 18–19; othering of slaves, 125; in right-to-life discourse, 67–68; selective amnesia about, 168; slave economy and sexual violence, 67–68, 114; and three-fifths rule, 166, 168
Snyder Act of 1924, 76
social contract, 10, 22–25, 50, 63–64, 193, 200
Soleimani, Qasem, 143
Solomon, 93
Southern Baptist Convention, 70
Southern Strategy, 169

Index   255

sovereignty: and Bill of Rights, 54; and expansion of rights, 22, 83; rhetoric of, beneficiaries, 201–5; rhetoric of, overview, 8–10, 46–48, 198–200; as term, 199. *See also* personhood; rights discourse
Spillers, Hortense J., 23, 24
The Spirit of Laws (Montesquieu), 120–21
state militias, 129–30
Stewart, Chris, 158
Stone, Anthony, Jr., 7, 167
Sunday, Billy, 26–27

terrorism, 34–37, 47, 69, 142–43
Tester, Jon, 179–80
Thanksgiving, 58
Third Amendment, 68
Third Persona: and bipartisanship discourse, 170, 174–77, 179, 187–88; defined, 51, 52; and inheritance, 193–94; negation of, and selective amnesia, 168–69, 170; negation of rights, 199–200; and othering, 193–94; and race, 52, 59, 68, 69, 84; and rights discourse, 58, 59, 60–61, 62, 68–69, 71, 77
Thirteenth Amendment, 22, 166
three-fifths rule, 166, 168
time and rights discourse, 71, 74–75, 77, 80, 82, 85
Toomey, Pat, 151
trained incapacity, 169, 188, 196, 198
tropes, agency of, 30–31, 197–98
Trump, Donald: and border wall, 181–82, 183; father rhetoric by, ix; and freedom of press, 77, 79, 80, 81; impeachment of, 1, 45, 92, 149, 150–61, 178–81, 186–88, 190; judicial appointments by, 105, 179–80; and popular vote, 159; and Putin, 175; and war powers, 143, 144, 145, 147, 176
Twelfth Amendment, 164–65, 190–91
Twenty-Third Amendment, 165
Twenty-Fourth Amendment, 72
Twenty-Sixth Amendment, 72

Universal Declaration of Human Rights, 56, 57
"uppity" discourse, 133–34, 178

Urbinati, Nadia, 8–9
use and enjoy property, right to, 20

VanDyke, Lawrence, 179–80, 183
Vargas, Juan, 155, 162
veneration: of American exceptionalism, 45, 92–95, 192–93; and bipartisanship, 46; and celebrations, 95–100, 106–9, 117, 199–200, 201; cynicism as counter-discourse, 44, 91–92, 110–17, 119, 205–6; overview of, 44–47, 91–92; and wisdom, 16, 45, 92–95, 99–100, 106–7
Vietnam War, 142
violence: and Christian nationalism, 201–2, 204; against journalists, 79–82; and "the people," 9; and white masculinity, 24–25, 201–2, 204; and white supremacy, 34, 35, 36, 47, 69, 201–2, 204
vote, right to: discourse on, 44, 53, 71–77, 205; and race, 22, 72; and women, 22, 72, 74, 76, 125, 127
Voting Rights Act of 1965, 22, 72–73, 75, 76
Voting Rights Advancement Act of 2021, 73

Walberg, Tim, 158
Walden, Greg, 160
Wander, Philip, 51–52, 168, 194
war powers, 128, 141–48, 161, 176, 183
Washington, George: in collective memory, 11–12; as father of country, 2, 17–18; in Loudermilk's discourse, 39–40; and nonpartisanship, 163, 164, 188
Washington, Martha, 11
Wayne, John, 27
Wenstrup, Brad, 64
Westmoreland, Lynn, 131, 133–34, 138–39
Weyrich, Paul, 27, 70
white American jeremiad, 101
white evangelical fear, 90–91, 118
Whitehead, Andrew L., 29, 90
Whitehouse, Sheldon, 102–3, 117
whiteness: and American exceptionalism, 89–91, 101, 106, 107, 117–19, 199; and bipartisanship discourse, 178; and Christianity, 17, 27, 118; and citizenship,

20, 50; and containment rhetoric, 135; as determining factor in early republic, 49–50, 193, 200; and "family" values, 47, 53, 83, 89, 119, 194, 198, 199–200; and inheritance, 18–21, 42, 43, 45, 50, 119; in Loudermilk's discourse, 32, 36–37, 39, 42, 43; and masculinity, 25–29, 201–2, 204; overview of, 6–7; and personhood, 21, 39, 42; as property, 10, 19–20, 27, 28, 52; and property ownership and rights, 18–20, 28; as rational, 134; and rights discourse, 58, 59, 71, 72, 73, 83–85; and Second Persona, 71, 194; and social contract, 10, 22–25, 50, 193, 200; and veneration of Founding Fathers, 45, 47, 193; and white saviorism, 147, 148

white supremacy: and Christianity, 27, 29, 70, 118, 207–8; and Christian nationalism, 29; and civilized *vs.* uncivilized discourse, 135–36; and containment rhetoric, 128, 135–36, 140–41, 148, 161–62; "fourteen words" mantra, 202–3, 204; and inheritance, 19, 46, 203; and masculinity, 207–8; and othering, 199–200; and "the people" construct, 9; and personhood, 22–23; privileging of, 6, 8, 10; and replacement theory, 46, 47, 69–71, 201–4; and rights discourse, 64, 67–71; and Southern Strategy, 169; unconscious use of, 198; and violence, 34, 35, 36, 47, 69, 201–2, 204; and white saviorism, 148

Whittington, Keith E., 150
Wicker, Roger F., 190
Wilson, Woodrow, 15
Winthrop, John, 101
wisdom: and Christianity, 93–95; and containment rhetoric, 128, 132; and masculinity, 93–94; and veneration of Founding Fathers, 16, 45, 92–95, 99–100, 106–7

women: and Christian nationalism, 201–4; and citizenship, 22, 125; and containment rhetoric, 134, 135; control of white women's procreation, 28, 201–4; and doctrine of coverture, 12, 18; and inheritance, 18; othering of, 125–27; and personhood, 22–25; and property, 18–19; and replacement theory, 201–4; and rights discourse, 61–62; role in Christian patriarchy, 28, 202–3; role in masculinity, 26; and sexist racism, 23–24; and social contract, 193; and Third Personae, 68, 69; and voting, 22, 72, 74, 76, 125, 127

World Press Freedom Day, 78, 80
Wyden, Ron, 80–82, 172

Yemen, military action in, 143, 147
Yoho, Ted, 65, 178–79